THE BLACK HAND
A CHAPTER IN ETHNIC CRIME

THE BLACK HAND
A CHAPTER IN ETHNIC CRIME

THOMAS MONROE PITKIN

FRANCESCO CORDASCO

ROWMAN AND LITTLEFIELD
Totowa, New Jersey

For
GIOVANNI CORDASCO and VINCENZO CORD
Who Lived, Unafraid, in the Shadows
of The Black Hand

Published 1977 by
Rowman and Littlefield

Library of Congress Cataloging in Publication Data

Pitkin, Thomas M.
  The Black Hand.

  Bibliography: p.
  Includes index.
  1. Black Hand (United States)—History. 2. Italian American criminals—United States—History. 3. Organized crime—United States—History. I. Cordasco, Francesco, 1920- joint author. II. Title
HV6791.P57 1977b   364.1`06   77-21966
ISBN 0-87471-886-4

Printed in the United States of America

Disproportionately, perhaps, yet surely, some part of the American attitude toward the Italians has been determined by their record in crime. If this history had in it less that is characteristic it might indeed count for less. For it is not so much the number of offences that has fashioned public opinion as the evidence they appear to give of an uncanny and fearsome disposition. Elemental natures seem to be at work. Abduction, kidnapping, rape, stand forth, and the newspapers glory in the details. The knife is used by men in their senses, by sober men; and a startling record of homicides or of attempted homicides appears. It is the Old World way. That the victims are themselves Italians, and that the roots of the dispute often lie in the past or in a misadventure of love, is insufficiently realized.

The strangest manifestation has been in the "Black Hand" outrages, which in their frequency and power of terrorization—but little else—recall the "Molly McGuire" doings of the Irish period of immigration. A man of means receives a scrawled missive bearing the sign of the black hand and the inexorable demand that a stated sum of money be privately conveyed to the nameless writer. The robber is as good as his word. Death by the knife or bomb, the blasted home or store, is the proof which comes too late.

Robert F. Foerster, *The Italian Emigration of Our Times* (1919)

TABLE OF CONTENTS

Preface

When William the Conqueror made his successful invasion of England in A.D. 1066, his army included not only Normans but also adventurers and mercenaries from different parts of Europe. More Europeans came in his wake, after the decisive battle of Hastings, to share in the spoils. The defeated Anglo-Saxons and Danes, themselves invaders in their time, were very unhappy but finally accepted the situation. British civilization became much richer for the experience. Already ethnically mixed, the United States was inundated with well over thirty million European immigrants from the end of the Napoleonic wars to World War I. They did not come in arms, but they probably brought lasting change as vital and as fertilizing as the hosts of William brought to England. We are still digesting the experience.

Most of these immigrants, especially when they were arriving in great numbers, met with prejudice. So it was with the Irish fleeing from famine in the 1840s and the economic changes that followed the starving time. So it was with the Germans, the Scandinavians, and others. With the shift in emigration from the north and west of Europe to the south and east toward the end of the nineteenth century, prejudice sharpened. A movement toward immigration restriction, that rose and fell but never ceased, developed in the United States. America's strong tradition as a refuge for the oppressed never was entirely obliterated, but it was submerged under the avalanche of massive immigration. Emma Lazarus's immortal invitation, "Bring me your tired, your poor, your huddled masses yearning to breathe free," was scarcely uttered when the movement to cancel it began to develop.

1

Slavs of all kinds, scarcely differentiated in the eyes of earlier-arrived Americans—Hungarians, Russian Jews, Greeks, Italians, and others included in what came to be called the "new immigration"—all met with a certain amount of disfavor at the same time as the rapidly growing American industrial complex demanded their services. Hostility was based on a great variety of grounds—religious, economic, political, and social—all the things that can be embodied in the word *stranger*. Discriminatory racial theories, imported from northern Europe and of domestic manufacture, emerged to justify it. As John Higham has pointed out, two of the newer groups suffered in particular. These were the Jews and the Italians. As the largest two elements in the swelling tide, they were inevitably prime targets for nativist attack. But there were already stereotypes that could be applied to both of them. The Jews were objects of age-old suspicion on religious grounds. There was also the long-standing image of them as rapacious money-grubbers, immortalized in Shakespeare's character, Shylock. South Italy, from which most Italian immigrants were now coming, already was fixed in the popular mind as a land of banditry and general turbulence. These immigrants "soon acquired a reputation as bloodthirsty criminals."

This view of the Italians was crystallized early in the 1890s by the murder of the chief of police in New Orleans at the hands, it was believed, of the criminal society of the Mafia, imported from Sicily. From that time on, news of Italian communities in the United States unfortunately tended to be dominated by accounts of their crimes, though it generally came to be recognized that most of these were strictly intramural. Americans aware of the richness of the Italian cultural heritage were outnumbered, outshouted, and ultimately outvoted.

As Italian immigration rose spectacularly at the turn of the century, extortion—usually by threatening letter—became a common practice in the Italian colonies of New York and other American cities. Italian ex-convicts followed their honest compatriots to the United States, resuming their customary practices. These included counterfeiting, kidnaping, and extortion. They often found willing accomplices among the youth of the poor and crowded Italian slum settlements. Extortion letters commonly were signed with the names of Old World criminal societies, notably the Mafia of Sicily and the Camorra of Naples. The usual threat for noncompliance with a demand for money was dynamiting or shooting. Such threats often were implemented.

Beginning in 1903 and following a case in Brooklyn in which the threatening letters were signed "La Mano Nera," the term *Black Hand*—or *Mano Nera*—generally supplanted the others. The term, and the symbol of a black hand as a threat, seem to have originated in Spain, where an alleged anarchist society using them was broken up in 1882. Italian extortionists had taken over the society. In the Brooklyn case, a reporter gave the Black Hand dramatic coverage in the *New York Herald*, and other journals followed suit. Italian newspapers adopted it, preferring it to the old labels, especially "Mafia," which for years had been applied to Italian crime and sometimes to Italians generally. The belief in an actual and powerful Black Hand society of criminals, fostered by both the press and the criminals themselves, came to have wide currency among both Italians and native Americans.

The Black Hand label soon was applied to almost any crime of violence in Italian neighborhoods in New York, Chicago, and other cities. Its use spread rapidly to the mining towns of Pennsylvania and other states, to labor camps in upstate New York, and to most communities where Italians were found in numbers. American police, often Irish, found Italian crime hard to combat. Witnesses could not be found, failed to show up in court, or declined to testify effectively for the prosecution. The American police and press generally attributed this to the code of *omertà*, or refusal to cooperate with law enforcement agencies, a supposed universal Italian tradition. Actually, such reticence among most Italians was little more than sheer terror.

Although American police were generally ineffective in combating such crime, often deliberately ignoring it, Italian detectives—notably Joseph Petrosino of the New York City force—were more successful. In 1909 Petrosino was sent to Italy and Sicily to arrange cooperation with the Italian police and other agencies in curbing the Black Hand. Italian law forbade the issuance of passports to ex-convicts, and American law forbade their admittance to the United States; but numbers of them were coming to America by one means or another. Petrosino was assassinated in Palermo; and Italian crime in New York and other American cities, which had been curbed to some extent, resumed an upward curve and soon reached new heights The growing belief that Italians, particularly those of the South, were a criminal race, was strengthened. This belief eventually was translated into law in the form of the discriminatory quota immigration laws.

The Secret Service, with its basic mission of combating counterfeiting, was for years the only federal agency that took part in fighting Italian crime. It had considerable success over the years, most notably in breaking up the Lupo-Morello gang of New York in 1910. This gang had operated for a long time and had contacts extending from Palermo—where it kept in touch with Mafia chiefs—to New Orleans and Chicago. It engaged extensively in extortion, kidnaping, murder, and other crimes as well as in counterfeiting. At about the same time, the postal authorities began bringing Black Hand cases before the federal courts on charges of mail fraud. In Chicago, the post office seems to have been the only agency that curbed the Black Hand to any extent for years.

In both New York and Chicago, municipal corruption extending deeply into their own forces greatly hampered the efforts of police administrators in all crime control. In both cities the Italian communities attempted to organize to protect themselves against the Black Hand, but these efforts were largely ineffectual. In New York the reform administration of Mayor John Purroy Mitchel (1914-1917), with Arthur Woods as police commissioner, set out to destroy the Black Hand and criminal gangs in general. These gangs—largely Irish, Jewish, Italian, and often ethnically mixed—had flourished under previous administrations. They often actually controlled municipal elections through dirty work at the polls, under the guidance and protection of corrupt politicians.

The efforts of the Mitchel administration, involving the

use of authoritarian methods, were for a time quite successful but were aborted largely with the coming of Prohibition. Black Handers and gangsters of varied ethnic origin turned eagerly to bootlegging, with its often spectacular profits. The Black Hand, as a symbol, as a technique, and as a supposed organization, soon disappeared. Chicago became most notorious in the gangland wars that resulted from competition for control of the illicit alcohol supply, but New York suffered almost equally. Corruption, under the gangster profits from bootlegging, grew worse than ever. Law enforcement throughout the country was affected disastrously. Italians were prominent in bootlegging and gang warfare; but the term *Black Hand*, along with *Mafia* and *Camorra*, dropped almost entirely out of currency. Gangsters of all ethnic origins usually were designated as just that or as "hoodlums" or "mobsters," though crime movies tended to depict them as Italians.

After Prohibition was over, criminal entrepreneurs, including numbers of Italians, developed new enterprises to replace bootlegging. In the years after World War II, the designation *organized crime* came into vogue to describe their activities. With investigations into organized crime by federal and state agencies from 1950 on, the term *Mafia* (briefly interrupted by *Cosa Nostra*) was revived. It has had wide currency since, especially in the American press. Although the symbol of a black hand as a threat had lingered for some time in Italian communities, the belief in an organized Black Hand society had faded even there. The term Black Hand has never been revived, except for occasional brief reference when it simply has been equated with Mafia.

Black Hand was the word for Italian crime in America for more than fifteen years, though members of other national groups often operated under its terrifying symbol. It dominated, unfairly and tragically, news of Italian America, as Mafia had done before and was to do again.

While I was working on a study of Ellis Island some years ago, I found that one of the problems of the immigration commissioner there had to do with the so-called Black Hand. The New York City police, in their frustration, charged the commissioner at the island station with letting in too many alien criminals, especially Black Handers, and with failing to cooperate in deporting them when they had been arrested by the police. The immigration authorities, of course, denied the charges vigorously. When the Ellis Island study was finished (it has since been published as *Keepers of the Gate: A History of Ellis Island*, 1975), I decided to follow up some of the problems resulting from the mass immigration through the island in the period just before World War I, including the Black Hand phenomenon. The present work is the first result.

Much of the material for this study had already been picked up in general research on Ellis Island, in repositories in Washington, New York, New Haven, and elsewhere. Additional research has been concentrated largely in New York, notably in the New York Public Library, the New York Historical Society, the Municipal Reference Library, and the Municipal Archives and Records Center. The professional staffs of these agencies have been invariably courteous and helpful. Unfortunately, I found that pertinent records of the New York Police Department had been systematically destroyed. Records of the New York County Court of General Sessions, in which many Black Hand cases were tried, still exist but are for all practical purposes inaccessible.

Moral support for this venture into an obviously sensitive field has been forthcoming from Italian-American scholars. These include Luciano J. Iorizzo, of the State University College at Oswego, New York, Rudolph J. Vecoli, of the University of Minnesota; and especially Francesco Cordasco, of Montclair State College, Montclair, New Jersey. Without Professor Cordasco's constant encouragement, the study might more than once have been abandoned. All three gentlemen felt that a study of the Black Hand was needed, but none can be blamed for any errors, either of fact or of interpretation, that may come to light in the present work.

NEW YORK CITY   THOMAS M. PITKIN

Foreword

There is little doubt that an ethnic revival has been under way for some time in the United States; the revival, of course, merely attests the ethnic presence in America. More accurately, the renaissance of ethnic identity is the rediscovery of diversity in our society, and the new ethnic affirmations have not been without controversy. Perhaps controversy was inevitable (and ineluctably pervasive), given the assimilationist *ethos* purposefully cultivated by American societal institutions. The very assessment of *assimilation* as a force in American society (whatever its genesis, motivations, and history) is not without difficulty. In attempting to harness the complex factors that explain the ferment attending the new American ethnicity, Andrew M. Greeley struggles with a still elusive social phenomenology:

> In America there is a profound distrust of diversity based on anything other than social class, which is the only "rational" diversity. American theory endorses cultural pluralism, but our behavior insists on as much assimilation as possible as quickly as possible. Most Americans feel ambivalent about the fact of diversity and also about their own particular location in ethnic geography. We are torn between pride in the heritage of our own group and resentment at being trapped in that heritage. This ambivalence is probably the result of the agonies of the acculturation experience in which an immigrant group alternately felt shame over the fact that it was different and unwanted and a defensive pride about its own excellence, which the rest of society seemed neither to appreciate nor understand. The superpatriot is the man who is proud of his uniqueness and yet simultaneously wants to be like everyone else, only more so. (*Ethnicity in the United States* [1974], 17)

The Italian American community, of course, has not been immune to the new ethnicity. As members of one of the largest American minority groups (estimates on the number of Italian Americans range between 16 and 30 million; no one knows for sure), Italians have vigorously participated in the contemporary ethnic affirmations; and not unlike other ethnics, Italians have proclaimed their newly discovered identity in a bewildering multitude of ways. They have issued defensive tracts and remonstrances (essentially congruent with a long-established tradition best epitomized in the work of the American Sicilian journalist, Giovanni Schiavo); and, in the contexts of the social volatility of the recent past, Italian Americans have gathered in the streets to vociferously acclaim both their disaffection and discontent. The *New York Times*, largely reacting to public demonstrations by Italian Americans in New York City, commented at length on the elusive identities of the city's Italians:

> They are not a closely knit group in any sense. The two great characteristics of the descendants of the immigrants is pride—frequently unarticulated—they take in being part of the great Romano-Italian civilization, although many of them know very little about it. But mostly, they share an overriding sense of responsibility as American citizens and in that, they are not Italian.
>
> There is disagreement over the number of people of Italian ancestry in the United States, but the best estimate is between 15 million and 20 million, with perhaps 1.5 million in and around New York City. Most are the descendants of immigrants who arrived penniless and illiterate from southern Italy more than half a century ago . . . . Who are these people and what have they become?
>
> Perhaps their identity has been more defined by motion pictures and television than by anything that might be considered truly Italian. The cinema has presented them as brown of eye, black of hair and red of temper. So great was the demand for swarthy Italian gangster styles some years ago that an Irishman named J. Carrol Naish made a fortune portraying them in Hollywood.
>
> Many Americans retain an extraordinary image of the Italian immigrant and his descendants as cultural aberrations who sing tenor and peddle fish, and who are romantic, oily, prudish, devious, faithful, sexy, clannish, open-minded, tolerant, intolerant, brilliant, anti-intellectual, unambitious and industrious—all at the same time.
>
> In New York, Italians are stereotyped as garbage collectors

who adorn their lawns with plastic flamingos and who sit behind aluminum storm windows in Queens and talk of how Negroes and Puerto Ricans must wait until they are qualified before they get good jobs. The image of the barber who keeps the Madonna on his dashboard remains alive and well.

These impressions have not been altered by the fact that anticlericalism is an older tradition among the Italians than dashboard Madonnas, or by the fact that a survey on race relations conducted recently for the Urban League suggests that Americans other than Italians are far more reactionary.

Whatever his image, the Italian from his very beginnings in America prided himself on how rapidly he was assimilated. Some immigrant parents refused to speak Italian in front of the children so that they could become American that much faster. . . . But on June 29 [1970], a remarkable thing happened to the people who have been described as being more American than the Americans. About 40,000 of them, according to the police estimate, gathered at Columbus Circle and waved the Italian tricolor. Perhaps the only Italian word many of them knew was "ciao," but they wore red, white and green buttons calling for "Italian power." After melting in the melting pot for all these years, they looked like they wanted to climb out.

Here was a group New York had taken for granted. But it was also a group that never really considered itself a group, for the Italians and their descendants are notoriously independent of one another. Even in the early days, when they worked for nickels and dimes and were called wops by the immigrants who had gotten there before them, their self-help societies had been weak.

But here they were, reflecting the American proclivity for group defensiveness, joining blacks, Puerto Ricans, Jews, Arabs, Mexicans, Indians, welfare recipients, the aged, conservatives, women, policemen, the New Left, drug advocates, homosexuals and Yippies in protesting for their rights.

If the speech-making at Columbus Circle was taken at face value, those who attended came because they felt that use of the word "Mafia" had smeared and made them suspect. And there is no question that many Italians, even those who did not go to the Unity Day rally, are upset by the use of the word. . . . Why, Italians wonder, is it no longer permissible in respectable circles to use pejoratives to refer to Negroes, Puerto Ricans and Jews, but almost fashionable to direct the same vulgarity at Italians, and expect them to laugh at "wop," "guinea," "dago" and other terms. (*New York Times*, November 9, 1970)

The Italian experience in the United States has been and continues to be extremely diverse; how diverse the experience has been is recorded in the two bibliographical registers in which I have attempted to define its archives: *Italians in the United States: A Bibliography of Reports, Texts, Critical Studies and Related Materials* (1972), and *The Italian American Experience: An Annotated and Classified Bibliographical Guide* (1974). The wealth of these archives is suggested in a core collection of texts and related materials that I assembled for the *New York Times'* Arno Press (*The Italian American Experience*, 39 vols., 1975).[1] Yet, the systematic study of the Italian American past has only recently begun (and this is true generally for American ethnic historiography both as a discipline and a field of study). As recently as the mid-1960s, Leonard Covello, Rudolph Vecoli, and I initiated the colloquia out of which emerged the founding of the American Italian Historical Association. The neglect of the study of the Italian American past is not unrelated to the very nature of the Italian experience in the United States. I have posed the question and attempted its answer: "How is the neglect of Italian-American past to be explained? The answer is complex, but a number of facts help explain the neglect. The majority of Italians who migrated to the United States during the period of the great migrations (1880-1920) were Southern Italian *contadini*, wretchedly poor and easy marks for manipulative oppression, discrimination, and cultural assault. Their tardy arrival in America made success and achievement elusive and more difficult than it had been for earlier peoples (*e.g.*, the Irish); their American-born children were caught in the maelstrom of adaptation (and were clinically studied by a varied cadre of psychologists, social workers, educators and sociologists). In a complex constellation of forces, Italians were the victims of a village-mindedness or provincialism (*Campanilismo*) that they had transplanted from their southern villages of Italy to the teeming ghettos of urban America; and Italians, mystically medieval Catholics, were inhospitably rejected for the most part by the American Irish Catholic church. Certainly, such a past was not to be envied or nostalgically pursued. And this oppressive burden of the past has been further exacerbated by the stigma of crime; as Alexander DeConde has noted: in the popular mind, the connecting of

1. The titles of the *New York Times*/Arno collection are noted in F. Cordasco, *Italian Americans: A Guide to Information Sources* (1977).

Italians with crime was as American as associating Jews with shady business deals, Irishmen with boss politics, or Negroes with watermelons." (*The Italian American Experience,* pp. vii-viii)

Against this background, the publication of Thomas Monroe Pitkin's *The Black Hand: A Chapter in Ethnic Crime* has a special importance. It is, of course, an important contribution to ethnic social historiography, and it has a particular importance for students of social deviance and, in a broader sense, for students of criminology. But for the Italian American community, *The Black Hand: A Chapter in Ethnic Crime* has a more profound significance. Acknowledgedly, it is a serious addition to the proliferating corpus of studies directed to the study of the Italian American past; but because it studies *crime* in the interstitial Italian American community of earlier decades, its appearance has a crucial importance for the psychosocial history of Italians in the United States.

When the American Italian Historical Association convened its third annual conference, its theme was "An Inquiry into Organized Crime," and the AIHA began its deliberations with the somber reflection that "For better or for worse no subject elicits such animated discussions about Italian Americans than the issue of crime. Reactions to the topic range from smiles of acknowledgement to bitter tirades against insinuations: from whatever dimension, the subject warrants serious and dispassionate consideration and study." And it was hardly unanticipated that the high seriousness of the AIHA conference's agenda was marked by tendentious assertions and polemical protestations:

> Objectivity, which was the hallmark of the formal presentations, began to give way to partisan and highly emotional reaction once the chair recognized questions from the floor. A sense of militancy, which has long been identified with the black movement in the United States was now being exhibited by a large number of the audience, many of whom represented the lay ranks. Those whose arguments could be interpreted as flattering to the Italian-Americans were solidly cheered. Those who gave a contrary impression could scarcely be heard over the disapproving hand-clapping and foot-stomping din of the crowd. One expert, with years of experience as a law enforcement officer, was known to have walked out in disgust.

Though some were obviously disappointed by the turn of
events (they undoubtedly have not been at historians' annual
meetings of late), many were pleased to have had the opportunity
to undertake a needed dialogue with representatives from diverse walks of life. The emotional enthusiasm which moved so
many in the afternoon meeting will hopefully act as a constant
reminder to all who were present for the need to continue the
serious work required in organized crime. (AIHA, "An Inquiry
into Organized Crime," *Proceedings* [1970], *Preface*)

What Thomas Monroe Pitkin has achieved in *The Black
Hand: A Chapter in Ethnic Crime* is of commanding importance. He has drawn from the shadows the dreaded *La
Mano Nera* whose terror dominated the Italian American
communities of the first two decades of this century. In the
verisimilitude of detail with which Dr. Pitkin has recreated
the turn-of-the-century immigrant community, the crimes associated with *La Mano Nera* are correctly perceived as that
social pathology undeniably part of a milieu in which crime
is related to the total configuration of a people's experience
in the isolated contexts of minority enclaves. In a word, the
"Black Hand" extortionists and terrorists were *Italians*
committing crimes against *Italians*, a phenomenon not in-
congruent with the patterns of contemporary urban crime in
which both criminal and victim are indigenous to the vast interstitial *barrios* to which a society's poor are consigned. Italian Americans were immune neither to poverty nor to its
deleterious consequences; in a larger sense, "Black Hand"
criminality was inevitable in contexts of social neglect and
exploitation. It was not Italian inclination to crime but Italian
vulnerability to crime that explains the short-lived phenomenon that was *La Mano Nera*, a fate that Italians shared in
common with other newcomers to America.

In a larger sense, *The Black Hand: A Chapter in Ethnic
Crime* has sharpened the perspectives in which the *Mafia*
and the infrastructure of American organized crime are to be
understood. Clearly, Dr. Pitkin's disciplined chronicles dem-
onstrate that *La Mano Nera*, if it is to be understood at all,
must be seen as a phenomenon with a life of its own, unen-
cumbered with the legacies of the Neapolitan *Camorra* or
the Sicilian *Mafia*. Strictly, allowing the interplay of very
complex social forces, the "Black Hand" phenomenon is, sui

generis, without comparable analogue. It is limited both in time and place; it is not an antecedent of the *Mafia*, and certainly it is not a prototype out of which organized crime emerges.[2] In Dr. Pitkin's words: "In summary the term *Black Hand* was generally applied to Italian crime and sometimes to the Italian community as a whole, for more than fifteen years. The basic technique and the label were imitated among other immigrant groups and even among native Americans. With the coming of Prohibition, and the opening of a vast and highly profitable new field of endeavor for criminals in general, the Black Hand began to go out of fashion, but it had a lingering death."

There is high drama in *The Black Hand: A Chapter in Ethnic Crime*, and this is nowhere more evident than in Dr. Pitkin's account of the legendary Giuseppe Petrosino (1860-1909) and his fateful mission to Sicily; only a social historian of first rank, immersed in immigration history, could successfully handle the *disjecta membra* of an episode in Italian American history more legend than fact and infused with uncontrolled speculation. And Dr. Pitkin has met the challenge successfully. Unlike Arrigo Petacco's *Joe Petrosino* (1974), a popular work by an Italian journalist (the book's English translation and wide circulation reaffirm the continuing attraction of the Petrosino legend), Pitkin has harnessed the legend and placed Petrosino in the tumultuous social contexts in which he (and the times that created him) are to be understood. In this account (as in much of the material in *The Black Hand: A Chapter in Ethnic Crime*), Dr. Pitkin has a clear advantage; his unrivaled knowledge of immigration history has, in a very real way, illuminated the chiaroscuro social milieu of the immigrant. Pitkin brings to this volume the same talents so clearly evident in his *Keepers of the Gate: A History of Ellis Island* (1975) of which I wrote: "Pitkin's chronicle is a painstaking assembly of the island's administrative history out of the archives in which it is entombed: informative, judicious, lucid, and illustrative of the Wilhelmine dictum of Ranke: *wie es eigentlich gewesen ist.*

---

2. Generally, for the greater context in which the Black Hand is to be understood, see, Humbert S. Nelli, *The Business of Crime: Italians and Syndicate Crime in the United States* (1976).

As such, it is vigorous historiography in which the scholarship of sustained investigations is everywhere apparent." (*Italian Americana*, 2: 123, Autumn 1975)

Thomas Monroe Pitkin's *The Black Hand: A Chapter in Ethnic Crime* will achieve a deserved success. Its readers will applaud its disciplined narratives and the skillfully orchestrated drama of its themes. But its greatest praise will come from Italian Americans who will perceive in its pages a congruence of design with the overarching patterns of American social history, and it is this that the new ethnic historiography has as a basic animus.

WEST NEW YORK, N.J.   FRANCESCO CORDASCO

CHAPTER I

A New Name for an Old Crime

On August 3, 1903, Nicolo Cappiello, a prosperous Italian contractor and dock builder of 107 Second Place, Brooklyn, New York, received a letter signed "Mano Nera" (Black Hand), ordering him to meet unspecified persons at a designated street corner the next afternoon, or "your house will be dynamited and you and your family killed." When he failed to appear, this was followed by another, indicating that he was marked for death unless he followed instructions. It was signed, "Beware of Mano Nera." Cappiello at first paid no heed, he said later; but several men, including some old friends and others claiming to be agents of a Black Hand order, soon called on him. They told him that though a price of $10,000 had been set on his head, they believed they could get him better terms. Involved and emotional negotiations followed in the presence of the whole family. He finally paid $1,000, but more was demanded almost at once.

Cappiello's nephew-in-law, Enrico Moresco, who had been in disfavor with him, now saw a chance to ingratiate himself. He went to two of the men, ostensibly to demand a share of the loot, and picked up enough information to cause the arrest of the whole group. Cappiello, at the urging of the Brooklyn police, brought charges against them. More Black Hand letters came, threatening him with instant death if he did not drop the charges. But Cappiello, though obviously terrified, was persuaded by the police to go ahead with the prosecution. In court, Cappiello and his family were described as "obviously fearful that the Society of the Black

15

Hand might blow them up with dynamite or cut holes in them unexpectedly," in spite of their police guard. In the course of testimony, he admitted that he had first conspired with the defendants to punish Moresco, who then heaped coals of fire on his head by rescuing him from their plot to ruin him. "Noble Enrico," he said, turning dramatically to Moresco, "this you did for me after I had plotted with these same men to work your undoing, when you married without my knowledge the heiress of my house." Indictments were returned by the September grand jury of Kings County against five men for extortion. Two of them, the self-styled Black Handers, were tried and convicted.

Cappiello and his friends were Neapolitans. Some of these friends had evidently undertaken to wreak vengeance on Moresco for eloping with Cappiello's niece. They had brought into the plot Annunziato Lingria, a Calabrian with a sinister reputation. Lingria seems to have taken over and changed the operation into an attack on Cappiello's fortune, estimated at $100,000. It was evidently Lingria who wrote the threatening letters with the Black Hand label; it was Lingria who posed as the agent of a secret society by that name. He and Biaggio Giordano, an associate, were those convicted.[1]

There were elements of comedy in the case of Cappiello. He was hoist with his own petard. But there was little that was comic in the general setting or in what followed. The case marked the beginning, not of a new type of crime but of the use of a new symbol for an old one, the long reign of Black Hand terror in the Italian communities of New York and other American cities. "For more than two years," the *New York Herald* noted at the beginning of the Cappiello affair, "the police of New York and Brooklyn have striven to break up the bands of blackmailers who, under such names as the Mafia, the Mala Vita, and La Società Cammorristi, have first terrified and then reaped a harvest from hundreds of wealthy Italians." The men engaged in this business were dangerous and would not hesitate to kill anyone who failed to meet their demands or who tried to bring about their capture. "Many doctors, lawyers, and business men in the Italian colony," the *Herald* pointed out, "who have received threatening letters from these bands have sent the money demanded for fear of incurring the penalty."

The *Herald* reporter obviously wrung all the drama he could get out of the case. Years later he was accused unfairly of having invented the Black Hand to keep the story going. He certainly did not invent the practice of extortion in the Italian community. That was already flourishing. It continued to flourish; and the name *Black Hand* quickly came to be applied to it, almost to the exclusion of the other terms. The *Herald* was first to use the name in print, but other newspapers soon picked it up. Threatening letters, among the Italians, usually were adorned with such devices as daggers, skulls, crosses, and coffins. Now a new device had been added. Apparently something similar had been used not long before to inspire terror, without attracting very much attention. "The black or bloody hand of Picciotto di Sgarro, the executioner of the Camorra," said the New York *World*, "has been invoked again over in Brooklyn for the old purpose— extortion under pain of death." The "Order of the Black Hand," it asserted, was "another name for the Camorra." The *World* had probably picked up the phrase about the Camorra and its executioner a few months before from agents of the Secret Service in another case. These men, who long had been tracking down counterfeiters among the Italians, seem to have regarded Mafia and Camorra as merely local designations of the same organization.[2]

The *Brooklyn Daily Eagle* did not at first use the new label in its treatment of the case, but soon printed a letter to Cappiello that its reporter had seen, signed "La Mano Nera." Thereafter it used the term *Black Hand* freely and commented on the breakup of an Italian gang of robbers in Brooklyn by naming it the Black Hand. "The 'Black Hand' is worldwide," the *Eagle* proclaimed, "and is known for the way it terrorizes and draws money from scared Italians." This sweeping assertion seems to have been based on the fact that one of the band had been held for the action of the Italian consul general, who had written to Italy to get details on the prisoner's connection with a murder there. The *New York Tribune* reported on the efforts of "the Italian secret society known as the Black Hand" to terrorize witnesses in the same case, involving the prosecution of four Italians. Finally, in effect setting the seal of approval on the new scare words, the *New York Times* referred to a threatening letter turned over to the police by an Italian, "purporting to come from the 'Black Hand Society.' "

The newspapers had popularized the sinister term, and blackmailers took to using it freely. Detectives of the New York police force began referring to "the 'Black Hand' gang" as "undoubtedly at work in this city." The annual report of the commissioner-general of immigration for the fiscal year 1904 expressed some alarm at "the introduction into this country of such hideous and terrifying fruits of long-continued oppression as the mafia, the vendetta, 'black hand' and anarchist societies." The Italian language press, in an effort to shake off the stigma of Old World criminal labels, took it up and caused a panic at schools in Harlem's "Little Italy" a few months later by publishing a rumor that the Black Hand was planning to blow them up. The new term spread quickly to Chicago, where it soon supplanted *Mafia* in both the American and the Italian press.[3]

The American public long had heard of criminal societies that flourished in south Italy, notably the Mafia in Sicily and the Camorra in Naples. As early as 1876, when the Italian government was preparing to move against the Mafia in force, readers of the *Atlantic Monthly* were told by a well-informed Sicilian ex-official of "the vast secret association of peculiar character called *mafia*" that engaged in smuggling, highway robbery, and other lawlessness but thrived mostly by levying blackmail on the wealthy and peaceful part of the population, "who from time immemorial have submitted to it, and do so still." In return, such persons were "protected by the mafiusi in their life and property better than they would be by the government itself." When they had paid their quota, "the mafiusi feel in honor bound to protect them, and do so . . . their *vendetta* would surely fall on any one who dared to pilfer in their province." The organization had its origin in hatred against the Spanish Bourbon government that oppressed Sicily for centuries; it still represented, in the eyes of the Sicilian people, resistance to outside oppression. They submitted to its exactions out of necessity but also took pride in it. "To be a mafiuso in its present significance among Sicilians," said the author, "means to be a brave man, a man who fears nobody; and many a good mother speaks of her boy as being a little mafiuso or malandrino, meaning by that a brave, bright boy."

"The *mafiusi, malandrini,* or *cammorristi* of Sicily, for they are designated by either of these three appellations," the writer said, "very seldom live together in armed bands." They were not ordinary highway robbers or brigands, though bands of these did exist. When they did plan a robbery or the seizure of a proprietor for ransom, the chiefs collected a number of men sufficient for the operation in view, "and as soon as it is accomplished, they disband and go about their business in the cities or the fields, as if they were the most honest and respectable laborers." They had a code called *omertà,* to which all adhered. The principal laws of this code were that "a man must seek redress by himself for injuries received," and that "no man should testify before a judge even if he is the injured party." In obedience to these rules even the most respectable among the common people would never testify if he had been spectator to a crime; not only that, "but he would consider it his duty and a worthy action to secrete an assassin from the pursuit of justice." According to the code, "it is not justice but the living that must avenge the dead." This was part of the law of vendetta.

"The mafia of Sicily is a regularly organized association," according to the author. Members were not admitted until after an examination of their past conduct and a trial of arms, consisting of a duel with knives. Membership was denied to anyone who had committed an infamous or cowardly act. Infamous acts were primarily violations of *omertà.* The aim of the organization was not robbery but domineering, being independent of and even above the laws and authorities. It had intelligent leaders in both the cities and the country. "In the country it is all-powerful, in the cities influential." The crimes committed by its members to maintain their baneful influence were enormous. Respectable men dared not be witnesses against criminals, juries dared not convict; all the peaceful and honest citizens were in awe of the power of the Mafia. Landowners were regularly taxed by it, and so was every branch of industry. The efforts of the Italian government to suppress it by force, the writer believed, would be futile. Only the spread of general enlightenment, economic development and land reform, and the conviction among the mass of the honest people that the protection of the liberal new government was more manly, honorable, and safe than that of the Mafia could with time destroy "this vast association which for centuries has gnawed the very vitals of industry in Sicily."[4]

In the following year a brief article in the *Times* described "The Capi-Mafia in Palermo." These Mafia chiefs, the author, one Franchetti, said, were all in good circumstances. They were themselves capable of murder but seldom had need to resort to it, as there were plenty of instruments at hand. "The *facinorosi* (atrocious ones) of the lower class are all in different degrees and under diverse forms clients of either one or the other of these Capi-Mafia." The chiefs organized operations and established "that unity of action in the perpetration of crimes which gives the Mafia its appearance of an implacable and invincible force." They maintained discipline and judged when circumstances required "a momentary suspension of violent acts or the multiplication of them, and whether a more ferocious character is to be given to them." According to the state of this market, they decided on the operations to be made, on the persons out of whom to wring extortions, and on the means to be used.

A few months later there was a two-column article in the *Times* from an occasional correspondent in Palermo. The article was based on the recent kidnaping of Alessandro Parisi, a young man of a rich Palermitan family. The writer, apparently an American artist living there, philosophized at some length on crime in Sicily and in America. "The knife is as ready here as in Arkansas," he said. Robbery and murder were common in Palermo and seldom punished. Witnesses could not be found. He referred to debates in the Italian parliament two or three years before, revealing widespread brigandage. "This was especially shown in the information given as to the existence of the *Maffia*. The *Maffia* is a secret union of evil-doers, extending throughout Sicily." It had no regular organization but was bound together in the common pursuit of gain by means of crime. It had its own code of justice, and its decrees were swift and inexorable. Many people joined it merely for their own protection. Italian friends had told the author "that the *Maffia* had ceased to exist," but he had objected the case of young Parisi. Americans often asked if it was safe to visit Sicily, though they never seemed to hesitate to travel to Arkansas or Colorado, where knife and revolver were freely used. He thought they were as safe in Sicily as in those states; he often moved about the city alone, sketching, and he had never been bothered.[5]

A few years later a writer in the British *Saturday Review* described the Neapolitan Camorra in detail. While many foreigners believed that this criminal society, which originated in the prisons of the Spanish Bourbons, was a thing of the past, "the society has never exercised a greater influence than it does at present," though its power was concealed. It was similar to the Mafia but more fully developed and more highly organized. It exercised almost unlimited control over the poorer classes in Naples, and there was also a Camorra "in kid gloves." The true leaders of the Camorra were men in the highest position; they were universally known as such in the city, but their names were only whispered. Recruiting and training of members from the adventurous youth of the poor were highly systematic, and there was a definite hierarchy, with district chiefs who put recruits through their paces in tests of courage and experience in crime, culminating in the grade of full member, or *picciotto di sgarro*. From there a member might eventually rise to the rank of district chief, or *capo*. "What his direct emoluments are," the writer admitted, "we cannot say, but he enjoys a position which for a man of a violent, arrogant, and commanding temper must possess a great charm." As long as he obeyed the commands of his superiors, he could treat the rest of the world pretty much as he pleased and rest assured that he would not be left without support in time of need. If a considerable number of the district leaders of the Camorra were exiled under police supervision, as the judges had power to do, the society would be crippled, but such action was highly unlikely.

In 1891 there was an article on the Camorra in the *American Catholic Quarterly Review*. "The meaning of the word Maffia," it said, "Sicilians can no more exactly define than the Neapolitans can define 'Camorra.' " The Maffia was confined to Sicily; but the Camorra flourished not only in the city of Naples, as many imagined, but also in neighboring provinces as far as Calabria, in the islands along the coast, and even in Sicily. The name might not have been adopted everywhere, but similar organizations existed, or did until recently, even in parts of north Italy. "Associations of criminals are not unknown in the United States. Every large city has its 'gangs.' These, however, are vulgar associations which no political party, no senator or cabinet officer would, even secretly, negotiate with and much less protect." But among the Italians, if the testimony of Italians was to be trusted, "the secret society has been more scientifically adapted to ends openly criminal than among other European peoples." Among these the Camorra easily held "first place in the annals of Italian associations especially devoted to the encouragement of crime and to the protection of criminals." No one could tell how or when the Camorra was first organized, the writer said. It was first discovered about 1820 at work in the jails of Naples.

At about the same time, when diplomatic relations between Italy and the United States had temporarily ceased and hostility to the Italian immigrant was at a high pitch, a well-informed article in the *Nineteenth Century* reviewed the circumstances calmly and objectively. Among other things, it told of the impositions practiced by the Camorra on emirants embarking at Naples. The society was engaged in "wholesale, cruel, mean pillage" of the emigrants passing through the port on their way to the United States or South America. But the worst feature of the relations between the Camorra and the emigration was that "they have an organization for 'shipping merchandise' which defies the police and the special agents employed by the Government to detect them." A criminal escaping from justice or a fugitive from the military draft, "one of their own number who has made the place too hot for him," sought assistance. The Camorrists had friends everywhere among those engaged in the emigrant traffic at Naples. If the fugitive could afford it, a Camorra agent procured him a passport under a false name, hid him until the last moment, and then accompanied him on board an emigrant ship. If he had no means, he was passed as a stowaway. "When he lands in the United States, or even elsewhere, it is more than likely that the association has adepts at the landing-places marked by cablegram—'so many bales will arrive by such and such a steamer.' " There were also other transports than emigrant ships, "and the Camorra probably avail themselves of these."[6]

There had been a considerable migration of Sicilians to New Orleans even before and especially after the Civil War, and it came to be generally believed that they had brought the Mafia with them. While some of the Sicilians prospered and became politically influential, a high rate of homicide developed in the community. In 1881 David G. Hennessy, a young detective on the city's police force, captured and was instrumental in deporting Giuseppe Esposito, a notorious Sicilian bandit who was badly wanted by the authorities in Italy. Esposito was believed to have assumed leadership of the local Mafia. Hennessy was dismissed from the force not long after; but in 1888, after a reform local election, he was appointed chief of police. He began compiling data on murders that he attributed to the Mafia.

Two gangs, or factions, had developed among the Sicilians—the Provenzanos and the Matrangas. They became engaged in a struggle for control of the New Orleans water front, and there was a number of killings. In 1890 the Provenzanos were tried for an ambush attack on the Matrangas. They accused the Matrangas of being a branch of the Mafia, and the Matrangas returned the compliment. The Provenzanos were convicted but were granted a new trial. The Matrangas believed that Hennessy had favored them, and he apparently had found evidence of perjury in the first trial. There had been threats against his life and in October, shortly before the new trial was to begin, he was waylaid and mortally wounded by shotgun blasts. Before he died, he was supposed to have said that "the Dagoes did it."

There was great excitement in the city, where Hennessy was a popular official. The entire police force was deployed and ordered "to arrest every Italian you come across." Most of the men picked up, however, soon were released. Official action centered on the Matrangas, who were popularly identified as Mafia and as the murderers of Hennessy. A mass meeting was called "to assist the officers of the law in driving the murderous Mafia from our midst." With the approval of the city council, the mayor appointed a citizens' committee to collect evidence. The Provenzanos were acquitted on their second trial in January. Nineteen Sicilians, some of them American citizens who were identified with the Matrangas, were indicted by the grand jury. All were kept in detention, and in February nine of them were put on trial for murder.

The accused had able counsel, and a protracted legal battle followed, "one of the most spectacular and sensational criminal trials ever conducted in the city." There were constant reports of attempted jury tampering and intimidation of witnesses, the whole city being bitterly arrayed against the prisoners. When, in March, the jury found six of the accused not guilty and disagreed on the other three, the belief was general that it had been terrorized or bought off. There was a mass meeting led by prominent citizens, a large mob formed, and eleven of the prisoners, who were all still in custody, were lynched at the parish jail. The sheriff had carefully absented himself.[7]

The Italian consul at New Orleans had kept his government in touch with the whole affair and had tried in vain to get local authorities to intervene. After the lynching, which caused a great sensation in Italy, diplomatic relations were broken off and there was even a brief war scare along the Atlantic seaboard. The United States finally paid 125,000 lire indemnity for the families of those victims who were still Italian citizens. The killing of Hennessy, however, had attracted national attention and roused hostility to Italians generally. The brutal avenging of the murder was noted, on the whole, with comparatively mild reproof. In New Orleans a grand jury refused to indict anybody for the lynching. In New York one or two newspapers condemned the affair vigorously. A *Times* editorial, however, observed that "while every good citizen will readily assent to the proposition that this affair is to be deplored, it would be difficult to find any one individual who would confess that privately he deplored it very much." An article from Rome in the *Nation* stressed the efforts of the Italian government to suppress the Mafia, and declared, "The organization is probably stronger today in Louisiana than in Sicily. . . . transplanted to a new and almost virgin soil, where, too, a certain old infirmity of the law has predisposed to violence and short roads to justice, it was certain that the Mafia would become a danger to society."

A sampling of opinion across the country indicated widespread belief that the Italians were a peculiarly violent people. "The Italian immigrant would be no more objectionable than some others were it not for his singularly blood thirsty disposition and frightful temper and vindictiveness," according to the *Baltimore News*. "We have seen a good deal of this sort of thing in this country of late and the fact has been vividly established that the lower class of Italians are a dangerous people—cruel, treacherous, vindictive and relentless." The *Indianapolis Journal* admitted that thousands of intelligent Italians had come to this country and become good citizens but declared that the bulk of the Italian immigration then coming in was anything but desirable. "Ignorant, suspicious and violent, nearly all armed with deadly weapons, naturally hostile to lawful authority, living in squalor and in the midst of the most repulsive vices, they are at war with social order." Americans called the Italians undesirable, the *Kansas City Times* declared, not because the "diplomatic incident"resulting from the affair in New Orleans had aroused dislike but because they were undesirable. "It would be too much to say that they give their stabbing and throat cutting practices to America, because Americans do not copy these Italian methods, but their ready murderousness does add to the difficulty and expense of our police protection."

The *New York Recorder* did not indulge in any such wholesale indictment of the Italian immigrants but did call attention to the finding of the New Orleans grand jury that a great many illegal immigrants had been coming in on Italian vessels, "criminals who are the ready instruments of the crimes of the Mafia." There was a surreptitious immigration "made up of fugitives from justice, whose evasion of the laws of their own country is winked at in order that they and their desperate dispositions and deeds may be transferred to the United States by their 'leaving their country for their country's good,' but to our great injury." Recent amendments to the federal immigration laws had tended in the right direction but were "totally inadequate to the reformation of the gigantic evil which threatens public order."[8]

More than two years before the New Orleans lynching, Inspector Thomas Byrnes, chief of detectives of the New York police force, issued a statement to the press announcing the solution of an Italian case of murder on the East Side. It was the work of the Mafia, he said. With the help of his two Italian detectives, he had grilled three reluctant witnesses, all Sicilians from Palermo, as were both the murdered man and the alleged murderer. Byrnes's interrogation methods were celebrated and usually successful. The men were rather intelligent and had some education, he reported. They admitted being fugitives from their native country, having been engaged in various crimes there. They had given him a detailed account of the workings of the society which, they said, had "two principal headquarters" in this country, "one in this city and the other in New Orleans." The murdered man, Antonio Flaccomio, had been a member but was in bad odor with the society for giving information to the authorities and had been singled out for destruction. The man they said they saw murder him, Carlo Quarteraro, had fled the country, but his brother had allegedly aided him and had been picked up. Byrnes evidently felt that he had an ironclad case.

The brother, Vincenzo Quarteraro, was later tried; but after many witnesses, both Italian and American, had placed him in Mount Vernon very close to the time of the murder the jury disagreed. Quarteraro testified in his own defense and evidently made a good impression. The defense counsel not only presented a very convincing alibi but also openly charged the three prosecution witnesses with actually having committed the murder themselves. He called attention to the high class of witnesses he had brought forward to prove Quarteraro's alibi, "and contrasted them with what he called the 'scum of Sicilian society' who had testified against the accused." When the jury failed to convict, Byrnes is said to have given up on Italian crime in the city in disgust, announcing that the Italian criminals could "go ahead and kill each other."[9]

Judging by the newspaper accounts of the affair, Byrnes may have learned much that was new to him about the Mafia but was cleverly hoodwinked as to the actual culprits. Having exposed his reputation as a great detective at the beginning of the case, he was understandably embarrassed by its outcome. Thereafter he downgraded the Mafia. After the New Orleans lynchings, he assured the *Tribune* that "No band of assassins such as the Mafia could be allowed to perpetrate murders in New-York." The police were perfectly capable of preventing anything of that kind, and anyway, "The Italians in New-York are mostly law abiding people. They live cheaply, work cheaply and save money." They seldom hurt anybody who was not an Italian in their fights. They were trying to better their condition and were improving all the time. "There are no portraits of Italian thieves in the Rogues' Gallery. Now and then some of the most ignorant of the Italians try to make counterfeit money on a small scale, but their efforts do not pay. As a class the Italians do not seem to be dangerous to the public in this city." The *Tribune* headed its account of the interview, "No Mafia in New-York City."

The *Times*, however, was alarmed and joined the rising chorus of the immigration restrictionists. The recent events in New Orleans, it said, "have compelled attention anew to the necessity of restricting immigration. For what that riot showed was that a band of foreign cutthroats had acquired such control of an American city as to kill officers of the law whom it failed to frighten and to intimidate a jury from bringing in a righteous verdict in a clear case." There was "no decent American citizen" who didn't feel that something must be done, it declared. A little later the New York *Sun* reported on a canvass of opinion in American cities conducted by its correspondents, in which both favorable and unfavorable opinions of the Italians were revealed. But in the same issue it also carried an article illustrated with pictures of knives, revolvers, and blackjacks, entitled "Weapons Italians Carry." It quoted an official at the Barge Office (where immigrants were being received while the new station at Ellis Island was under construction) as saying that two-thirds of all male immigrants landing there were armed with deadly weapons. There was no law permitting the immigration authorities to disarm them. The police said that "ninety-five out of every one hundred Italians are armed with some sort of deadly weapon." "The past year in New York and the immediate vicinity," the *Sun* declared, "there has been a daily average of at least two crimes of violence, such as shooting or stabbing, committed by Italians." The Italians "bore the mark of Cain" in American eyes, as John Higham has put it in his *Strangers in the Land*.[10]

Two years after the New Orleans lynching, the *Times* observed editorially that a recent shooting in Brooklyn was probably "the work of one of those criminal societies that are the pests of Italy and the pests of Italian immigration in this country." The violent passions of Italians and their readiness to resort to deadly weapons for the settlement of trivial quarrels made them very troublesome neighbors, it affirmed, and it was almost impossible to convict an Italian on Italian testimony. As long as Italians confined their murderous attentions to one another, the writer commented cynically, "Americans are not likely to pay much attention to their performances, although nothing can be more demoralizing to society than the immunity of criminals." But the Italian criminal societies, he pointed out, had no scruples about the nationality of their victims. "If these societies exist among us it behooves the detective force and the public prosecutor to do their utmost to stamp them out, lest they lead to some such a tragedy as the massacre at New-Orleans."

A few days later the *Times* modified its hostility considerably, after an interview with a former assistant district attorney. This gentleman was confident that the lawless element among the Italians, though existing, was by no means dominant and was yielding to the influence of the better class of immigrants. The bulk of the Italian immigration, he was sure, was made up of "hard workers, frugal, and generally temperate" and would be assimilated in the course of a generation. At the same time, as was made clear in a report by the Sanitary Aid Society on the Italian quarter centering in Mulberry Street, the dangerous element was made more dangerous by being crowded into unsanitary slums, within a rifle shot of the city hall. If these tenements were cleared out, many of the temptations to crime would be removed.[11]

Jacob Riis, crusading journalist, already had made the elimination of this slum district one of his major objectives. In his classic study of the New York slums, *How the Other Half Lives*, first published in 1890, he had noted that "Where Mulberry Street crooks like an elbow within hail of the old depravity of the Five Points, is 'the Bend,' foul core of New York's slums." Not many years before, the whole district, already notorious, had been heavily Irish. The "in-rush of the Italian tide," he noted, had "ever since opposed a stubborn barrier to all efforts at permanent improvement." Around "the Bend" clustered tenements that even the Health Department classified as "altogether bad." The persistent crusade that Riis led eventually brought about the demolition of the worst housing in the area and its replacement by a small park. Slum conditions continued, however, nearby in this and other Italian colonies as well as in the Jewish and other immigrant neighborhoods of the East Side. The relationship between the slum and crime, as cause and effect, has become a sociological commonplace since Riis's time.[12]

In 1893, *The Illustrated American* also took up the theme of Italian crime. The Italian element in New York, it argued, was hardly representative of Italian immigrants as a whole. Those who came to America with any sort of equipment for life in a new country preferred to make their way to the far West and South. These were mainly from the northern provinces. "But the riffraff and ragtag from Calabria, Naples, and Sicily, often men exiled by their government because of crimes of rapine and murder, prefer to take their chances in New York or the large cities nearby." *Il Progresso Italo-Americano*, one of the leading Italian newspapers in the city, took the *American* sharply to task, and the *American* published its protest. *Il Progresso* asserted with undoubted truth:

Every time that a poor, ignorant Italian laborer, whether in a drunken brawl or when tormented by one of those miserable

loafers who would try the patience of a saint, or as sometimes happens, provoked to defend his life, uses his knife or
revolver to wound, or alas! to kill his adversary, the American papers in relating the fact never forget to add to the name
of the criminal or murderer the word "Italian", as though it
were an absolute necessity to state the nationality of the culprit and almost as though to be an assassin one could not be
other than an Italian.

The mayor of Chicago, *Il Progresso* pointed out, had just
been murdered by a man whose name was obviously Irish.
Why didn't the newspapers say he was Irish? The *American*
tried to turn off this counterattack with a bitter jest. The
editor of *Il Progresso* evidently did not keep up with the
times, it said, as the name of his paper suggested he should.
He was a quarter of a century behind the times if he had not
learned that "the American republic has ceased to exist; that
to-day we are enjoying the beneficent rule of Irish dic-
tators."[13]

As a matter of fact, New York City had been under the
control of the corrupt Tammany regime for many years, and
since the downfall of Boss William M. Tweed in the early
1870s, its leadership had been Irish. The Irish-born Richard
Croker was its leader during the 1890s, and a large proportion of his underlings were Irish. When the different
boroughs were united under a single city government on
January 1, 1898, the elected mayor of Greater New York was
Robert Van Wyck, scion of an old Dutch family, but the orders were given by Croker, the Tammany boss. There was at
the time a bipartisan board of police commissioners, which
had done some good service to the city while it was under
the presidency of Theodore Roosevelt, during a reform administration that had interrupted Tammany rule. Early in
Van Wyck's administration the Republican members of the
board were ousted and replaced, and the reorganized board
retired the honest, incumbent chief of police on a pension.
Deputy Chief of Police William S. Devery, a lifelong Tammany man, a personal friend of Croker, and a police officer
with a very spotty record, was made acting chief of police
and later confirmed in the position.

Under Croker, Van Wyck, and Devery, who dominated
the police board and the single commissioner who succeeded

it, the city probably reached the lowest depths of corruption that it touched since Tweed's time. The biggest graft money, as usual, was in city contracts. As for law enforcement, the great concentration of gambling joints, cabarets, saloons, dance halls, and whorehouses in mid-Manhattan, known as the Tenderloin, offered the best sources of revenue. Officers with Tammany connections supervised operations there, levying tribute on all. A lesser but rowdier center of profit was the Bowery district, dominated by "Big Tim" Sullivan, a rising power in the Tammany organization. Honest cops found themselves assigned to duty elsewhere. There was some protection to the more polite neighborhoods, but very little attention was paid to what went on in the scattered Italian settlements in Manhattan, Brooklyn, and the Bronx.[14]

Giovanni Branchi served as Italian consul general in New York from 1895 to 1905. Replying, after his retirement, to an article in the London *Times* on the depredations of the Black Hand in America, he wrote from Rome:

> At that time we had certainly 250,000 to 300,000 Italians within the limits of Greater New York. Whole parts of the town, whole streets, were inhabited by Italians only, with their shops, cafes, etc. All these places were virtually without police supervision with the exception of the regular Irish policeman at the corner of the street, who did not care a rap what Italians did among themselves so long as they did not interfere with other people and as long as they voted the regular (Tammany) ticket. At that time there were on the force only two or three policemen who spoke or understood Italian, and the man who directed any detective or police operations among Italians (an excellent man, by the by) was only a sergeant. He many times told me that he had so many cases, so many inquiries, thrown on his hands that he could not possibly attend to half of them. As to other authorities, they did not trouble themselves at all about it, so much so that in nine cases out of ten any Italian committing a crime was nearly sure of going unpunished if he only escaped a few days from arrest.

Branchi and his government had tried to remedy this situation by arresting in Italy emigrants who, after committing crimes in New York, had escaped and returned to their native land. But even this was futile, "owing to the apathy and indifference of the New York authorities." In one case of murder, though everybody knew of the case and who the culprit was, the police had not taken the trouble to get out a warrant against the man. In another case where proceedings had been instituted, when Branchi informed the district attorney that the man would be prosecuted in Italy if the district attorney would supply him with the evidence, Branchi "was met with a demand for an exorbitant sum for the copy of the proceedings, etc. So I sent him word that the man would be set free and that New York would soon have the benefit of such a deserved citizen."[15]

A student of the Italians in Chicago has pointed out that they brought with them Old World traditions both good and bad. There was intense family loyalty and pride and a strong tendency for fellow townsmen to migrate together and to reproduce, as far as might be, their old communities. Loyalty did not go much beyond the old town group, however, and even within it there were sharp class cleavages and old .feuds. "The south Italian peasants," he notes, came not only with their virtues but "also brought with them to Chicago some of their less attractive customs." Ancient vendettas were fought out in the streets of the American city, and family honor was preserved, or its violation avenged, bloodily. Quite aside from these crimes of passion were the depredations of the Black Hand. "After 1900 the practice of extorting money under threat of death became so common as to cause a reign of terror in the Sicilian settlements."[16] So it was in New York and on a larger scale.

The upsurge of blackmail in the Italian districts of New York and other American cities followed hard on the heels of the tremendous rise in immigration from south Italy and Sicily that began around the turn of the century. Beginning with the fiscal year 1900, Italian immigration to the United States reached one hundred thousand; it remained in six digits steadily for fifteen years. Returning prosperity in this country after years of depression offered the pull; continuing poverty at home furnished the push for this migration. But the efforts of the Italian government to stamp out brigandage in Sardinia, Sicily, and Calabria also had something to do with it. America offered attractions to the brigand as well as to the honest laborer. There was no ubiquitous *carabinieri* to watch him here. There were likely to be fellow townsmen and former associates to shelter him. There were hundreds of thousands of susceptible fellow countrymen at work or in small businesses to prey upon.

The favorite method of enforcement of extortionist demands was the use of dynamite. Italian labor was used very extensively in the flourishing construction going forward in and near New York and other cities. Dynamite had replaced blasting powder in excavation work. A watchful pick-and-shovel man often could pick up a few unexploded sticks at the end of the day. There was always a profitable market for them among the blackmailing gangs. As late as 1917, when tight regulations on the sale and use of dynamite long had been in effect in New York, the police commissioner was warned that "workmen at the 14th street subway are 'getting away' with 2 or 3 sticks of dynamite daily."[17]

The extortionists who operated in New York were probably largely Sicilian, as they were in Chicago, and from the region around Palermo, "where the criminal element known as the *mafia* had thrived for decades." Mainland Italians in New York liked to think that this was the case. At a time when the police department had been considerably improved, there was organized a dragnet in search of all Italians carrying concealed weapons, after two plain-clothes policemen had been killed by a young man not long from Palermo. The county coroner, who first considered homicide cases, was himself an Italian. He received a letter signed by 200 Italian women protesting the action. The Sicilians had done the shooting, they said: "The Sicilian is blood-thirsty man; treacherous; thief; overbearing; vindictive; liar; counterfeiter. He belong to Black Hand. He exercises blackmail. Is a dynamiter, and by blood a coward." If the government wanted quietness in America, the letter advised Coroner Acritelli, "we must suppress the immigration from the Sicily. Then you will see if the Italians in America will not be mentioned any more criminally." Obviously there was no love lost between peninsular Italians and Sicilians. When police at headquarters heard about the letter, they said their orders had been to pick up Italians and admitted that they couldn't tell the difference between Sicilians and mainland Italians anyway.[18]

There was one flaw in the blistering indictment of the Sicilians by the Italian women that might have been pointed out at the time. The prize catch in the police roundup of weapons-carrying Italians had been Enrico Alfano, otherwise known as Erricone, recognized head of the Neapolitan Camorra and definitely *not* a Sicilian. He had been in New York hiding from a murder charge against him in Italy. While he may not have indulged in any nefarious activities during his sojourn here, he obviously was not a very savory character by any ordinary standards. The Italian government wanted him badly, and he was quickly deported.

If the extortion then going on was largely Sicilian and directed against Sicilians, it did not long remain within these strict limits. When a very active and diversified Black Hand gang was cracked a few years later and some of its members talked freely, they were found to be neither all Sicilians nor even Italians. The point was made clear that they preyed on anybody they could reach who seemed to have a little money or on anybody they were hired to attack by bomb or pistol. Their operations "shaped themselves into the system of a carefully directed organization. The bombs were exploded, either for the purposes of extorting money from the small merchants suspected of prosperity, or because the gang had been hired to throw them to satisfy the enmity of some one willing to pay the fee that sometimes was as high as $150." Sicilians and Neapolitans, one gangster volunteered, were likely to give money at the first threat, but "the Calabrians were apt to run to the police with the letter."[19]

For years Italians and Jews alike also had been moving into the world of the East Side fighting gangs, long the peculiar preserve of the Irish. Kate H. Claghorn, writing a chapter on the immigrants in New York for the U.S. Industrial Commission about 1900, spoke well of the Italians and the Jews but said they were being influenced for evil in the Bowery district by "the corrupt remnants of Irish immigration which now make up the beggars, the drunkards, the thugs, and thieves of those quarters." What the sociologists have come to call "ethnic succession," in crime as in other fields, was at work.

Perhaps the most powerful of the gangs of the lower East Side in the early 1900s, the Five Pointers, was led by Paul

Kelly, whose real name was Paolo Antonini Vacarelli. The chief rival of the Five Pointers was the Monk Eastman gang. Eastman, born Edward Osterman and of Jewish origin, sometimes called himself Edward Delaney, or William Delaney. While there was often friction on ethnic lines, Irish prestige in the underworld was great. The Five Pointers were largely Italian and the Eastmans largely Jewish, but contemporary accounts of their activities indicate that both gangs and their successor groups on the East Side were ethnically mixed. They included not only Irish, Italian, and Jewish elements but also reinforcements of native American roughs who wandered into the Bowery area from the West and South, liked the climate, and stayed. As Police Commissioner Theodore Bingham pointed out in 1908 when he was seeking funds and legislation to strengthen his department, the New York police had many problems to deal with that the greatly admired London police did not have to face. In London the alien population was not so large as to cut a serious figure in the statistics of crime, while the New York police "are compelled to deal with the predatory criminals of all nations, including our own." Most of the city's crime, Bingham contended, was committed by aliens, but they had no monopoly. "In spite of Federal laws the criminals of the Old World enter with comparative freedom at this port; many gravitate here who enter from other directions."[20]

These gangs, which sometimes fought bloody battles with each other and lesser satellite and independent gangs in various parts of town, enjoyed a large measure of protection from Tammany politicians and their allies in the city's police and judiciary. They thrived on prostitution, gambling, robbery, burglary, assault, and murder but made themselves useful on election day by voting repeatedly for approved candidates and intimidating the opposition. The gangs were composed largely and increasingly of second-generation immigrants, but they often were reinforced by newcomers with a criminal background. A confidential report presented to the police commissioner in 1908, prepared by an Italian criminologist "well versed in the ways of Italian criminals in this country and abroad," called attention to this. Many of "the most desperate Italian criminals," he declared, "after living in America a short time, associate themselves with some political gang for which they do work and receive in exchange unlimited protection." He often had heard in the case of a narrow escape from a criminal conviction: "Nothing doing against him. He is a Tammany Man."

The parole agent for the Prison Association of New York, to whom were paroled young men who had served short terms in the Elmira reformatory, reported in 1908 that it was mere poetry to speak of such men as first offenders. They were young toughs from the toughest section of the toughest city in the United States. "Some of them are native born, but a considerable number have come to our shores from Southern Italy, from Sicily and Calabria. We have now on parole two Italian blackmailers of the 'black hand' type,— and they look it." When serious offenders were sent to Elmira, it raised the question of what consideration influenced the courts. The reformatory had not reformed them, but merely restrained them from plundering the public for thirteen months. "When paroled to us, they are directed to go to a place to work which we have with considerable pains investigated and approved for them. Instead, they probably take a bee line for some Bowery dive where they meet their old pals and concert schemes for a new career of crime."[21]

Both John Torrio, born in Naples in 1882, and Al Capone, born in Brooklyn of Neapolitan parents in 1899, afterward leaders in Chicago's gangland, served at one time or another in the Five Points and successor gangs. So also did Lucky Luciano, born Salvatore Lucania in Sicily, who later became the most powerful figure in New York's underworld. In 1910 the keeper of a notorious hotel and bawdyhouse at 58th Street and Third Avenue, a former policeman dismissed from the force and apparently an Irishman, was heard to boast that nobody could touch his place, not even Mayor Gaynor. He had pull, he said, and "If anyone says anything he can have them hushed up in 4 hrs. on account of a gang of young Italians he has." Of the four gunmen executed for the murder of gambler Herman Rosenthal in 1912, three were Jewish and one Italian. Most of the characters involved in the case were Jewish, but Jewish gang leaders had no hesitation about hiring Italian gunmen. Luciano, though he served occasionally in established gangs, apparently began developing his own criminal organization as a boy on the lower East Side. It seems to have included Jewish as well as Italian members from the first. The Melting Pot seemed to be working, at least in New York's underworld.[22]

The Tammany–Van Wyck administration came to an end in 1901. Appalling conditions of vice had been revealed on the East Side, and a Citizens' Committee of Fifteen had roused public opinion against the machine. Boss Croker, alarmed by the growing revolt of reformers in his own party and their momentarily effective fusion with the Republicans, put up a clean and respected candidate for mayor, but he was beaten. Croker left politics and retired to his estates in England and Ireland. Seth Low, once mayor of Brooklyn and later president of Columbia University, was the winning Fusion party candidate and took office at the beginning of 1902. He set about reforming the police department at once. His first choice for the post of commissioner (which had replaced the former board) was John N. Partridge, who had served him in the same capacity in Brooklyn some years before. Partridge brought in new assistants and made a number of promotions, demotions, and transfers to try to break up the massive system of corruption in the department; but he did not move fast enough to suit the reformers. Low was put under pressure to replace him, and Partridge resigned loyally and without protest at the end of the year. He was replaced by General Francis V. Greene, a professional soldier with a distinguished record who had retired and gone into business. Under Commissioner Greene there was a thorough shakeup in the police department. "Discipline returned to the force," a student of Low's administration says, "the bribery system was largely abolished, and the red light districts lost their glow."[23]

Greene concentrated on the hardy, perennial problems of vice, gambling, and liquor control, with accompanying graft in his department, but he did give his few Italian detectives his active support and encouraged their cooperation with federal authorities. One of the most spectacular cases yet to come up in the Italian community, and one that gave the press a field day on Italian crime in general and the Mafia in particular, occurred during his term. A badly mutilated body was found stuffed into a barrel on East 11th Street in Manhattan. The case reminded police of the murder the year before of Brooklyn grocer Giuseppe Catania, whose partially dismembered body had been found in a sack on the beach in Bay Ridge. Catania's murderers had not been found, but the motive had been traced to a criminal case in Palermo twenty years before in which Catania's testimony had sent a number of men to prison for a twenty-year stretch. Police were convinced that it was the work of the Mafia, which "permeates every branch of activity throughout Sicily," according to the *Brooklyn Eagle*.

This time there were quick arrests, and it developed that both the Secret Service and Detective Sergeant Joseph Petrosino, "the Italian sergeant," who came from the Salerno district, had kept a gang on Elizabeth Street under surveillance for months as suspected counterfeiters and blackmailers. Some of the members had already been convicted on counterfeiting charges. The murdered man had been seen in the company of gang members only a day or two before his body was found. City and federal officers joined in the roundup, and Petrosino identified the body through an interview with a convict serving time for counterfeiting in Sing Sing prison. It was that of Benedetto Maduena (or Madonia), allegedly a former member of the gang who had been hiding out in Buffalo. He had returned to New York, said the convict, his brother-in-law, to get their share of the gang's loot. Petrosino believed that the gang was responsible not only for the Maduena killing but also for that of Catania.[24]

The term *Black Hand* had not yet come into vogue. All of the arrested men were Sicilians, and Agent William J. Flynn of the Secret Service was convinced that the gang was a local branch of the Mafia, "perhaps the most secret and terrible organization in the world." His staff had, he said, "a surprisingly vast amount" of knowledge of the Mafia, which had been active in New York as counterfeiters as early as 1884. Secret Service men had tracked a gang of counterfeiters to New York in the spring of that year. The murder of Flaccomio four years later, as a supposed betrayer of secrets, had been the work of this gang. "The police were not at that time familiar with all of the facts," Flynn told a feature writer for the *Sun*. "They did know, however, that a Mafia counterfeiting band had killed Flaccomio" and were responsible for other deaths. The word "Mafia," originating in Sicily, was taken up here, according to Flynn, when the Italian counterfeiters began to organize in bands all over the country. "It connected these bands like the links of a chain, and they began to acknowledge a certain ill-defined obedience to the chiefs or influential members." Secret Service men had tracked them from one city to another, now and then discovering a counterfeiting den and sending a batch of counterfeiters to jail. But as fast as one band was broken up, another was organized. There were several bands or branches of them in New York. They had operated in Boston, New Orleans, and Chicago but seemed at last to have established central headquarters in New York.

Flynn may not have been exaggerating the facts about the Italian counterfeiting gangs, and the Secret Service had evidently accepted the Mafia label for them for some time. In 1896 its agents had rounded up a gang of Italian counterfeiters in New York, and "May Be Mafia Leaders" was the heading in the *Times*. William B. Hazen, then chief of the Service, had captured with them correspondence that convinced him that Nicolo Taranto and Candelara Bettini, the principal figures in the gang, "were leaders of the Mafia, whose criminal deeds have from time to time startled peaceable communities in the United States." The correspondence captured in Taranto's apartment then was translated and "besides connecting the men with the Mafia, [it] showed that from this city Italians in Philadelphia, Baltimore, Scranton, and other towns in the coal regions of Pennsylvania engaged in passing counterfeit bills were supplied with the bad notes."

There was a general society in Italy, Flynn now affirmed, with a branch in each province. Emigrants coming to America preserved their affiliation, scattering to various cities but banding together in them "for the purpose of committing crimes for gain." The *Herald* gave the barrel murder extensive coverage and freely referred to the arrested men as "the Mafia band." At first, it found, Italians would not talk to reporters about the case. "A veritable reign of terror has been inspired throughout the various Italian colonies in Greater New York . . . . Sources of information which have always been open to newspaper men have been absolutely closed so far as it relates to the Mafia band." It was obviously hated and feared by Italians. A little later, however, a persistent *Herald* reporter did get statements from leaders in the Italian community:

> Certain prominent Italian-American citizens have felt constrained to declare and even publish a denial that there is anything akin to the Sicilian Mafia at work in the metropolis. On the other hand there are certain other Italian-Americans here who regard this as false patriotism, and who prefer to have the whole truth known . . .
>
> These men not only assert that the Mafia is operating here, but that it has developed dangerous powers. While confessing a shame in the acknowledgement of these things, these men profess a pride in the true Italian civilization and desire to clear its reputation by proving that not all Italians here are banditti by nature or through opportunity.

Such men were quoted as admitting that "the Mafia is at work in New-York to-day." It had been suggested that the matter might be brought before the Italian Chamber of Commerce. The facts, the *Herald* admitted, were as hard to get at as proof of political corruption.

No doubt there were great differences of opinion in the Italian community. Some weeks before the barrel murder case there was a meeting of the Get Together Club at the St. George Hotel in Brooklyn, where the subject of discussion was "The Italians in New York." Prominent Americans, including Dr. Lyman Abbott and Dr. Eliot Norton, as well as local settlement workers took part. Dr. Lorenzo Ullo, who had been on the legal staff at Ellis Island, reviewed the history of Italian immigration. According to him, the earlier Italian immigrants had been largely political refugees and of the better class.

"During the seventies an entirely different element came here, after the unification of Italy. It was made up of the bandits, outlaws—Mafia, if you will—who had been protected by the old regime. These characters gave my race a bad name, which it has been difficult to wipe out." But the

Mafia, he stated positively, was a thing of the past. The *Bollettino della Sera*, whose editor had attended the meeting, was certainly not alone in resenting the fact that "that odious word 'mafia' is continually thrown in our faces," and in calling attention to Kentucky mountain feuds and other American lawlessness.[25]

Ignazio Lupo, one of the gang members picked up after the barrel murder, was supposed to be the treasurer of the local branch of the Mafia. Much literature of the society had been picked up in his apartment, it was reported. Giuseppe Morello was the leader of the gang and was believed to be "the head of the Palermo Society of the Mafia in this country," directing its affairs in many cities. Counterfeiting, Flynn said, was the chief crime Secret Service agents had found them to indulge in all over the country. In some places, as a sort of side line, they practiced blackmail. "The local authorities," said the *Times*, "now believe that the gang they have under arrest engaged in this business more extensively than they had supposed previously and that the power of the gang was very great."

The Italian police had to deal regularly with secret criminal organizations, the *Brooklyn Eagle* noted. "It is the most natural thing in the world when leaders of these organizations find their home haunts too hot for them that they should emigrate to this country." Until very recently Italian colonies had not been under systematic or skillful observation here, and the chance for an outlaw from home to conceal himself among them had been excellent. "Once here it is extremely unlikely that these leopards would change their spots, and we may as well accept the existence of the Mafia in more or less effective organization as one of the facts with which our police and criminal courts will be called upon to deal."[26]

Gino C. Speranza, a New York lawyer of Italian ancestry who was involved in a number of activities looking to the well-being of the Italian community, took issue at once with this interpretation. The *Times* had given an account of the Mafia, he noted in a letter to the editor, and made the statement that "Italians of all stations" feared to talk about it. But there was not a man in a hundred thousand among the Italians, with whom he identified himself, who was afraid of the Mafia or of talking about it. He would be glad to give the police "all that is known about the Mafia since the time of the Sicilian Vespers several centuries ago." He would advise Flynn of the Secret Service to take a trip to Italy to study the Mafia on the spot "and see if it is 'a general society,' with a branch in each province." It was not surprising to him that certain yellow journals should give publicity to such police vagaries, but it was strange "that the *Times* should consider such stuff 'news that's fit to print.' " As a lawyer and student of criminal problems, he had "no hesitation in characterizing the police talk about the Mafia as arrant nonsense." The police would do better to devote their energies to detecting criminals than to turn their talents to the production of fiction.

But the newspapers continued to refer to the Mafia as the principal source of crime among Italians. The Mafia, the *World* declared, was "now almost as strongly entrenched in New York, New Orleans and Chicago as in its Sicilian home," but a complete history of the order would never be written. Its records were scattered or locked up in the minds of men who knew that death was the certain fate of he who told. "Unlike other societies it has no fixed organization, no permanent laws, no supreme director, no central headquarters." It existed in a chain of small coteries, all pledged to the Mafia greed of illicit gain. It had spread all over the civilized world "wherever Sicilians have settled in numbers." In the fact that the Italians in New York had contributed a large fund for the defense of Morello and his confederates the *Tribune* saw an indication that there was "an institution on this side of the Atlantic of the same degree of criminal terrorism, and a distrust in the efficacy of protection by the law and the police as prevails on the other side of the Atlantic."[27]

A *Times* reporter sought interviews with informed Italians on the subject, as the *Herald* did. His story appeared under the headline, "Declares Mafia Cry Is a Police Fiction." Some Italians admitted that there was once such an organization as the Mafia in Sicily but said that it was now dead, "with its elements remaining only in various unassociated bands of criminals, such as exist among all nationalities." Speranza, identified as a director of the Prison Association of New York, was among those interviewed. He said that he was not surprised that the American people should accept the Mafia as a reality. People in Italy were equally ignorant of America. "For instance, there everybody imagines that justice in America is dealt out by a great supreme Judge called Lynch." At a time when lynchings, usually of Negroes but sometimes of Italians and other foreigners and occasionally of native whites, were of almost daily occurrence in the United States, this was a shrewd thrust. As for the Mafia, it had never existed outside Sicily. "At the present time," Speranza said, "I would call it a sort of Tammany Hall in its worst form and dealing with its own problems in its own way. It is largely confined to Palermo and does not assassinate except in extreme cases. It is more political than criminal, and numbers both rich and poor among its members."

Speranza, though American born, was highly sensitive on the subject of the Mafia. In the following year the social service periodical *Charities* prepared a special Italian issue and submitted all the proposed material to him for review. After some argument, he saw to it that an intended article on the Mafia did not appear. In a brief article of his own, he was highly critical of the American press for playing up stories on Italian bandits and running "half-page headlines on the mafia," but never a word on progress in modern Italy. "One result of the unfriendliness of the popular American press," he declared, "is that it drives Italians to support a rather unwholesome colonial Italian press." Why should Italians read American papers that told only of the misdeeds of their compatriots? It was better to support a local press that, however poor and often dishonest, "keeps up the courage of these expatriates by telling them what young Italy is bravely doing at home and abroad."[28]

Not long after the excitement over the barrel murder had begun to die down, there was an attack on a former Italian Secret Service officer who had been in this country only five days. A young Italian came up behind him on a Brooklyn street in daylight and cut his throat with a razor. The young man was captured. His victim, who was terribly gashed but lived, asked him why he had done it. "I do not know you," was the reply, "but you were pointed out to me. I was ordered to kill you." At once the cry of Mafia was raised. A report was sent to Commissioner Greene. Greene indicated only that he would do everything possible to solve the mystery of the attack, but the *World* headlined the story, "Greene Will Stamp Out the Mafia Here." Effectively squelched in New Orleans by the public uprising that followed the murder of Chief of Police Hennessy, "the death-dealing society has seemingly moved its headquarters to New York." A list of Mafia atrocities for even the current year, it said, "would far exceed the limits of newspaper space."

Sergeant Anthony Vachris (Vaccarezza) of the Brooklyn detective force, who came from Genoa, was assigned to the case. He was struck by the fact that the men involved were not Sicilians but Calabrians. He thought the case was one of mistaken identity, the work of what he called the "Strong Arm" gang, who had been levying blackmail on Italians who had means. They were "a desperate lot of fellows," he admitted, and their favorite form of punishment was to slash the face or neck with a razor. Vachris, who a few months later handled the Cappiello Black Hand case, did not identify them as Mafia. A little later an article in the Sunday *Eagle* on Italian immigration discounted the society's existence in this country. The author had consulted, among others, "An Italian whose work has made him conversant with the doings of the criminal class in this country." This gentleman, who may possibly have been Speranza, was quoted as saying that the coming of large numbers of mostly illiterate Sicilians and Calabrians meant more trouble. They went in fear of American roughs and armed themselves as well as they could. But, "As for the Mafia, there's nothing in it. I've known all classes of these people for years, and I tell you plainly there is no Mafia in America." Most of the killings amongst Italians occurred in fights, he said, and the men who were mixed up in them would stand by one another. Anybody who gave information to the police was likely to be killed. It was true that they did have a word for a bad man, "mafioso," but it meant about the same thing as "tough guy" on the Bowery.[29]

In the light of this information, coming from presumably

well-informed sources, it is perhaps not surprising that the New York metropolitan journals seized on the new term *Black Hand*, when it was offered to them a few months later, as a more colorful substitute for Mafia, one perhaps less offensive to Italians. Neither is it surprising that the new scare words should have first come into use in New York just when they did, in 1903. Charles W. Heckethorn, a British writer who made the history of secret societies a lifelong study, published a two-volume work on the subject in 1875. In it he told of the Camorra of Naples, but made no mention of Black Hand or even of Mafia. In another edition, more than twenty years later, he elaborated his account of the Camorra, described the Mafia, and told of a Black Hand, or Mano Negra, society that had existed in Spain, beginning about 1835. It was organized among agricultural laborers who had been deprived of communal rights when large estates had been broken up and sold. It was, he said, strictly secret and highly organized and inflicted death and other penalties on its own members and on landlords and usurers. It later degenerated into criminality. It was active in Andalusia around 1880 and was suppressed by the Spanish government.

In 1903, after reports of Black Hand activities in New York had circulated in Europe, a French writer, Marcel Colliere, attempted to account for the name. He said that the Spanish society, the Mano Negra, was invented out of whole cloth by a provincial chief of gendarmes in Andalusia. This was done to help incriminate the anarchist organizers of the local peasantry in their struggle with the oppressive landlords. He had drawn his inspiration from seeing black hands printed in ink on village walls to indicate a road to be followed. His chief assistant had providentially found the constitution of the society hidden under a stone, showing it to be an association that "dreamed only of massacre and pillage." In 1882, following a local murder, there were criminal proceedings resulting in a number of executions and many prison sentences, mostly on charges of belonging to La Mano Negra.

Gerald Brenan's informative study of the background of the Spanish Civil War tells of the growth of the anarchist movement in Spain and of the Mano Negra trials in 1882.

"Thousands of arrests were made"; he says, "there were three hundred sentences of imprisonment and, after the usual tortures to obtain evidence, eight executions. Yet the very existence of the *Mano Negra* has been disputed." The circumstances of the criminal proceedings indicated that the whole thing was an invention of the police, but later evidence made it appear that there were secret societies at work. What was also certain was that "the police enormously magnified the whole matter and took advantage of it to condemn the leading Anarchists of the district without any regard to whether they were innocent or guilty."

The Mano Negra, real or imaginary, came to be known and admired in Sicily. It was reported a few years later that the "Fratellanza of Girgenti" was modeled on it. A British criminologist in 1899 took the Spanish society seriously and stated that at one time it had more than forty thousand members. "The operations of another society, that of the 'Fraternal Hand of Sicily,' " he said, "which was inoffensive and even philanthropic in its origins, a society intended for mutual help, degenerated into criminal courses."

It seems likely that Don Tomas Perez Monforte, chief of gendarmes of the province of Jerez de la Frontera, had simply revived a symbol already known in Spain to meet his own immediate needs. David Chandler, in his recent rather startling study of criminal brotherhoods, has shown that the symbol of a black hand was actually used for extortion purposes in Louisiana as early as 1855. A mixed Spanish and Italian criminal gang in New Orleans was broken up a few years later, and nothing further was heard of the Black Hand there for many years.

Chandler has traced what he calls the Black Hand briefly to New York and other cities in succeeding years. Certainly there seems to have been sporadic blackmail in Italian colonies, whether the name or the symbol of the black hand was used or not. In 1882 some Sicilian extortionists were arrested in New York after they had demanded $500 from an Italian fruit merchant on pain of death. They had not used a black hand but a revolver cartridge as their threatening symbol. Contemporary newspaper accounts made no mention of Black Hand, though the police evidently believed that the extortionists belonged to some larger group. The *Sun* called

their efforts only a "Picturesque Attempt to Extort Money."
The Italian detective who had made the arrest told reporters
that "this sort of attempt to extort money was a popular
proceeding in Italy until recent severe enactments for its
suppression by the Government." He assured them that the
men under arrest were "not cowards like the American
blackmailers, but desperate fellows who would have put
their threats into execution had they not been frustrated."

Black Hand was not a recognized terrorist symbol in New
York for many years to come, and extortion seems not yet
to have been a common practice among Italians in the city.
By 1893, however, the editor of *Il Progresso* could speak of
"those miserable loafers who would try the patience of a
saint"—by which he evidently meant extortionists—as at
work in the Italian community. He did not call them Black
Handers.

Dwight Smith, in his new and scholarly study of the
growth of the Mafia legend in the United States, calls attention to a Black Hand Society in Puerto Rico. The American
troops occupying the island after the close of hostilities with
Spain in 1898 discovered a secret society at work back in the
mountains, using the black print of a human hand as a symbol and committing atrocities against Spaniards and former
collaborators with the Spanish authorities. This society was
presumably purely Spanish in origin, an echo of the Andalu-
sian brotherhood. It was said to have been in existence on
the island before the beginning of the Spanish-American
War.

Revival of the Black Hand, under its Italian name of Mano
Nera, came in 1903 and was probably associated with the
fresh publicity given to the Spanish society. In 1902 a series
of articles appeared in a Madrid labor periodical exposing
the Mano Negra trials as a terrible miscarriage of justice.
These articles were reprinted in left-wing journals all over
Europe. Early in 1903 the Spanish minister of justice was
forced to bring the cases of the surviving prisoners up for
review. Any literate Italian laborer arriving in the United
States at the time had probably read of Mano Negra. Any
Italian immigrant of a criminal bent, newly arrived or resident, might have thought highly of such an organization with
its terrifying symbol.[30]

CHAPTER II
A Growing Police Problem

The gang that had been rounded up after the barrel murder escaped the penalties of the law. At the morgue they all denied knowing the deceased. None of the accused could be broken by questioning, which was prolonged and undoubtedly severe. Flynn of the Secret Service, who took an active part in the proceedings, later criticized the police for having made the mistake of locking up the gang together, "so that they could speak and plan together." When the magistrate at Jefferson Market Court refused to hold them any longer, they immediately were rearrested by order of the coroner and held for his court. Coroner Scholer had great difficulty in forming a jury for an inquest. "Italians called as witnesses showed utter lack of knowledge of things they were known to have seen," the *Tribune* reported, "and even denied being acquainted with friends." It appeared that "fear of the Mafia and its blood thirsty gang here has led to the forced collection of a fund for the defense of the prisoners and caused uneasiness in men called to serve on the jury." A coroner's jury of prominent businessmen was finally impaneled, with not an Italian name on the list.

The inquest, which was long and grilling, was the nearest thing to a trial that most of the men received. The jury, after prolonged hearings, finally held seven of the men as accessories to murder but declared itself unable to designate the assassin. Later most of the seven were released. The murder charges were concentrated on one Tommaso Petto, known as Petto the Ox because of his physique, or Petto the Bull

("Il Bove"). A pawn ticket for Maduena's watch had been found on him. The watch had been redeemed, and Petrosino had taken it to Buffalo, where it was identified by the victim's family. A question of Petto's identity had come up, however. Petrosino's biographer says that an actual substitution had been made and that the man held for murder was not Petto at all but one Giovanni Carlo Costantino, who recently had come to the United States and changed his name to Giovanni Pecoraro. The district attorney himself was quoted by the *Eagle* as saying that the man held for murder was not really named Petto but was Giovanni Pecoraro—that he used Petto as an alias. The real Petto, the *Herald* understood, was still at liberty but had no connection with the case.

Nevertheless, a grand jury brought an indictment for murder in the first degree against the man under the name of Petto. Whoever he was, he was finally discharged for lack of evidence and disappeared at once. The real Petto, Flynn said later in his book about the barrel murder, was eventually traced to Pittston, Pennsylvania, by the Secret Service. He began Black Hand operations among the Italian miners there but was murdered, in revenge for the Maduena killing as Flynn believed. Several members of the gang, rearrested by United States marshals on counterfeiting charges, also slipped through the fingers of the federal authorities. But Flynn, and Petrosino as long as he lived, kept their eyes on the gang. Flynn had found that they all came from a single town, Corleone, in western Sicily, and that they had frequent contact with fellow townsmen in Chicago, New Orleans, and other cities. As they had contacts in distant cities, so did the Secret Service have informers. Most of them eventually were rounded up as counterfeiters, bringing a period of relative peace to the vicinity of Elizabeth Street.[1]

The gang headed by Ignazio Lupo (later always referred to by the press as "Lupo the Wolf") and Giuseppe Morello certainly had great influence in the Italian community of New York. Some of the proceedings against them in 1903 suggest that it was not without influence in other circles. It was far from omnipotent, however, even among Italians.

When the gang was hauled into court, there was a forced collection for its defense throughout the city and even in New Jersey, but there was also considerable resistance to it. "Many Italians of Newark have bought second-hand revolvers and guns in the last few days," the *Tribune* reported late in April, "and about every house in the several Italian colonies there now looks like an arsenal. The Italians, it is said, have armed themselves for fear of the Mafia, for which they refused to contribute for the defense fund for the men held in this city in connection with the 'barrel murder mystery.'" A committee from New York had canvassed Newark for the purpose but got very little. The committee then vowed vengeance. "Now, every Italian house is guarded day and night. At different hours of the night shots are exchanged from windows as a sort of warning."

The shakedown extended into the Bronx. Giovanni Bancale, of 802 East 187th Street, applied to the Morrisania magistrate's court for a permit to carry a revolver. He had had five Italians arrested "on charges of trying to extort money from him to defray the expenses of the prisoners in the barrel murder case." All that night Italians whom he had never seen called at his house and told him that if he did not withdraw the charges "he would be punished by the Mafia as Benedetto Madonia had been, besides being subjected to horrible torture before he was actually killed." He appeared distracted with fright. The magistrate referred him to the precinct police captain. Not all the Italian community, by any means, was prepared to submit tamely to the shakedown, Mafia or no Mafia. Some, like Bancale, sought redress through the courts in the approved American manner. The Newark Italians formed a vigilance committee, following, consciously or unconsciously, another good American tradition.[2]

Mayor Low was charged with loading up his Fusion administration with Republicans, and many of the reform Democrats who had helped put him in office began drifting back into the ranks of the regulars. He was cold and rather abrupt in manner, lacking in what is now known as charisma. Lincoln Steffens, who probably understood the inner workings of American cities better than any other man of the time, testified to the reality of good government under the Low administration. But business interests, he believed, had concluded "that good government hurt business in New York, somehow," and the voters as a whole had had a surfeit of reform. The efforts of the occasional reform administration, such as that of Low, to close the saloons on Sunday and to stamp out gambling entirely inevitably produced a reaction. Landlords, including aristocratic churches, that collected higher rents from their tenement properties when they were used for illegal purposes were naturally tepid at best in their reform enthusiasm. Hotels, of course, suffered when "the lid" was lowered on gambling and prostitution.

The Tammany organization had evolved new leadership in the person of Charles F. Murphy. Thoroughly schooled in the spoils system and certainly no knight in shining armor, Murphy was a man of force and organizing ability. He was also a good Catholic churchman with certain scruples, morally a considerable improvement over the ruthless and cynical Croker. In 1903 Murphy picked George B. McClellan, Jr., son of the Civil War general, as Tammany's candidate for mayor. McClellan accepted reluctantly. He was a lifelong Democrat and had served several terms in Congress, where he was more or less out of the recurring scandals of Tammany Hall, though sponsored by the organization. He was a gentleman and a scholar, and honest Democrats could support him with a clear conscience. The votes of all those connected with what then was called the "System" of protection to illegal activities were his without question. Low and Police Commissioner Greene had made their lives difficult. McClellan easily defeated Low's bid for reelection. There was wild rejoicing in the Tenderloin when the returns came in. "We have slid back into the black slime and ooze of the Van Wyck administration," the *Times* commented sadly.[3]

McClellan's choice of police commissioner, in which Murphy did not interfere, made the *Times* feel better about the new administration. William McAdoo, who had served in Congress and had been assistant secretary of the Navy under President Cleveland, was "a man of courage, of probity, and of positive force of character," it admitted. "If he can equal the record Commissioner Greene has made he will be successful," but he would have to count on the deadly hostility of the evil and really controlling elements in Tammany Hall. The Tenderloin, which had expected a return of wide-open rule like that of Big Bill Devery, was bitterly disappointed. McClellan, writing to the *Times* representative in London, assured him that " 'The Lid is screwed on tight' and I propose to keep it on as long as I am Mayor."[4]

This promise proved to be a little more than he could make good, but under McClellan, Commissioner McAdoo made valiant efforts to cut down corruption and enforce the laws relating to gambling, vice, and liquor control. District Attorney William Travers Jerome of New York County, who had come into office on the reform wave two years before and had cooperated actively with Commissioner Greene, gave him a high rating early in his term. McAdoo was "certainly the best police commissioner New York ever had," Jerome told a *Times* reporter. McAdoo also made an attempt to cope with the rising tide of extortion in the Italian community.

In 1904 a number of such cases made headlines. Early in March, Cologne Decaneine, living at 342 East 40th Street, received a letter written in red ink from the "Black Hand Society." He was instructed to meet a member of the society at the Brooklyn end of the Brooklyn Bridge the same night and to have with him $100 in cash. He was informed that "If you do not keep the appointment prepare for death within ten days." The letter was covered with sketches of daggers, pistols, skulls, and crossbones. Decaneine took the letter to the East 35th Street station and turned it over to the police.

In May the Italian colony at Fourth Avenue and 20th Street in Brooklyn was thrown into panic when the house of Antonio Bartolatta, a grocer, was bombed. "Their demands for money ignored by their intended victim," the *Times* reported, "Italian blackmailers in Brooklyn attempted . . . to blow the victim and his house to pieces with dynamite, and almost succeeded in totally wrecking the house." The man picked out for death escaped unhurt. Bartolatta had received three letters demanding $500 but had decided to ignore them. The last letter said he and his family would be "put out of the way." He insisted that he had no idea who the perpetrators were. The next day he received another letter saying that if he continued to assist the police he would be immediately assassinated. This letter was signed only with a cross. The Black Hand name and symbol were becoming popular but were not invariably used by the extortionists. "Bartolatta was on the verge of collapse" when he reached the police station with the letter. He declared that a man the police had arrested on suspicion was a good man, a neighbor, and wanted to furnish bail for him. The police always rushed out and arrested somebody, he said, without evidence and without waiting.

Poggioroale Ciro's little grocery store at 252 Elizabeth Street, in a Sicilian neighborhood, was wrecked in July by a dynamite bomb after he had turned over to the police a blackmailing letter written in red ink, with a skull and crossbones at the top and signed with a black hand. Ciro had been receiving the letters for some time. They all demanded $2,000 on threat of blowing him and his wife into atoms. A *Times* reporter talked to Captain Martens, in charge of the local police precinct. Martens said he had had at least fifty cases of blackmailing brought to his attention since he had been in charge; predatory bands composed almost exclusively of Sicilians had been making a good thing out of blackmailing prosperous Italians. "There is very little hope, in my mind," said the captain, "of ever breaking up these secret bands, from the fact that the Italians of all classes are in such mortal terror of the blackmailers that they do not dare to give the police any assistance whatever for fear that they will be marked for vengeance and murdered." Ciro, whose store had been blown up, though he had dared to take one threatening letter to the police, soon quit talking, telling detectives "that it would be as much as his life was worth to do any further talking along that line."[5]

In August, Ruggiero Nicosia, a barber of 214 Second Street in Manhattan, received two Black Hand letters threatening to kill him and his family if he did not pay $4,000. He turned the letters over to the police, and Sergeant Petrosino and one of his men laid a trap. Giuseppe Massaro called on the barber in his shop, and Nicosia gave him a roll of marked bills. The detectives jumped out and seized Massaro with the marked money on him. Then they went to Massaro's rooms on East Third Street and arrested his brother Filippo. Nicosia courageously appeared against them in court. They refused to let Petrosino act as interpreter for them, and bootblacks and laborers passing on the street were brought into the court to act in this capacity. "These recruits showed no little fear of the 'Black Hand', particularly those who were born in Sicily. They tried their best to show that they did not understand the dialect." Nevertheless, the magistrate held the Massaros in lieu of $2,500 bail to answer to the charge of extortion.[6]

Shortly afterward Antonio Mannino, the little son of a Brooklyn Italian contractor, disappeared. The young man who had led the boy away was captured and confessed, but it was soon recognized that he was only a tool. His statement turned up some suspects and even a possible link with the gang suspected of the barrel murder the year before. Italian colonies were combed and some fruitless arrests were made. The father and his partner, who indicated that they were making a search of their own, soon stopped talking to the police. The boy turned up unharmed. The police tried to have him identify the house in Harlem where he had been held captive, but without result. The Brooklyn police precinct captain had already been warned by post card signed, "The Black Hand," to "Stop chasing us or you will be killed." After the boy was returned the captain received another "anonymous letter of the 'Black Hand' variety," threatening to blow up the station house with dynamite unless the hunt for the kidnappers was abandoned. Mannino had paid the ransom for the boy, the police were informed, and would never appear against any of the suspects. Another kidnapping in the same neighborhood was promised soon.[7]

A feature article in the Sunday *Tribune*, entitled "Italian Crime and Police Incompetence," now noted that the city's detectives seemed "utterly unable to unearth the 'Black Hand' conspirators."

> The city is confronted with an Italian problem with which at the present time it seems unable to cope. Citizens are waking up mornings to read "Black Hand" letters demanding extortionate sums of money, to be deposited in some out of the way rendez-

vous or else a pistol shot or dynamite bomb will end their days.
Some of these letters have been turned over to the police, but it is
believed that not one-tenth of them have been made public.
Besides such threats, there have also been acts of violence and
even of death. Boys have been kidnapped and held for ransom.
Homes have been wrecked with dynamite on the failure of their
tenants to pay blackmail, and not long ago an Italian was murdered and his body thrust into a barrel and abandoned because he
had aroused the vengeance of a gang of conspirators.

In its efforts to grapple with these forms of crime the Police
Department has shown itself especially incompetent. Officers
make a series of theatrical arrests, only to be compelled to let
their prisoners go. Mysterious witnesses are unearthed, who,
after many dark hints, leave Police Headquarters as mysteriously as they went there. In the case of the "barrel murder," after
the city had gone to great cost in "scouring the East Side," in
arresting "alleged cutthroats" and in "giving them the third
degree," it was at last requited by seeing the whole gang go free.
In much the same way the police allowed the kidnappers of
nine-year-old Antonio Mannino to slip through their fingers while
following clews which led one moment to a Pittsburg slum and
the next to a Hoboken cave.

As the police have shown themselves more and more helpless,
the criminal Italian element has become bolder, until the better
class of Italians have become thoroughly alarmed. Meetings
have been held by some of the more prominent Italian citizens to
devise some way of purging the Italian name of the obloquy with
which certain vicious members of their colony have defamed it,
and a few have taken special personal precautions against the
kidnapping of their children . . . .

The *Tribune* thought that the barrel murder had had "the stamp
of the Mafia" and the Mannino kidnaping the "thumbmarks of
the Camorra." A *Tribune* reporter had toured the district around
Elizabeth Street with "an Italian detective," who pointed out a
number of men he knew to be Mafia but against whom he could
prove nothing. The detective did not think that they had been
able to reorganize here, however, though the reporter thought
this would be simple and easy.

A *Times* editorial a few days later, "There Is a Way," took a
strong line on Italian crime and its prevention. Noting that the
police had failed to find the kidnapers of the Italian boy who was
so mysteriously returned to his parents, it strongly suspected
that the father of the boy had compounded with the felons by
complying with their demands for money. "That is another

illustration of the Italian habit of getting along without the law or the police." It was notorious that Italian crimes were the most difficult ones American detectives had to deal with. "We have too many bad Italians already, and since the good Italians so generally refuse to give any information to the police which might assist them in their efforts to run down criminals of their race, we may be unable in any protective measures we adopt to distinguish in every case the good Italian immigrant from the bad Italian immigrant." But we must protect ourselves. "The imported Italian variety of crime, notably kidnapping and murder," said the *Times*, speaking as though these were Italian monopolies, "has begun to flourish here quite beyond the limit of toleration." If Italians domiciled in the United States thought it good policy to shield from police pursuit criminals of their race, "we may find it necessary to stop immigration altogether from Southern Italy and Sicily."[8]

Some weeks later Commissioner McAdoo announced some changes in the police department. A number of so-called detectives who had been appointed to headquarters at the end of the Devery regime, who had been "worse than an incumbrance to the detective force," were to be demoted and banished to the precincts. A new departure consisted in the organization of an Italian branch of the police force, "to deal with the peculiar problems constantly arising in the Italian districts." Petrosino had no doubt been urging such a step for some time, as his biographer states. This change was to go into effect at once, and McAdoo had high hopes of its success. "I have made arrangements to utilize the Italians on the police force in the congested Italian districts," he stated. "We have also established a small staff of Italians for general work under the direction of Detective Sergeant Petrosino."

There were not many Italians on the force, he noted, and he would be glad to see more of them take the civil service examination for patrolman, to make their numbers more proportionate to the large Italian population. An Italian criminal sought refuge behind racial and national sympathy, he said, not mentioning the sheer terror that was the usual motivation, "and many of his countrymen, otherwise honest, believe it a sort of patriotic duty to shield him from the officers of the law." Police work would not get the results desired unless it was followed up by a moral movement on the part of the better class of Italians and the Italian newspapers. They must be made to understand that the police were not their enemies but their friends.[9]

The most sympathetic and factual account of Italian immigration that so far had been published in the United States, *The Italian in America*, came out the following year. It bestowed a large measure of praise on Commissioner McAdoo and the new "Italian Department" of his detective force. "An admirable object lesson to every community plagued by blackmailers is offered in the method devised last year by Commissioner McAdoo in New York City for the detection and arrest of blackmailers and criminals of every stripe in the Italian quarters of Greater New York." This new unit of his detective force was "headed by one of the most competent members of his staff, Detective Sergeant Petrosino." This force was made up of "alert, keen and trustworthy men of Italian descent thoroughly familiar with the Italian quarters." They were quick to pounce upon the rascals that had been infesting those quarters and furnishing the newspapers with visions of an imported Mafia. The commissioner did not believe in any such bogy organization, but he was determined to stamp out the blackmailing pest "in every guise in which it appears." McAdoo reported "a gratifying reduction" in blackmailing and other crimes in the Italian colonies. "No measure of the Commissioner's administration has been better conceived and more signally successful," said the authors. The mass of Italians had confidence in Petrosino and his men; the device should have been applied years before.

After he left his post, McAdoo himself wrote a book justifying his administration. In it he took great pride in his innovation. The Italians were a hard-working, honest, peaceable, law-abiding, and thrifty people in the great majority, he noted. They should not be held accountable for the bad acts of the criminal element among them. But there was a great deal of public indifference to crime among them as long as it was confined to Italians. This was all wrong. The community could not hope "that lawlessness thus encouraged and tolerated will always confine itself to this neighborhood and among these people." There were no people in New York who would welcome a vigorous enforcement of the law so much as the large majority of the Italians. When they saw the law authorities indifferent they naturally became terrorized at the dangerous element among their own countrymen.

"That there is such a thing as a thoroughly organized, widely separated secret society which directs its operations in all parts of the United States from some great head centre, such as the Mafia or Black Hand is pictured," said McAdoo, "I have never believed in the light of the facts presented to the police." That there were groups of criminals—desperate ones—whose blackmail if not acceded to was followed by violence, "there can be no doubt." For the purpose of dealing with these Italian criminals he had found it most effective to create a special squad under the command of Detective Sergeant Petrosino. The results had been most gratifying from the beginning. "These men were Italian-Americans who were regular policemen, and were at once put in plain clothes and intelligently directed by Petrosino, working in all parts of Greater New York. The very existence of this secret service among the Italians had a deterring effect on the professional criminals."[10]

Early in 1905 an objective and judicious article in the Sunday *Times*, "True Story of Origin of The Black Hand," discounted the existence of a Black Hand organization. It noted that hardly a week now passed without the publication of some piece of police news in which a mysterious secret society known as the "Black Hand" was mentioned. Italians were invariably involved. Italians believed in the existence of the society, "formed and maintained for the purpose of vengeance, for blackmail, for extortion and for war on society in general." Police officers were more skeptical on the whole but still seemed to believe that such an organization existed. Actually, the Black Hand was not Italian in origin at all, but Spanish. The author recounted in considerable detail the story of La Mano Negra, as described by a French writer in 1903. The name *Black Hand* had "probably passed into the consciousness of the Latin mind as bound up with organized anarchistic or terroristic warfare on society," he observed, "and on that account the name is used whenever an Italian with criminal tendencies, if not record, starts out to even up some old score or to get a slice of some other man's cake."

In other words, the name and the emblem had become accessories to the criminal profession among the imaginative Italians. But letters threatening punishment in the name of an alleged Black Hand organization "may be treated as ordinary attempts at extortion, with a dramatic touch added in order to give more point to the threat." Reports that criminals under arrest were members of such an organization had "about as much foundation as similar reports had a few years ago, when every Italian charged with some crime of violence was supposed to be an agent of the Mafia."[11]

Activities of the Black Hand type may have diminished for a time, as McAdoo reported, and Petrosino's squad no doubt did excellent service; but alarms continued. Petrosino's services were in great demand. Sam Fassett's barber shop at 1143 First Avenue was bombed early in the year. Sam, his two assistants, and his customers were hurled to the floor. He screamed for the police, shouting "The Black Hand" alternately in Italian and English. He had received Black Hand letters and had turned them over to the police. The last letter had said, "You miserable cur. You did not show up. Now we will blow up your shop and kill you." Members of Petrosino's squad were put on the case.

Rocco Agaglio, a banker of 705 Fourth Avenue, Brooklyn, received a letter signed only with a crude black hand, informing him that if he failed to pay $15,000 his home would be blown up and he and his family killed. When a second letter came, he went to the police, called his son home from Cornell, and hired two private detectives. They guarded the house night and day while the police were searching for the letter writer.

Dr. M. Lambardo, of 97 Middleton Street in the Williamsburg district of Brooklyn, received three letters in one week demanding money and threatening the use of dynamite. He took the last one to the police, and they tried to induce him to meet the blackmailers as directed, accompanied by detectives. He refused, and a guard was placed on his house. A barber in the same neighborhood had recently had the front of his house blown up for refusal to meet similar demands.

The Williamsburg area was a favorite Black Hand target. In August, Salvatore Doranna, an Italian merchant of 683 Flushing Avenue, got tired of Black Hand demands after paying $100 twice. He reported a third extortion attempt to the police, a trap was laid, and the Black Hander was captured by detectives disguised as Italian workmen. The prisoner gave his name as Gastino Figard and said he lived in Tiffany Place, Brooklyn. "The prisoner was expensively dressed," the *Tribune* reported, "and the police are of the opinion that the man lived by extorting money from wealthy Italians." There was no suggestion that he had any accomplices or was a member of an organization.

The Italian colony in East Harlem was also receiving a good bit of attention from the extortionists. "A bomb thrown against the house of Michael Palladina, a rich contractor living at No. 417 East 116th St., at midnight, shattered the front doors, smashed the windows and drove all of the people from that and surrounding houses to the streets." Some of the neighbors thought that a gas tank had exploded, but most believed the explosion to be Black Hand work. Palladina himself had no doubts about it. He said that he had received five threatening letters, each demanding $2,000. Recently a man had warned him on the street. The last letter came just a few hours before the explosion. After the explosion, he saw a man run around the corner and believed him to be the bomb thrower.

Downtown Italian settlements had their full quota of alarms. Dr. Vincent Sellaro, of 203 Grand Street, founder of the Sons of Italy, received six letters from a gang of blackmailers, warning him not to inform Petrosino. The police were impressed by the daring of a gang that would threaten "a man so well known and regarded among his countrymen." The last letter was signed, "The Champions of the Black Hand." A few weeks later the tenement in which Sellaro lived and had his office was shaken by a dynamite blast. The final letter, which like the others he had ignored, had warned him that some day, "when you feel most secure, you will feel the mighty vengeance of the Black Hand."

"Our society is composed, besides Italians, of policemen and lawyers," a passage in a letter to Serrino Nizzarri, a baker of 98 Bayard Street, said, "and if you make known its contents to the police we shall know of it at once." Petrosino quickly picked up the writer of the letter, a young man who had worked for Nizzarri and had been fired. He later had assaulted his former boss. He seems to have been an amateur, working alone, but Petrosino, said the *Times*, would "investigate to see if the statements regarding the existence of the society are true."

In October Petrosino and three of his men laid a trap and caught Frank Ursetti, a tailor, of 142 Elm Street, in the act of taking Black Hand money. Michael Scancarelli, a contractor of the same address, had received letters signed, "The Black Hand," threatening death to him and abduction and maltreatment of his family if he did not place $600 at a designated spot in Centre Street. Petrosino and his men captured Ursetti when he picked up a dummy package wrapped in a $5 bill. When he was searched there was found "a slip of paper containing the names of many well-to-do Italians."

On another case Petrosino told a *Times* reporter that there were 400 Italian criminals in New York, a figure that he expanded greatly later. The immigration laws were lax; there ought to be a detective bureau abroad to seek out the real criminals who intended to emigrate. "The trouble with my people," he said, "is that they have such faith in the United States that they believe that the Government can absolutely protect them in their private lives. They are timid, and will not give information about their fellow-countrymen." If they would form a vigilance league that would drive Italian malefactors into the hands of the police, "they would be as safe as anyone else and not have as the penalty of their industry and prosperity the payment of large sums to the idle and worthless." Until there was such a league as he had suggested, "families will be endangered."[12]

In October also the grocery store kept by the Gimbaleo brothers in Stanton Street on the lower East Side was wrecked by a bomb. The place had been occupied as a butcher shop by Vito Laduca, one of the men mixed up in the barrel murder mystery, and it was believed that Maduena had been killed there. "There was a hoodoo on the place for a time," the *Tribune* understood, "but the Gimbaleo brothers had come from Sicily, and opened a successful grocery recently." After word got around that they had paid off part of their loan, they received demands for money. They turned over a letter to Petrosino, the bombing followed, and there was great excitement in the neighborhood. Petrosino got on the trail of the bombers, but he seemed close to desperation. "In my mind the only remedy is deportation," he told reporters. He could pick out a thousand Italians who should be deported for the good of the city. There had been sporadic instances of blackmailing all along, "but it is now epidemic." The penal code and ordinary police procedure were useless because of the fear held by the victims. He soon picked up a prime suspect in the Stanton Street bombing but practically admitted that the problem was getting out of hand. More reliance on the Secret Service, which had done much to break up counterfeiting among the Black Hand gangs, and on the immigration authorities at Ellis Island, might help. "According to Petrosino," said the *Tribune*, "the name of nearly every man engaged in blackmailing, or who is a secret member of a 'Black Hand' society, is known either to himself or to the Secret Service agents."

His squad, nevertheless, continued to have its successes, Late in the year they discovered a new method employed in Black Hand operations. Angelo Cuneo, an Italian banker of 28 Mulberry Street, received a letter signed, "The Black Hand," telling him to mail $250 to a legitimate address. The name was given as "Al-Sig. Am.," care of *L'Araldo Italiano*. Marked mail was left there, and one John Duncovitch came to pick it up. Detectives followed him to Nicolo Abati. Both were arrested. In Abati's room were found letters in handwriting similar to that in the letter to Cuneo. The prisoners were arraigned in Tombs Court, and Abati was held in $2,000 bail to await grand jury action. Duncovitch, obviously a tool, was discharged. Abati evidently had thought that the use of a non-Italian agent would give him good cover. The designation of a bona fide address, however, had offered an excellent lead when an intended victim had the courage to report a blackmailing letter.[13]

The *Times* now took to lecturing the Italian community on its failings in regard to the Black Hand. Its quiescence in the light of a long series of "assassinations, kidnappings, arsons, and blackmailings in which a minute fraction of our Italian population is indulging" was a criminal attitude. The city was confronted with "the amazing spectacle of associated bands, composed of men whose identity is perfectly well known to thousands of our citizens," going about openly demanding tribute from carefully selected victims and deliberately killing the few who refused the demands or were slow in granting them. The gravity of compounding and concealing felonies should be strongly impressed on the un-Americanized Italians by sending a few scores of them to prison for long terms. "The Black Hand organization appears to be well known in its personnel among all resident Italians." Sometimes they were bold enough to report to the police and sometimes they took measures of their own, but in general they were restrained by terror. "It was hoped that the Italian annex of the Police Department instituted some time ago might put a brake on this kind of industry, but so far it does not appear to have done it."[14] The *Times* did not appear to have any better solution than the rather remote threat of prosecution for collusion.

While there was definite strain between Tammany Boss Murphy and Mayor McClellan over patronage and policy, there was as yet no real break. Murphy suggested to the mayor that he would send him back to Congress if he would withdraw as a candidate for re-election, but McClellan chose to run. The Tammany organization was forced to support him. He was re-elected in 1905, after a hard fight with William Randolph Hearst, running as an independent. This time it was for a four-year term, as the city's charter had been amended to this effect. Only a month before the election the mayor had assured Police Commissioner McAdoo of his confidence, but McAdoo was replaced at the beginning of the new term. This was part of a general restructuring of the administration that did mark a real break with Tammany. McClellan later credited McAdoo with some useful reforms, which he claimed to have suggested himself, but was dissatisfied with the police commissioner personally.

He reached outside the city for a new commissioner and brought in General Theodore A. Bingham, an Army officer whom he had known in Washington. Bingham recently had lost a leg in an accident and been retired from the service, but he was still full of energy and military zeal. The *Times*, which had generally supported McAdoo's regime, welcomed his successor. Bingham had been superintendent of public buildings and grounds in Washington and, as such, had created a police force to protect the parks. He also had been ex-officio chief of protocol at the White House but had quarreled with President Roosevelt and been transferred to a minor military post. He brought to his new office, according to the *Times*, "one of the best organizing minds in public life to-day." One of his tasks would be to strengthen the detective force, it said; McAdoo had made a gallant effort in this direction but had not been very successful.[15]

Bingham entered on duty with something of a flourish, haranguing the assembled inspectors and captains and banging the platform with his cane, telling them that "you've got to deal with me on the level, as I shall deal with you." He startled headquarters by showing up on Saturdays and by demanding smart military salutes. He made wholesale transfers and imposed heavy fines for infractions of discipline. He reduced the numerous special duty details sharply and abolished a number of special squads. He began reforming the departmental records, introducing the card file system, and strengthened the recruit training program. Like his predecessor, he asked for an enlarged force, and pointed out the peculiar problems of New York City, where "the struggle for life" was more intense than elsewhere, because of the congestion of new immigrants, and where the great concentration of wealth attracted the vicious and the criminal.

As expected, law enforcement effort was concentrated on the Tenderloin, which was increasingly subjected to spectacular raids; but Bingham also was compelled to give attention to the special problems of the Italian community. Petrosino operated under severe handicaps. He had only a few men, and despite their plain clothes, they became well known on sight to criminals as well as law-abiding citizens. Black Hand activities became more prominent as the year 1906 wore on. The Italian immigrant tide was still on the rise, bringing a certain percentage of scum with it. Black Hand outrages continued in Brooklyn, Manhattan, and the Bronx, and this type of criminal was found to be active in Jersey City, sometimes from a New York base. Black Hand gangs based on Manhattan were found to be operating far afield, among Italian laborers in upstate construction camps and elsewhere. Petrosino and his men scored a good many successes, and occasionally an intended victim shot his tormentor; but as the year drew to a close the situation became critical. Bingham took action, with a good bit of publicity.

"Recognizing the inability of the present small force of Italian detectives to drive out these criminals," the *Times* reported in December, "Police Commissioner Bingham ordered yesterday the organization of a secret service which is expected to be recruited and conducted as secretly as the operations of the men against whom it will work." Eligible for this squad were all the Italians in the city police force. The best of them would compose the squad, but not even any of its members would know all the others. There were about fifty men in all the boroughs who spoke Italian. Selection was to begin at once. Petrosino's existing squad had been struggling along under great difficulties. "Hardly a day has passed in the last two months without a batch of Black Hand letters being delivered to Petrosino or without at least one case of murder, attempted murder, or dynamiting." Petrosino himself had seen little of his home and family for six months. He had been unable to handle the situation. "His blotter records a large number of cases that he may never hope to reach." The gathering of a special and ample force to work "underground" against the increase in Italian crime was his only hope. Commissioner Bingham had now given him a free hand in the formation of such a force.

Editorially the *Times* took the credit for having suggested the move to Bingham and approved his action, but it also wondered how effective it would be. The new force could hardly be kept secret from the Italian community for long. But Bingham, it admitted, had to use the material and methods at his disposal. Apparently all that was happening was that more men were being assigned to Petrosino. "There is not much promise in a mere increase of a force that hitherto has been a rather dismal failure, but the added number will of itself do something toward interfering with the operations of what is called the Black Hand."

Taking note of the same move at police headquarters, the *Herald* reported that Bingham had sent out a notice to all commanding officers to send him the names of all Italians on their rolls. It was said that these would be turned over to Detective Sergeant Petrosino, who had charge of the Black Hand investigations. "So numerous have been the outrages of the 'Black Hand,' so many threatening letters are being sent to wealthy men and so many assaults and other crimes are charged to them that Petrosino and his staff of eight or ten men have had no success." It had been suggested to Commissioner Bingham that the men under Petrosino were being overworked. As a result of Bingham's action, Petrosino's force was increased to about thirty men, and a similar but smaller squad was created in Brooklyn under Sergeant Vachris. Petrosino himself was promoted to the grade of lieutenant.[16]

Early in the year John Foster Carr had presented in the *Outlook* a highly sympathetic picture of the Italian immigrants. "Thanks to the secluded ways of Italians," he said, "the actual facts of their life among us are almost entirely unknown. In common with Mexicans and Jews, they are pilloried by insulting nicknames. They are charged with pauperism, crime, and degraded living, and they are judged unheard and almost unseen." Actually, their rate of pauperism was surprisingly low. Carr cited a formidable battery of statistics on the subject, showing them to rate far above the Irish in this respect. So it was in the matter of most types of crime, according to the latest statistics available:

> The one serious crime to which Italians are prone more than other men is an unpremeditated crime of violence. This is mostly charged, and probably with entire justice, upon the men of four provinces, and Girgenti in Sicily is particularly specified. It is generally the outcome of quarrels among themselves, prompted by jealousy and suspected treachery. The Sicilians' code of honor is an antiquated and repellent one, but even his vendetta is less ruthless than the Kentucky mountaineer's. It stops at the grave. Judged in the mass, Italians are peaceable, as they are law-abiding. The exceptions make up the national criminal record; and as there is a French or English type of criminal, so there is a Sicilian type, who has succeeded in impressing our imaginations with some fear and terror.
>
> The Mafia is the expression of Sicilian criminality, and here, as in Italy, the methods of the Sicilian criminal are the

same. For some of his crimes he is more apt to have an accomplice than most other criminals. But there is no sufficient reason for believing that a Mafia, organized as it often is in Italy, a definite society of the lawless, exists anywhere in this country. No one who knows the different Italian colonies well will admit the possibility of its existence. The authorities at police headquarters scout the idea. As with the Mafia, so with the Black Hand. I went to Sergeant Petrosino, who is said to know every important Italian criminal in New York. He disposed very summarily of the bogey: "As far as they can be traced, threatening letters are generally a hoax; some of them are attempts at blackmail by inexperienced criminals, who have had the idea suggested to them by reading about the Black Hand in the sensational papers; but the number of threatening letters sent with the deliberate intention of using violence as a last resort to extort money is ridiculously small."[17]

Perhaps Petrosino had changed his mind in the course of the year, or he had himself begun to succumb to the rising hysteria that Carr had sought to combat by quoting him. Perhaps Carr had read too much into his statement about threatening letters. Certainly amateurs were already entering the field in numbers, and pranksters were using the Black Hand symbol for their own amusement; but there was undoubtedly a hard core of professionals at work, and their numbers seemed to be increasing.

Some of the Black Handers evidently had a hand in the importation of prostitutes, the "White Slave trade" as the traffic was coming to be called, as well as in extortion and counterfeiting. In November, Enrico Pavone shot and killed Nunziata Legato, "reputed agent of the Mano Nera, or Black Hand Society," at Mott and Grand Streets. Pavone was chased by a mob and picked up by the police. They found a revolver on Legato's body. Pavone told them he was glad he had shot Legato. "He tried to hound me and would have killed me if I hadn't shot him first. I want to see Detective Sergeant Petrosino." He was taken before the coroner and then sent to the Tombs without bail to await the inquest. Coroner Acritelli told reporters that the dead man had been a witness at inquests, that he was a prominent member of the so-called Black Hand, and that he was known as a clever counterfeiter. Pavone told the coroner that the dead man "had threatened him with a loaded revolver because he—the prisoner—refused to go to Ellis Island and swear that a woman there who had come in on a vessel was his wife."[18] It was standard procedure for procurers of different nationalities to have prostitutes they imported met by men who would swear to being close relatives and so get them past the immigration authorities. Since Legato's body was immediately recognized by the coroner as that of a known criminal, he probably was known also at the island and so unable to perform the errand himself. He seems to have been a professional of long standing and varied interests.

Broughton Brandenburg, a free-lance writer and student of immigration, had issued dire warnings in 1904 in a *Collier's* series about criminal immigrants of varied nationalities, with particular emphasis on the Mafia. The society was now in political control of Sicily, he said. There were numerous bands of the lower Mafia (*mafia bassa*) and some few fugitives of the higher Mafia (*alta mafia*) in this country, he held. They awaited only "the electrifying touch of executive power from the *alta mafia* and then will come—hell. That is the truth about the 'mafia' in the United States." Since then Brandenburg had concentrated on a study of the Black Hand. In 1906 he placed a sensational article on the subject in the *Tribune Sunday Magazine*. Responsible and influential Italians, he noted, declared that there was no such society as the Black Hand. They were, of course, interested solely in preserving the good name of the Italian people. But the Black Hand did exist. "The old Mafia is dead, but from its ashes has arisen a hydra-headed anomaly that is the fifth curse of Southern Italy. In the United States the transplanted seeds have sprouted into a flourishing institution that bids fair to become the greatest criminal organization of the world's history."

The Black Hand was not an organized society, Brandenburg explained, with an individual head or a governing board, a roll of members, a treasury, a common code, and the like. It was the popular name for a body of many thousands of Italian criminals organized in gangs wherever there was much Italian population. "The principal man in each gang, the *capo*, has usually been in a gang in Italy or New York." The older criminals kept the newer gangs in touch with each other, and there was a dreadful day coming when some mastermind, or several masterminds, would "arise and weld the hundreds of scattered gangs into a new Mafia as organized in detail for campaigns of crime as an army is organized for war."

The existing terrorism had its beginning in New York, according to Brandenburg. "The Barrel Murder Gang of New York was one of several that were preying on the Italian colony several years ago," combining counterfeiting with their Black Hand methods. They all had been picked up after the barrel murder but were all turned free. A carnival of crime resulted. "Detective Sergeant Giuseppe Petrosino, the noted central-office man who has charge of all Italian cases, backed by a number of other officers and public-spirited persons who were not afraid to risk their lives in the case, forced the formation of a secret squad of Italian detectives to combat the spreading evil." For a time there was consternation among the gangs, and they went elsewhere but "took their Black Hand propaganda with them." Since then there had been a reign of murder and terror in the mining districts of Pennsylvania and elsewhere. "The dispersed villains recruited new bands, and when at last they ventured back to New York, after all of Petrosino's men were spotted and known, their reconcentration effected the state of organization which I have described."[19]

News accounts from varied sources tended to lend credibility to Brandenburg's alarmism. Activities of the Black Hand type long had been reported not only from Chicago and other large cities but also from the mining towns of Pennsylvania and elsewhere, and from nearby Westchester County. There the Croton waterworks were being expanded, and wealthy men were building elaborate estates, both involving extensive use of Italian labor. As early as 1899, Dr. Egisto Rossi, chief of the Italian Bureau that had been set up by the Italian government to curb the padrone evil and then was operating at the Barge Office, testified that although passports were denied to men with criminal records, he knew many Italian criminals were coming in illegally by way of foreign ports. They came by way of Antwerp, Hamburg, Marseilles, and Havre, and he hastened to add, "as you know, the Italian Government can have no control of that."

These gentry undoubtedly came in increasing numbers in the following years, as economic recovery burgeoned in the United States. Some of them presumably found honest work, but a large percentage unquestionably resumed their old habits, spreading all over the land wherever their countrymen could be found in numbers. A little before the barrel murder, the *Tribune* reported that the police of several towns in Westchester County were after a band of Italians who for months had been holding up their more prosperous countrymen and compelling them under threats of death to pay ransoms. The great obstacle to obtaining convictions, it was understood, was the reluctance of the victim to testify against the outlaws. "They exonerate the prisoners in court, asserting that the accused came to them merely to borrow money or to ask them to contribute to some charitable cause. Privately they say that they have been held up by men armed with revolvers and knives and compelled to contribute money to the band, which calls itself 'The Society of the Bad Life.' " In some cases the money was collected in installments of so much a week, with the victim being threatened with death if he divulged the secret. "The men promise him that when he has paid $100 he will be made a member of the society, and that it will guarantee him protection if he wishes to prey on others."

The *World* reported on a letter that Chief of Police Timmons of New Rochelle had received from a victim of the society, posted in New York and unsigned:

> You are informed that in your city and the cities of White Plains and Port Chester exists the most treacherous association that has ever been heard of, organized under the name of "La Società Della Malavita," or the "Society of the Bad Life." Some of us honest citizens of America thought it advisable to notify those different cities so we can destroy the cruel association from existing on the face of the earth or in this beautiful country.
>
> We beg Your Honor to act at once before this association advances in numbers, because they are forcing good, honest citizens to join them. You can find something of this truth by inquiring at different business places in New Rochelle, espe-

cially saloons, where some of the members have been there for money, and if the sum from them asked is not submitted in such time, or they refuse to submit same, they report to their association and appoint a committee to go and slay the man.

The police had made inquiries about the society and found that it was "probably the same as a secret society in Sicily made up of brigands and murderers." Already charged to it were a half-dozen bold holdups and one murder. The murder was committed in New Rochelle, and the victim was found lying in the street with his head cut off. "The police of Mount Vernon, White Plains, New Rochelle and Port Chester have decided to co-operate in an effort to locate the secret meeting place of the bandits and bring them to justice."

Another group, or possibly the same one, called itself the "Carbonari." These brigands, the *Herald* said, had been particularly active in Westchester County, but the society had also been at work in New York City. Inspector McCluskey, the chief of detectives, was determined to put a stop to their work, "and he has the advantage of having as an assistant Detective Sergeant Petrosino, whom he regards as one of the most able members of his staff." The Italians had attempted to add dignity to their society, the *Herald* explained, by taking the name of Carbonari, "which less than a century ago was an organization of patriots banded together for good government."[20]

By the next year the term *Black Hand* and the technique characteristically associated with it were in use in Westchester County. Father Cenozo Cigalaino, in charge of Italian missionary work in Port Chester, who had been active in efforts "to stamp out the 'black hand' letter writers and blackmailers there," was assaulted and knocked unconscious. The priest's nephew, Urbano Alletti, was arrested and charged with being his assailant. Joseph Pagano, a baker of Tuckahoe, received a letter signed, "President Black Hand Society," demanding $100 or his life in ten days. "It is believed," the *Times* reported, "that the writer belongs to the same gang that has obtained by threats more than $1,000 from Italians employed on the watershed in Northern Westchester."

Black Hand levies on the camp of 500 Italians working on

the dams in northern Westchester continued in 1905. Every payday members of the band, it was said, demanded from one to five dollars from each man. Threatening letters were sent to those who refused. Sheriff Merritt and District Attorney Young of Mount Vernon had arranged for a reward for the arrest of "the leaders of the Black Hand society." They also had taken the unusual step of swearing in many Italians as deputy sheriffs, so that they could carry firearms. These men, they said, intended "to shoot every Black Hand outlaw they find."[21]

Much of the Black Hand activity in Westchester County flowed out of New York City. Giovanni Barberri, a baker of Mount Vernon, received letters signed "Black Hand" demanding that he send $500 to a designated address in the city. The last letter said that if the money was not forwarded at once one of the band would come to Mount Vernon and kill him. When Antonio Fotti, alleged agent of the Black Hand Society, came to follow it up armed with two revolvers, Barberri had prepared himself with a shotgun loaded with birdshot. Fotti took him by surprise and drove him into the street. There neighbor women seized Fotti. He struggled and fired two shots, but the women held on. Barberri went back into his shop, got his shotgun, and told the women to let Fotti go. Then he fired both barrels at the Black Hander. Fotti ran all the way to Yonkers, dripping blood, and reported to St. Joseph's Hospital. The police trailed him there.

In the following year a labor camp near Armonk was raided on payday by "five 'Black Hand' men," who demanded the men's wages. When the laborers refused, the robbers opened fire, and three men were wounded. The men wore masks, and the whole operation resembled those of the "road agents" of the American West. Perhaps the gang had been reading American dime novels. They were labeled Black Handers, however, since they were presumably Italians. Many of the workmen, who were employed by a contractor building macadam driveways at the summer home of C. R. Agnew, a banker, abandoned their work and returned to New York. Sheriff Merritt organized two posses, "to search for the bandits and also to protect the hundreds of Italians who are employed on the New York City watershed, the state roads, and other improvements." Merritt had tried to obtain the services of Petrosino and his staff from police headquarters in the city but found this to be impossible. A contractor working on state roads told Merritt that nearly all his workmen recently had received letters from the Black Hand. Many of his men had left, and he would be unable to continue his work unless something was done to protect them. Workers on the dam on Cross River, near Katonah, were abandoning their camps and returning to the city "seeking a padrone who could get them work anywhere where they would not be threatened by the banditti."

The murder of an Italian had been reported from New Rochelle shortly before. "Because he spoke sneeringly of the Black Hand Society, Donato Zarrillo, an Italian living in West New Rochelle, was shot and killed in the street by two men early this morning," the *Times* learned. His brother Tommaso was also shot and left for dead but was expected to recover. The assassins fled to the woods and had not been captured, although the police of three cities had been looking for them. About a month before, it appeared, Zarrillo had remarked in a saloon that the Black Hand were a lot of cowards and he would kill them if they tried to blackmail him. "This is the sixth murder in Westchester County this month, and Sheriff Merritt has called on the police to disarm all foreigners as far as possible." Evidently Merritt had decided that the deputizing of Italians so that they could carry guns had been a mistake. Perhaps Zarrillo had been one of his deputies and had felt overconfident.

After more murders attributed to the Black Hand had taken place in Westchester County, Sheriff Merritt established a system of mounted patrols to protect the Italian workmen on New York City's water-supply system. The *Times* approved. "According to the best authorities," it editorialized, "there is little or no organization among these murderers and thieves, and they have brought with them from abroad nothing of the Black Hand except its name and the terror that can be inspired by its use." Organized or not, they could and did kill when their demands for money were not obeyed, and they had created something like a reign of terror among their potential victims. "But though the mounted patrolmen can do something against these bandits, the real remedy lies elsewhere." The Black Hand trusted to and exploited a peculiarity of the lower-class Italian, "his distrust of the police and his feeling that it is somehow treasonable or dishonorable either to ask its aid in defending himself or to assist it in its war against crime." What was needed was a change of ideas. The attitude of these Italians was easily explicable by the student of their national history, but it was out of place and time here; and "their enlightened friends should make every effort to convince them of these facts." The editorial made no mention of what had happened to Zarrillo.[22]

A little later Petrosino and his men rounded up a gang in the city and captured account books in the hands of one Francesco Santori, with lists of his associates and also the names and addresses of Italians who were paying the gang every week, along with the amounts they were paying. "The list covered four pages, and showed that at least sixty men employed in labor camps in various parts of the state were paying to someone sums ranging from $1 to $3 a week." Nine men were arraigned in Jefferson Market Court, while Petrosino's men hunted for the rest of the twenty men on Santori's list of his presumed associates. Witnesses were to be brought to the court from Poughkeepsie, where a Black Hand gang had been operating in the nearby railroad camps. Petrosino was optimistic. He had never before gotten such evidence as a book of accounts, he told reporters, as the Black Hand chiefs seldom carried documents. The case fell apart, however, when "the cloud of witnesses that should have appeared was reduced to a single terrified laborer who had been dragged here from Poughkeepsie, much against his will," the *Times* said, "and as soon as he could swear that he never saw any of the prisoners he hurried away." All that could be done was to hold four of the men for carrying concealed weapons and to discharge the others. "This is a lamentable outcome of weeks of work, apparently as good as could be done. It seems impossible to convince Italians of the class exploited by these loosely organized bandits that the police are powerful enough to protect them."

When the growing city reached out to tap the upper waters of the Delaware in 1908, and began work on the Ashokan dam with its aqueduct to reach 108 miles, the Board of Water Supply set up its own police force "to patrol the Catskill watershed of New York City and the camps which will be established while the work of construction on dams and aqueducts is going on." The initial force was to be fifty men, temporarily appointed pending a civil service examination; but it was estimated that when all the contracts were under way it would consist of from fifteen hundred to two thousand men. Presumably its function was to be to protect the workmen from the Black Hand, as well as to protect the communities along the way from the workmen.[23]

In 1903 a story from Scranton, Pennsylvania, told of the arrest at Carbondale of two men on the charge of extortion. Information had come from a committee of Italians who alleged that the men had been soliciting money from miners as contributions to the Mafia Society. The usual demand was for ten dollars under threat of a cut throat. Letters were found from one Frank Costi of New York. "Giuseppe Colandi, one of the complaining committee, who was formerly a chief of police in a town in Italy, and who was influential in bringing about the arrest of 143 members of the Mafia, told Mayor O'Neil that Costi was a leader of the Mafia." By the following year the term *Black Hand* was in vogue in Pennsylvania as elsewhere. When an Italian picked up a little girl in Pittsburgh and started walking away with her, the cry of "Black Hand" was raised, and he was in danger of being lynched before the police arrived. In 1905 a story from Monessen, Pennsylvania, told of the bombing of the fruit store and home of Vincenzo Palumbo with a charge of dynamite said to have been exploded by members of the "Black Hand" society. Palumbo had received two letters demanding $5,000 and threatening death if he failed to comply. He had ignored them.[24]

Early in 1906, Robert J. Black, the ex-mayor of McKeesport, got a letter from the "Black Hand Society," demanding $3,100 in gold and silver coin, or his life would pay the forfeit, his house would be blown up, and his family ruined. Here was evidently a new refinement in the Black Hand technique; the gang wanted to avoid the use of paper money, which could be and often was marked and used to bait a trap. In the same year a troop of the state constabulary was called out on the appeal of the mayor and chief of police of Monongahela "to break up the Black Hand Society, which has been terrorizing the country, and which, it is believed, has been responsible for twenty-one murders committed within the last year." Warrants had been sworn out for the arrest of 140 alleged Black Hand members in Monongahela City and nearby towns. "Troop A of the State Constabulary will be asked to make the arrests," it was reported, "as the local authorities are wholly unable to cope with the situation." Later in the same year a story from Punxsutawney told of a pitched battle between Troop D of the constabulary and Italians, alleged Black Handers, surrounded in a house at the Florence mine. Two troopers had been killed and two wounded, and more action was expected. "The position of the watchers is a perilous one to-night," the excited local reporter said, "as there are many treacherous members of the Black Hand in and about Florence mine and the surrounding mines."[25]

A story from Plainfield, New Jersey, in the following year told of the arrest there of Nicolà Lobianca and Joseph Novetta. They had been tracked there from New Castle, Pennsylvania, by private detectives of the Pinkerton agency. Chief Kiely of the Plainfield police and the Pinkertons were quoted as saying that they believed they had "two ring leaders of the 'Black Hand' who have terrorized the residents of New Castle . . . in the last six months." They were believed to be members of a band who had extorted large sums of money from their countrymen and was suspected of being implicated in several murders committed in that city. They were said to be agents of one John Jati, who was believed to be the head of the American branch of the Mafia and a partner of "Mussilino, the bandit, for whose capture the Italian Government has offered large rewards." The Pinkertons had been hired by private employers in New Castle, whose Italian workers had been demoralized by Black Hand activities. They had been searching for the suspects for months and had traced them to Plainfield.[26]

A little later Pennsylvania state police arrested fourteen alleged Black Handers at Marion Heights, near the middle of the state, where a meeting of the supposed society was being held. Many others escaped. A local Italian resident had tipped off the troopers. The group was described as "every bit as desperate as the Molly Maguires," and the prisoners were held without bail by a local magistrate on conspiracy to murder and other charges. The capture of the two Black Handers from New Castle in Plainfield, New Jersey, evidently had not cleared up the situation there. There was a roundup at Hillsville, near New Castle, where Black Handers had been shaking down Italian quarrymen systematically every payday for months. Private agents of the U.S. Steel Corporation and local authorities were assisted by an Italian detective from Pittsburgh who had infiltrated the group. Twenty-one suspected Black Handers were picked up and lodged in the county jail at New Castle. There were soon alarming rumors of a plot to dynamite the jail, and a troop of constabulary was sent there.

Shortly afterward two Italians were hanged for murder in Pittsburgh. They had been "imported from the slums of New York to murder at so much per job," it was said. They had been convicted of murdering an Italian merchant who had given the authorities information about the Black Hand. Two other Italians from New York had been picked up on charges of planning to blow up the Allegheny County jail and liberate them. The hanging was called "the first real blow against the Black Hand" in western Pennsylvania, where for three years it had been "terrorizing that district and Eastern Ohio." Toward the end of summer, dispatches from Harrisburg announced that "Effective war is being waged against the Black Hand throughout Pennsylvania by the State Constabulary." Operations in half a dozen counties across the state were cited. It was believed that "the troopers will soon rid the Commonwealth of the murderous organization."

In New Castle in October, trials were held, and twenty-three Italians "arrested in connection with numerous Black Hand outrages" were convicted or pleaded guilty and were sentenced to a total of seventy-one years in the Western Pennsylvania Penitentiary at Pittsburg. The local sheriff and a squad of the state constabulary took them there. Italian extortionists continued to be active in Pittsburgh itself, however. In December, after prosperous Italians in that city had organized to defend themselves, there was a gun battle in the produce yards of the Pennsylvania Railroad, reported as "White Hand Fights With Black Hand." M. Rei, a Black Hand chief, was killed and his lieutenant wounded, as was Joseph Sunseri, wholesale fruit dealer, from whom they had tried to extort $1,000. The fight raged over three adjacent blocks, and hundreds of shots were fired, before police reserves broke it up. Sunseri, Ernest Bisi, a macaroni manufacturer, and Mariano Cancelleri, editor of a local Italian newspaper, had organized the defense society, probably inspired by similar action in Chicago. Both sides evidently had been prepared for the contest, with reserves at hand. A few days later the Pittsburgh police swooped down on a large group of Italians in the nearby Allegheny Valley Railroad yards and captured sixteen of them. A number of concealed weapons were found on them, and they were, of course, labeled "Black Hand" members.[27]

In 1906 there had been reported captures of Black Hand extortionists in Greenwich, Connecticut, in Baltimore, Trenton, and Jersey City. In the Baltimore incident, members of the family of Michael Lanasa had received one letter signed, "The Mafia Association," and several signed, "The Head of the Black Hand and Company," all demanding $5,000. Mrs. Lanasa had replied to one of these, and when a young man came to collect, she called a policeman. The young man, Ignazio Castalano, was captured after a chase, and another, Rosarto Romeo, was picked up later. Castalano told police he came from New York, sent by four men he knew only by their first names. Romeo said he had been employed to deliver some of the letters but had no knowledge of their contents. Quite often, it appeared, there was a New York City angle to such affairs, and Petrosino's men knew that young "greenhorn" immigrants were often employed on blackmailing errands.[28]

Late in 1903 there was a report from New Orleans headlined, "Government to Run Down Mafia Leaders." The deadly vendetta had broken out again there, it was said, "when Giuseppe Imposatto, a wealthy local macaroni manufacturer, was shot and killed by Italians believed to be members of the Mafia." The New Orleans police, aided by the Secret Service, were cooperating with the police departments of New York, Chicago, Philadelphia, Boston, and Baltimore to suppress it. "This is the first time that a concerted movement has been organized by the detectives and police organizations of the principal cities of the United States to run down the Mafia," the *Times* noted. The fact that the federal government was the moving spirit in the plan, it observed optimistically, indicated that it would be vigorously prosecuted and would bring about the conviction of the Mafia leaders who were "known to be operating in New York and Chicago." Simultaneous raids in several cities were predicted. An inquiry at police headquarters on Mulberry Street, however, drew a blank. The New York police knew nothing about such a plan, they said. There was no further report on this; if any such plan had been devised, the advance publicity given to it presumably spoiled the operation.

In 1907, when there was an Italian kidnaping in New Orleans, it was reported as the work of "a Black Hand gang." Peter Lamana, a wealthy undertaker, had refused to pay a ransom of $6,000 for the return of his nine-year-old son Walter, and "ignoring the instructions of the Black Hand," had placed the case in the hands of the police. The gang, including several men and women, were captured, and one of them confessed; but the boy meanwhile had been killed and his mutilated body thrown into a swamp. There was intense excitement in the Italian quarter, and threats of lynching were made freely. "These demonstrations came from the foreign element," it was noted. The populace generally was stirred up. "Seldom since the Mafia lynchings, sixteen years ago," the *Tribune* learned, "has New Orleans been so stirred with threats of violence as to-day." However, the law-and-order element was much stronger than it had been, "a large number of leading citizens having pledged themselves to prevent violence." This time the jail was heavily guarded.[29]

Next to New York City, the concentration of Black Hand activities was greatest in Chicago. Late in 1907 there was

formed by leading members of the Italian community the
"White Hand" Society. Its object was to serve the colony in
its need for "peace and the good name of Italians" by action
against the Black Hand type of crime. It had the support of
the Italian Chamber of Commerce and was encouraged by
the Italian consul, who seems, in fact, to have been a prime
mover in the organization. Its formation was received with
"unanimous applause" by the American and Italian press.
The Italian ambassador in Washington endorsed it and so did
the Ministry of Foreign Affairs in Rome.

The society employed detectives and undertook extensive
investigations not only in Chicago but also in Italy and Sicily
to dig into the past of notorious Black Handers with a view
to their deportation. Where information for prosecutions was
obtainable, it was turned over to the police, and Stephen A.
Malato, the society's attorney, succeeded in securing indictments and even convictions against a number of them.
At the end of the year an encouraging report·was issued.
The American press, the society asserted, had been forced
to take a new tone toward the Italian colony, and the timid
within it had been given courage.

As for the Black Hand, which the American newspapers
had been using "almost as a generic name for the Italian
immigrant in this country," it did not exist. What did exist,
the society's report said, was a class of criminals, "the sad
relic of the old Mafia or of the Camorra." These men were
either compromised in their native land or were lured by the
vision of a profitable field for their exploits and migrated to
the United States, where they had greater liberty of action.
To this type, the frequency with which crime went unpun-
ished in this country made it appear "a fertile vineyard, easy
of cultivation." There was no "vast organization" of these
criminals, but there was a bond of mutual sympathy and
mutual interest among them that extended widely throughout
the country.

After a promising start, the White Hand Society lapsed
into inactivity. It found that the Black Handers were allied
with "certain vicious and lawless saloon-keepers in the Italian districts" and that these saloon-keepers were active in
precinct and ward politics and had the favor of the local

bosses. The result was a "let alone" policy toward Black Hand crime on the part of the police. After issuing its report and urging that more Italian policemen be added to the force, the society seems to have remained dormant for some time, with a brief and futile revival of activity two years later. Rudolph Vecoli, in his study of the Italians in Chicago, attributes the collapse of the society largely to factionalism and growing lack of interest among the well-to-do members of the community who had founded it. Humbert Nelli, covering the same ground, lays more stress on the belief among the Italian working class that funds collected by the society were to be used "to defend the lives and wealth of the prominent men of the community." The workers cared little for the protection of the good name of Italians in general. Many of them expected to return to Italy and had no roots in the city. They were accustomed to crime and political corruption and did not believe that the society could eliminate these ills.[30]

Early in 1910, ten members of "A Sicilian Black Hand organization" were convicted in federal court in Toledo, Ohio, and hurried off to prison at Leavenworth, Kansas, to serve sentences of from two to sixteen years. Two indicted members of the band were believed to be in hiding in Italy. The charge had been "conspiracy to use the mails to extort money from Italians living in Ohio and Indiana." The gang had had its headquarters in Marion, Ohio, and its agents had operated clear across the state and far beyond its borders. Large postal money orders sent from Marion to Sicily had been an important clue. Government officials believed that they had "effectually broken up Black Hand operations in the Middle West."[31] This proved to be unduly optimistic, but the postal authorities were becoming active in the suppression of all types of mail fraud. This was their first major operation against the Black Hand, and it had been highly successful. Not long after, Federal Judge Landis in Chicago began handing out maximum sentences in Black Hand cases brought before him by post office inspectors.

In New York City the Italian Squad, considerably expanded, had plenty of work to do and made some notable captures. When there was a roundup of weapons-carrying

Italians in the spring of 1907, after the murder of two plainclothes men, it was Petrosino that recognized Alfano, the Camorra chief, from a photograph supplied by the Italian government. Alfano's arrest and prompt deportation produced a sensation in Naples. There, a report to the *Times* stated, he was considered by the populace "in the light of a demi-god; he was thought to be invulnerable to bullets and able at all times to escape his pursuers." He had been a well-known figure in Naples, where he "used to drive around in his own carriage, fashionably dressed, while on his criminal business." At his instigation the Camorra had condemned his rival Cuocola to death. Cuocola and his wife both were murdered. Alfano had remained in Naples for a time, trying to cover up the traces of the crime. When he found that he was in serious danger he fled to the United States. He had been in New York for about six months when Petrosino picked him up on Mulberry Street. Alfano made no effort to conceal his identity.

Shortly afterward, the Italian Squad rounded up "a Black Hand gang of five Sicilian men and two women" for the kidnaping of a seven-year-old boy named Salvatore Saitta. They were said to have lived for several years "upon money obtained as ransom from parents of children kidnapped in Little Italy." Their leader, Pietro Pampinella, was identified in part through the new fingerprint method, his fingerprints corresponding to those on letters demanding ransom. The boy identified him and one of the women as the two who had kept him prisoner for eight days. One of the gang talked and said that he had been forced into kidnaping the boy under threat of death. Petrosino and his men regarded Pampinella as "one of the keenest Sicilians in the colony here" and believed him to have written "most of the Black Hand letters received by well-to-do Italians here in the last year." He was convicted along with one of his confederates, and both of them were sentenced to terms of fourteen years and ten months. On the recommendation of the district attorney the woman was discharged.[32]

The Italian government had some time before offered a large reward for the capture, dead or alive, of a celebrated Sicilian bandit named Francesco Varsalona. A head had been turned in to the authorities soon after, and the reward had been paid. Later it was rumored "that the money was paid for the wrong head, and that Varsalona took his to the Argentine Republic." However this may have been, his band had been broken up, and several of its members left for the United States. Among them were two trusted lieutenants, the brothers Pelletieri—Giuseppe and Giovanni. Arriving in New York in the fall of 1906, they found a fertile field for their professional operations. They promptly launched a program of kidnaping, blackmailing, and murder, attracting a considerable following. Petrosino collected much evidence against them but hesitated to bring them to court for fear of having his witnesses murdered.

On July 1, 1907, however, a new immigration law went into effect. One of its many provisions was that foreign criminals could be deported up to three years after their arrival in the United States. The law also created an immigration commission to study the whole problem of immigration. This commission promptly began checking on foreign criminals, concentrating its first efforts on Italians in New York, cooperating closely with the police department. At its request, the Italian authorities sent over a list of fifty or more desperate criminals who recently had left for America. The list was turned over to Police Commissioner Bingham, and Petrosino found the Pelletieri brothers at the top of it. They were wanted by the prefect of police in Palermo. Although he believed the law to be inadequate, since it did not touch such long-resident malefactors as Lupo and Morello, Petrosino sought to try it out.

He went to the immigration commissioner at Ellis Island, who readily approved of the deportation of the Pelletieris. Thereupon Petrosino promptly arrested the brothers on a blackmailing charge. The magistrate, when the case was explained to him, discharged the prisoners in the custody of the detectives. They were taken to Ellis Island, along with their Italian criminal records and proof that they had been in this country less than three years. Petrosino appeared before the Board of Special Inquiry there and told them what he knew of the men. Although the Black Hand label for years had been most commonly applied to violent Italian crime and though Petrosino, like most Italians, usually shied away from the term, the Pelletieris were identified as Mafia. He told reporters that they were the heads of an American branch of the society numbering more than a thousand members, most of whom were in New York City. The action of the immigration authorities was not all that had been hoped for. One of the brothers was deported, but the other was freed.[33]

Much the same thing happened in a number of other cases, as Petrosino tracked down one after another of the men on the Italian government list. Some were deported; others were turned loose again to prey upon the Italian community of New York. There were loopholes in the law, and the immigration authorities at Ellis Island were bound by its interpretation as handed down from Washington. Petrosino, now Lieutenant Petrosino, had accomplished much with his little band, Commissioner Bingham told a *Times* reporter early in 1908. "There have been one thousand arrests for Black Hand crimes in a year," he said, "and of this number 500 were convicted and given sentences in prison of various lengths." Bingham was given to pulling startling statistics out of thin air in order to dramatize his very real problems. Petrosino, who received a great deal of attention from the press after his part in the barrel murder mystery of 1903, got into the same habit.

These criminals could not be run out of the country, Bingham informed the *Times*. "The minute we try it we run up against the immigration laws, and there is all sorts of trouble. After a man has been over here three years, no matter what we find to have been his previous record, here he stays." Bombings continued, and in February a dismembered body identified as that of Salvatore Marchione, who lived in the Union Street Italian settlement of Brooklyn, was found in a desolate section of Flatbush known to the police as "Pigtown." It was learned that he had come from Palermo two years before. Vachris's whole detective squad was put on the case, which at once was put in the Black Hand category, presumably revenge for some action in Sicily.[34]

Bingham now blasted the immigration authorities in general and Commissioner Robert Watchorn at Ellis Island in particular. In an interview with a *Herald* reporter he charged that Watchorn not only failed to deport criminals but also failed to cooperate in keeping them out. He "expressed the opinion that murders such as that of Marchione will continue in this country until a Commissioner of Immigration is appointed who will keep the bars up against the criminal class." Watchorn defended himself vigorously. He had enforced the law so severely, he said, that criminals now avoided New York and came by way of Quebec and remote ports in the South. Watchorn had, in fact, "earnestly requested" cooperation with the police department some time before, "in endeavoring to deport these criminals who bring such discredit on the Italian communities," as former Police Commissioner McAdoo admitted in his book. As for deportations, Watchorn now told the press, Bingham didn't often send over enough information on which to build a case. The law might be weak, but that was not Watchorn's fault.

At the same time there was a revival of the recurring fear of anarchism. An avowed Italian anarchist shot and killed a priest at the altar in Denver, and a young Russian anarchist attempted to assassinate Chicago's chief of police. President Roosevelt was roused and ordered a vigorous campaign against "all alien Anarchists and criminals," looking to their deportation. This campaign was launched by an order from Secretary of Commerce and Labor Oscar S. Straus, directing all immigration officials to cooperate with the Secret Service and with local police authorities to this end. Anarchists in New York were highly indignant when their known haunts were raided by the police. Alexander Berkman, a leading figure in the movement, was out of town, but his secretary declared that "the anarchists are being blamed for many things which should be put up to the Italian Black Hand gangs."

Watchorn said he thought the menace from anarchists was greatly exaggerated; there were not more than 300 of them in the country. The problem of alien criminals was another matter. Ellis Island had been vigilant, within the law: "We deported 35 criminals in 1905, 200 in 1906, and 319 in 1907." Most of these deportations, he said, were of fugitives from justice about whom foreign consuls general had information. All countries, Watchorn declared, should be compelled to furnish penal certificates to their emigrants, and there should be summary power to deport the alien criminals already in the country. But Bingham continued his attack; and Secretary Straus, who had great faith in Watchorn, soon sent him on a fact-finding mission to Europe, probably to get him out of the line of fire. Soon after, a senior Secret Service agent appeared in New York from Washington, armed with a number of deportation warrants and orders to cooperate with the local police. "With the arrival of Mr. Hazen," said the *Herald*, "it is presumed that a concerted move will be made to round up alien criminals, many of whom are known to the police and have been kept under surveillance since their appearance in this country."[35]

While Watchorn was gone, Gaetano D'Amato, deputy commissioner of licenses in the McClellan administration and former president of the United Italian Societies, placed an article in the *North American Review* proclaiming the Black Hand a myth. It was not strange, D'Amato said, that most Americans believed that a terrible organization named the Black Hand existed in Italy and sent its members to establish branches to plunder in the United States, "since nearly every newspaper in the country conveys that impression to its readers." But the term was scarcely known in Italy. It had been used for the first time in the United States, regrettably damaging the good name of the Italians here:

> In the United States the "Black Hand Society" is a myth, in so far as the phrase conveys the impression that an organization of Italian criminals exists in America, or that the Camorra or the Mafia has become naturalized here. By reason of the laxity of the immigration laws, there have crept into this country some thousands of ex-convicts from Naples, Sicily and Calabria, along with millions of honest and industrious Italians; and, owing to the inefficiency of the police in various cities where these Italians are domiciled, the criminals among them are able to live by robbery and extortion, frequently accompanied by murder, their victims being the more helpless of their fellow countrymen.
>
> These fugitives from justice and gallows-birds, from whom it is America's duty to protect the law-abiding Italians who are doing yeoman service in the building of the Republic, are

members of the Italian race that have brought disgrace upon
the others, and upon whom the sensational press has conferred the title of "Black Hand Society." How many of these
criminals there are in the United States it is impossible, for
obvious reasons, to estimate with any degree of accuracy.
Lieutenant Petrosino, who is in charge of the little Italian
Squad in the Police Department of New York and probably
knows more about the predatory brotherhood than anyone
else, says that they may number as many as from three to
four percent of the Italian population. They are no more organized, however, than are the many thousands of lawbreakers of other nationalities in America.

Italian outlaws were able to reach this country almost as
easily as the honest Italians, D'Amato declared. It was true
that an ex-convict could not obtain a passport from the Italian government and sail on an Italian ship, "but there is
nothing to prevent his crossing the frontier and leaving from
any port outside Italy to which he may make his way." The
Neapolitan, Sicilian, or Calabrian desperado, "once he has
reached these shores, finds the conditions ideal for levying
tribute upon the feebler folk among his countrymen." In
nearly all the large cities, particularly of the East and Middle
West, he would find them living in colonies by themselves:

> Conditions are much the same in these colonies all over the
> country. They are generally located in a poor quarter of the
> town, which is not policed as well as those where the native
> American lives. The newcomers, moreover, are timid in their
> strange surroundings; they are ignorant of the law of the land;
> few of them can speak English, even if they dared to com-
> plain of outrages perpetrated upon them. And when the hum-
> ble and respectable Italians do appeal to the police and find
> that the law cannot, or will not, protect them, they are re-
> duced to a pitiful extremity that has driven scores of potential
> citizens back to Italy, kept many an industrious resident in
> actual bondage to the lawbreakers, and in some instances
> even forced hitherto honest men to become criminals them-
> selves.

Aside from the urban Italians, D'Amato pointed out, there
were some five hundred thousand laborers of the race distributed throughout the United States, working in mines and
vineyards or on railroads, irrigation ditches, and farms, who
were equally victims of their rapacious countrymen. "In

fact, there is scarcely a point throughout the length and breadth of the country where a few Italians are gathered together that some criminals of the race have not fastened themselves upon them." Every reader of the newspapers was familiar with the outrages that, in the name of the "Black Hand," had been perpetrated among the Italians, beginning about ten years before and increasing coincidentally with the Italian immigration. "Murder has been a common crime, and the dynamiting of houses and shops, the kidnapping of children, with every species of blackmail and extortion, was of so frequent occurrence that the mind became dulled to the enormity of these offences." In New York conditions had been worse than anywhere else; and yet, with half a million Italians in the population, "there are to-day only forty Italians in the Police Department." During his twenty-nine years of residence in New York, D'Amato had found two causes that operated to the blackening of the Italian name in respect to crime: the sensationalism of the yellow press and the ignorance and recklessness of the police in recording arrests. Almost every dark-skinned European not speaking English, he charged, was put down on police records as an Italian. The attitude of a part of the American press with regard to the Italian could be comprehended only if "the theory is accepted that the truth is a consideration secondary to the publication of sensations that are calculated to increase the day's sales."

The term *Black Hand*, D'Amato said, had first been used in this country about ten years before, probably by some Italian desperado who had heard of the exploits of the Spanish society and considered the combination of words to be high sounding and terror inspiring. "One or two crimes committed under the symbol gave it a vogue among the rapacious brotherhood; and as it looked well and attracted attention in their headlines, the newspapers finally applied it to all crimes committed by the Italian banditti in the United States." Thus the press actually facilitated the commission of crime among the Italian ex-convicts by making it appear that their work was that of a single powerful society. Criminals were still coming in, he noted, and only stricter immigration laws would keep them out. He thought that all foreign ex-convicts who could not prove that they were making an honest living should be deported and that there should be consular inspection overseas to keep any more of the criminal class from coming.[36]

Watchorn, in company with William B. Howland of the *Outlook*, one of the founders of the Society for the Protection of Italian Immigrants, was received by the king of Italy. The talk turned to the problem of recent bomb outrages in New York, which had been attributed to the Black Hand. The king "frankly declared his belief that the Black Hand and similar alleged organizations were for the most part mythical." Even the Mafia and the Camorra were nonexistent, "at least non-existent as organized bodies with rulers like those of a hierarchy and the definitely defined purposes which the imagination of novelists and popular tradition attribute to them." As for the Black Hand, it was merely a gang of detached malefactors that had happened to come into existence among Italians, as in the past other organizations of malefactors had been formed among the people of other nationalities. He advised the two Americans to study the statistics on crime in Italy while they were in Rome. These data showed a wonderful diminution of crime over the last twenty years. Watchorn and Howland were reported as enchanted with the king's cordiality. They were indebted for their kind reception to the Duke of the Abruzzi, whom they had met on the *Lusitania* on the voyage from New York to Liverpool. The duke had written to the king requesting that he give them an audience.

Seizing on D'Amato's article, the *Times* declared the Black Hand myth exploded. "There is no regular organization of these criminals outside the columns of the yellow press," it proclaimed. Informed by cable of Watchorn's interview with the king, it gave the story extended treatment. The *Herald* snorted in disbelief. "Black Hand murder, Black Hand bombs, and Black Hand letters," it said, were reported from several places in New York City at the same time that the king of Italy was assuring New York's commissioner of immigration that no such thing as Black Hand crime existed in that country or America. "Lines must be crossed somewhere."[37]

Commissioner Bingham, roused by a new wave of Black Hand outrages and the activities of an Armenian extortionist and terrorist group known as the Hunchakists in the summer of 1907, had meanwhile been in a prolonged struggle with the Board of Aldermen in an effort to get an appropriation for a secret detective force to cope with the problem of foreign crime. In an article in *Harper's Weekly* that autumn, he noted that the existence of great foreign colonies in New York enormously complicated the problems of the police department. This brought to the city "the predatory criminals of all nations," he declared, "as well as the feuds of the Armenian Hunchakists, the Neapolitan Camorra, the Sicilian Mafia, the Chinese Tongs, and other quarrels of the scum of the earth." What he wanted, he said in his official report at the end of the year, was a branch in the Detective Bureau "composed entirely of 'civilians' engaged and discharged at will by the Police Commissioner, to be composed of the best men who can be found anywhere in the world, regardless of any conditions but efficiency." The Black Hand menace he felt to be most pressing. There were some fifteen or twenty groups of foreigners "who work the Black Hand racket," he told a *Times* reporter. They were known to exist, but it was hard to get the goods on them. Much had been done by Petrosino's little band, now numbering thirty to forty men, but there were simply not enough Italian policemen to protect the community, which now included about half a million people. Editors of Italian newspapers confirmed this, giving the *Times* "the same cry of lack of protection for the Italian quarter of the city."

Members of the Board of Aldermen began attacking Bingham, demanding his resignation, and he replied in kind. In a speech at the dinner of the Police Lieutenants' Benevolent Association he defied the aldermen, charging that crime could be bought from politicians, and declared that he would not quit. His remarks were received "with great applause." The next day he told the *Times* that there were "crime factories" in Manhattan protected by men in the board. If he had $100,000 for his secret detective force he could clean up the city, but the aldermen did not dare give him the money to hire the men who could root out crime. Only a few weeks before, Petrosino had told a *Times* reporter, "It would surprise the public if it knew the names of some of the men in both parties who have come to me to intercede for some Italian criminals."

Some time later Bingham appeared before the finance committee of the board to renew his application for funds. "Little Tim" Sullivan, chairman of the committee, said he thought "this Black Hand business is all a fake. I don't believe in it." "You come up to my office and I'll show you some Black Hand data that will make your hair stand on end," the commissioner replied. The committee finally recommended an appropriation of $25,000, but the proposal was defeated by the full board the next day. Some members, said the *Times*, "talked in a way to justify a slight suspicion that their real objection to the plan was fear of its possible efficiency." It admitted that there were good arguments against a secret detective force but noted that Attorney General Bonaparte was just then asking Congress for a regular detective force for the Department of Justice, instead of paying Secret Service men "by the job." This, the first move toward the establishment of what eventually became known as the Federal Bureau of Investigation, the editor approved. He thought that the city could use a similar force to its advantage for special cases, under an adequate system of checks.[38]

While Bingham was seeking funds to create a secret service to deal with the Black Hand, the Italian community was moving for its own protection. As early as 1904, when little Tony Mannino had been kidnaped, Antonio Zucca, ex-coroner and president of the Italian Chamber of Commerce, had called a meeting of the executive committee of the chamber. To the Italian businessmen of New York, the *Tribune* noted, this kidnaping "came nearer home . . . than any of the minor outrages which the blackmailers have perpetrated." The committee demanded more Italians on the police force, and some members urged that the police be given powers similar to those in Italy, where they could stop any citizen and ask his business. "This land has too great liberty for the criminal class," Zucca declared, "and for that reason many find it easier to write blackmailing letters than to work." One member urged that every immigrant be compelled to show a *fedina penale*, or moral passport, signed by the prefect of police of the district from which he came.

Nothing further seems to have been done at the time. The elder Mannino, apparently, paid the ransom, the boy was released, and everybody relaxed. The Italian press continued to dramatize the crime problem, however, throwing the blame for Black Hand operations on the Americans for admitting too many Italian criminals and charging that the American police and court systems were defective in comparison with the Italian ones. But as the American press seemed to find "Black Hand" as good a stick as "Mafia" to beat them with, editors began shifting Black Hand stories to inside pages and advising Italians not to communicate details to the American reporters but to the Italian consul general. When the roundup of weapons-carrying Italians took place in 1907, Zucca, now on the Board of Assessors, told a reporter that he knew of no movement to aid the police. James E. March, a wealthy Italian active in Republican politics on the East Side, said he thought the police should keep at the job and arrest men who carried weapons, whether they were Italians or not. "I have tried to get up a society among the Italians for the purpose of giving information against blackmailing Italians to the police," he said, "but nobody will join it." Merchants and businessmen in the community seemed to be afraid. "Some of them would rather pay blackmail, and thus encourage the Black Hand scoundrels, than give information against them."[39]

But as the problem continued to grow and blackmail became epidemic, the editor of the *Bollettino della Sera* tried again. Early in 1908 he reprinted a statement that Petrosino had given to the *Times* to the effect that "The United States has become the refuge of all the delinquents and the bandits of Italy, of Sicily, Sardinia, and Calabria." He charged that when the French authorities had cleaned out the criminal element in Tunis, thousands of Italian criminals who had taken refuge there from the home authorities departed for the United States and were admitted. There should be better inspection of Italian immigrants. There was no central organization of these criminals called the Black Hand, he had

said. It was made up of small bands, usually headed by a
man who had been a bandit in Italy or Sicily. These bands
were not connected and were usually bitter enemies. It was
the newspapers that had created the idea that there was one
big criminal club. The Italian population was not so much
afraid to give evidence against them as it was unable to act
in concert. Italian immigrants didn't know what to do with
the freedom that was given them. Petrosino had gone so far
as to say that the so-called Black Hand outrages in the city
would never be stamped out "until some restrictions are
made in the admission of Italian immigrants to this country."

Following the bombing of Pasquale Patti's bank on
Elizabeth Street, a meeting was called at 178 Park Row
above the *Bollettino* office, "in order to devise some means,
similar to the 'White Hand' Society in Chicago, to suppress
Black Hand outrages." The meeting was in response to a
Bollettino editorial warning that the doors of this country
would be closed to Italians unless something was done to
put a stop to the crimes that were besmirching the Italian
name. A society with over three hundred members was
formed—Association de Vigilanza e Protezione Italiana—and
Frank L. Frugone, the editor, was made president. The
Times hailed the move as looking toward the regeneration of
the Italian community. The meeting seemed to have had
some moral effect when in March, Patti's bank was visited
again by what he said were threatening Black Handers. Patti
and his son-in-law shot and killed one of them. What had actually happened, it developed later, was that there had been
a run on his bank after it was said that Lupo the Wolf was
after him. There was some sort of row and Patti started
shooting. The man killed seems actually to have been a de-
positor. Patti soon disappeared with all his depositors'
money. Four years later the police were still looking for him.
But for the moment he was hailed as a hero.[40]

By the end of April, the combined efforts of federal and
local authorities, with the help of Frugone's society, were
beginning to show results. A good many of the criminals on
Commissioner Bingham's list had been rounded up, and
Commissioner-General Frank P. Sargent of the Immigration

Service was working hard with Secretary Straus to process deportation warrants. Five Italians with criminal records were deported in one day. "It is likely," said the *Tribune*, "that several more on General Bingham's list will be deported as soon as the inquiry into their cases is ended." Watchorn returned from Italy a few days later and, on Straus's directive, went at once to confer with Commissioner Bingham. He was reported as enthusiastic about the Italian system of police registration of all citizens and evidently foresaw active cooperation with the authorities overseas. That day he signed two more orders for the deportation of men whom the police had gathered up.

The principal snag in deportation was the date of arrival, the *Times* understood. A criminal or an anarchist could not be deported if he had been in this country three years. Another problem, Watchorn explained, was names. Lieutenant Petrosino had been active in gathering information about objectionable aliens, but in many cases the name he sent to Ellis Island was as common in Italy as John Smith is here. A dozen men of the same name might be found in the records as having arrived at about the same time. That put it up to the police "to prove just which owner of that particular name they seek to send out of the country." Watchorn did not mention the use of aliases, which was common and must have complicated the problem further. The time limit on deportation of criminals should be abolished, he urged. "If the law were so amended, deportation would not depend on a record of landing here but on the record of their evil deeds."[41]

There already had been an effort to strengthen the 1907 immigration law by adding a literacy test, which was dropped from that measure after a hard fight. The proposed amendment was frankly directed at Sicilians and South Italians. Congressman John L. Burnett of Alabama, a member of the House immigration committee, had been in Sicily with the commission created by the new law to study the whole question of immigration. He thought the amendment would keep out 50 percent of the Sicilian immigrants. These people were breeding much of the crime in the large cities of the Northeast and the Middle West, he said, "so that they have had in New York to establish a special detective bureau for the purpose of arresting the Italian criminals, and Mr. Joe Petrosino is the chief of the bureau, himself an Italian, I believe." Petrosino had said in an interview that there were "132 of them doing time in Sing Sing prison on account of the 'Black Hand,' and you cannot pick up a newspaper, Mr. Chairman, without seeing an account of these 'Black Hand' atrocities in Pittsburg or Chicago or New York or some other of the great cities."

Another member of the committee mentioned the Molly Maguires among the Irish and thought the Black Hand would disappear as they had done. Burnett did not think this was a good parallel. The Molly Maguires had operated in the hard coal region of Pennsylvania at a time when the whole region was demoralized. The Sicilian bandits had been operating at home for centuries and were merely continuing their traditional practices in the great cities of America. "You were not with us, I believe," he told the chairman, "in the trip to Sicily; but down there we had read and heard of the acts of the brigands of southern Italy and of Sicily, and we asked them, 'Where are your brigands now?' They said, 'They have all gone to America.' "[42]

This effort to amend the law failed as earlier and later efforts to create a literacy test for immigrants did until 1917. There were also recurring attempts to do away with the three-year limitation on the deportation of criminal aliens, as Immigration Commissioner Watchorn had urged, and to make aliens subject to deportation for crimes committed in this country. Congressman William S. Bennet of New York, a member of both the immigration committee and the immigration commission, was no such nativist as Burnett of Alabama, but he was concerned about the alien crime problem. He, too, had been in Italy and Sicily as a member of the commission in 1907. "In view of the frequency of the so-called 'Black Hand' outrages in various parts of this country," the *Washington Herald* had observed at the time, "especial interest" would attach to a statement of his. "Congressman Bennet," it declared, "is reported to have made the discovery that the return to Italy of so many Italians from the United States is due to the fact that they are safer in Italy from the secret societies."

Bennet confirmed this later. He had just received a pamphlet, he wrote, which said there was no such thing as the Black Hand. But there was a Black Hand. Possibly it was not an organization like the Molly Maguires, with a grip and a password, but "an organization with a very thorough understanding." Readers should ask the ordinary, well-to-do Italian about that and see what he said. In Italy he had found a condition that was new even to the Italian government: men who had returned to the village of their youth because they had been threatened by the Black Hand in the United States. "There was an old baron in Galina, down in Calabria," said Bennet, "who shook his finger at me across the room in a council chamber in the village and asked why we did not enforce the law in the United States so that decent, self-respecting Italians that came here could stay here, and I did not have any answer for him for the moment."[43]

In March 1908, Bennet sought to have the House rules suspended and a bill passed to make aliens deportable when convicted of felonies here. Immigration officials strongly favored such a measure, and the National Liberal Immigration League had circularized to the press a somewhat similar proposal in the previous summer. The league had fought the literary test and helped to defeat it but urged "a drastic policy against those who abuse the hospitality of this country." It was making efforts "to secure the deportation of members of the Black Hand and of criminals of all races." Instead of being held in our prisons as a burden to the community, "all new arrivals who become criminals should be deported." This was being done with those who became public charges, it argued, and criminals were a real public charge. The League's proposal had met with wide acceptance by newspapers from Maine to Virginia and from Brooklyn, New York, to Lincoln, Nebraska. Bennet's bill, however, would have made alien criminals serve out their terms before being deported.

There was considerable debate on the proposal. One member thought that the administration of our immigration laws must be very lax to permit men who had a criminal record at home to enter the country. Bennet replied that if he had the time he could explain four different ways in which foreign criminals could get in without reflecting in any degree on our administration of these laws. But he wanted to say that this was one of the objects of the bill, "so that the criminal abroad will not have, as I find that some of them do have, as I am told by chiefs of police in foreign countries they do have, the idea that this is an asylum of refuge for criminals. It is not and ought not to be, and if you pass this law it will deter the criminal class from coming." The bill failed to pass, and later efforts along the same line, including attempts to tighten up the law regarding stowaways and alien seamen, were fruitless. While a wave of national hysteria over the so-called White Slave trade brought drastic legislation against foreign prostitutes and procurers, nothing further was done about other types of alien criminals until the general revision of the immigration laws in 1917.[44]

The commissioner-general of immigration, in his annual report for the fiscal year 1908, called attention to the circular issued in March, directing active cooperation with local authorities in the location and deportation of alien criminals and anarchists. In this field of administration, he noted, "the most discouraging obstacles to even comparative success are met." However, "while doubtless many aliens of said classes have succeeded in passing the inspectors and many others are still in this country, much has been accomplished and the foundation has been laid for even better results in the future." In spite of more intensive inspection of immigrants, made possible by the slackening of immigration following the panic of 1907, the statistics did not show any increase in rejections of criminals but rather the reverse since the previous year. This was due, the commissioner-general believed, to either the fact that the criminal class had been discouraged from embarking by the campaign against them or that its members had become more efficient in concealing their identity and status.[45] A simpler answer, not mentioned in the report, might have been that criminals were discouraged from coming during a period of depression, just as were honest immigrants. The proliferation of blackmail in the Italian colonies of New York, Chicago, and other cities had followed hard on the heels of the tremendous Italian immigration that began around the turn of the century. Criminals followed their victims to the greener pastures of America in prosperous times. In a year when alien departures from the United States for a time came close to balancing arrivals, it does not seem at all strange that fewer potential Black Handers should have come here.

Criminals of the Black Hand type remained active in New York City, however, in spite of the intensified campaign against them and in spite of the fact that hundreds of thousands of their potential victims were leaving the country, at least briefly, in the depression year 1908. In July, Petrosino's men arrested the man they claimed was the master bomb-maker for the Black Hand and at the same time raided a saloon in East 11th Street that was believed to be a principal Black Hand headquarters. In a style that a later generation has come to recognize in connection with the campaign against narcotics, police spokesmen gave out that these raids were "considered the most important ever made by Headquarters against the Black Hand." But only a few weeks later Salvatore Spinella, who owned several tenement houses in East 11th Street, told a *Times* reporter in the office of the *Bollettino* that one or another of his houses had been bombed five times since he told the Black Hand to go to hell with their blackmailing demands. "My business is ruined," he said. "My tenants leave, all but six of thirty-two families." His whole family lived in terror. A policeman was posted in front of his house, but what good was he? Spinella and his brother Francesco kept armed watch, but how long could this endure?[46]

Editor Frugone thought that the situation was a disgrace. Activities of the Black Hand type could be ended as they had been in Italy, he believed. What was needed was a secret police. They could be recruited from Italians who had served in the army and the *carabinieri*. Frugone said that since the meeting the winter before of Italians to protest against the Black Hand he had received visits from dozens of such men who understood the problems thoroughly. He and his friends were organizing a secret committee to cooperate with the police. If Commissioner Bingham could get funds and authority to form such a force, he would have no trouble in getting the right men. The *Times* editorially endorsed the plan. "The case of Mr. Spinella may be repeated in the case of any American resident of New York," it warned. "The Italian detectives and plainclothes men are known, they are evaded, they are useless. What would the Board of Aldermen suggest? Can its members longer deny Commissioner Bingham's request?"[47]

The muckraking periodicals that formed the cutting edge of what came to be called the Progressive Movement for years had been happily exposing one evil after another in American society. They did not neglect the Black Hand. "The Skull and Crossbones flag of piracy is gone from the seas," the editor of *Everybody's Magazine* now noted in introducing an article by Lindsay Denison on the subject. "But in our cities flourishes the Black Hand, a symbol every bit as significant of greed and cruelty—even more an emblem of cowardice and treachery. The scoundrels who lurk behind the terror of the Black Hand wax fat and daily grow more arrogant in their contempt for American law and order." The article itself, though more subdued in tone, was sensational enough:

> A letter shoved through the crack under a door or dropped in a tenement letter-box, bearing the dread symbol of the Black Hand and the signature *La Mano Nera*, and containing a demand for money under threat of death or disaster. A few weeks later, if the demand in the letter is ignored, a knife-thrust in the dark, or, more commonly, the explosion of a crude bomb, which wrecks the first-floor front of the house. That is the Black Hand.

Black Hand extortion was evidence that our immigration laws were not stringent enough to keep out the very worst of the bad people that they were intended to exclude. "It represents the transferring to this country of the most lawless men and methods of the Camorra of Naples and the Mafia of Sicily." Its existence and growth were not only a disgrace to our system for maintaining public order. "It is an affront to the hundreds of thousands of useful, honest, happy-tempered Italians who have come to this country to take up the work from which the prospering Irish immigrant turned a generation ago." It was a deterrent to their progress; the price of prosperity in any decent business was a blackmailing demand from the Black Hand.

But the Black Hand did not exist. "The law and the police have not been battling with a great, complicated, and secretly united murdering graft-machine, but with individual products of the opportunities for criminal education afforded by Southern Italy for hundreds of years." It was true, as well as amusing, that "this murderous system was presented with its name by a reporter of a New York newspaper." There had been a secret society in Spain by this name as far back as the days of the Inquisition, which fought the government and the church. "It passed, and the secret societies of southern Italy were its heirs." Twenty years or more ago a report had been raised in Spain that it had been revived. "The story lingered in the brain of a *Herald* reporter," said Denison, garbling the facts, and one fine day he tried to rejuvenate waning interest in an Italian murder case by speculating on the coming to life of the Black Hand among Latin immigrants in America. "The other newspapers seized on the idea eagerly, and kept it going."

There were in New York then, and had been for many years, a great many Italian criminals. They did not form two percent of the Italian population, perhaps, "but nevertheless there were more of them than would have been allowed at large in Italy. There were blackmailers, swindlers, counterfeiters, kidnappers, robbers, and murderers among them." They were mostly from the same ports in southern Italy, and there was some general intercommunication among them. There were chiefs among them, as at home, but they had no hours of meeting, no lodge rooms, and no gang names. They had no prestige as a body. "And along came the benevolent and intelligent New York newspapers and gave them a name and then exploited it. And did the inchoate Italian criminal gangs grab the chance and keep it going? For an answer glance over the headlines of any New York newspaper any day."

It was hard for the native-born American to fathom the psychology of the respectable, hard-working Italians who submitted tamely to Black Hand impositions, Denison knew. The answer was to be found in Italy. The secret society of Sicily was the Mafia. "It is a criminal machine like our own Tammany Hall. Nobles and men of high standing belong to it, as well as leaders of gangs of bad men. It is by the actions of these gang leaders that the Mafia is known on this side of the ocean." One explanation was that the gentlemen among the Mafia had tried to restrain their brethren "and have so far succeeded that the worst and wickedest of the 'Low Mafia' are now in and about New York and Chicago, St. Louis and Denver." The Camorra of Naples was very much the same sort of organization. In both societies, members who had been caught and served a sentence were helped to get out of Italy. So was the Black Hand in the United States recruited. The Black Hand crimes reported in the newspapers represented only one out of a hundred or a thousand efforts at blackmail, because refusals of demands were few. The extent of such crimes could not be computed, but "there is hardly an Italian, from contractor to fruit-stand keeper, who has not been coerced into paying blackmail." Presently the Black Hander would be looking for victims outside the Italian-born population.

Denison described in detail the methods used by the criminal societies of Italy to get their ex-convict members out of the country and into the United States. Here conditions were highly favorable to their customary operations:

> And so it is that the Italian criminal does get out of Italy and into the United States despite both governments. And in the fullness of time it has come to pass that there are more Italian ex-convicts at large in the United States than there are in Italy—that all the daring, reckless, unreformable desperadoes of Italy are in this country, taking not only the purses but the good names of their former compatriots by means of the Black Hand.

The Black Hand gangs had only a very loose and fluid organization. The American police had not been able to make much headway against them. But it was disgraceful that except for Commissioner Bingham of New York, hampered as he was by "a trivial and stupid board of aldermen," no intelligent warfare had been made on Black Hand crime. Denison's remedy was more Italian police, both in uniform and in secret detective units. Along with these there should be more active cooperation with the Italian government. Italy was willing to take back its criminals. Money spent on this side to hunt them out "would clear our Italian settlements of a shameful scandal and terror."[48]

Bingham himself added to the hysteria by an article in the *North American Review*. Some months before there had been set up at police headquarters a new card file of detailed individual information on alien criminals. Now the commissioner, presumably drawing heavily on this new file, proclaimed that while the Hebrews in New York City were probably resonsible for 50 percent of the crime, and the Italans for only 20 percent, "the Italian malefactor is by far the greater menace to law and order." Of the five hundred thousand Italians in New York, 80 percent were from the South—from Naples, Sicily, and Calabria. While the great bulk of these people were among our best citizens, "there are fastened upon them a riffraff of desperate scoundrels, ex-convicts and jailbirds of the Camorra and the Mafia, such as has never before afflicted a civilized country in time of peace."

Kept under the strictest kind of surveillance at home, Bingham noted, Italian ex-convicts seized the first opportunity to slip away to America, where conditions were perfect for them, and live on the more helpless of their honest fellow countrymen. Here the newspapers had given them the terror-inspiring name of the Black Hand Society, and although they were actually without organization, "the individual criminal need only announce himself an agent of the Black Hand to obtain the prestige of an organization whose membership is supposed to be in the tens of thousands." It was impossible to exaggerate the enormity of the offenses committed by these transplanted malefactors, by whatever name they might be called. Murder, arson, kidnaping, bomb-throwing, blackmail, and robbery were of frequent occurrence in the Italian colonies throughout the United States. The audacity of these desperadoes was almost beyond belief. "Arrested for crimes that, proved against them, might give them capital punishment or life terms of imprisonment, they will obtain bail and return to the scene of their depredations to jeer at and threaten their victims."

The Sicilian bomb-planter was extremely difficult to catch, Bingham said. Moreover, "Petrosino and the members of his staff are the best-known men in New York to the Italian criminals, who naturally attempt to acquaint themselves with the person of every member of the squad before proceeding to the commission of crime." As for the deportation law, the immigration authorities placed the burden of proof of length of residence on the police. "Owing to deficiencies in our laws, dangerous foreign criminals whom the police have sent to Ellis Island for deportation have been set at liberty there, and have of course returned to continue their depredations." To add to the trials of the Italian Squad, three Italian ex-convicts who had been certified for deportation had escaped from the island after having been given into the custody of the immigration authorities. Bingham asked again for a secret service arm for the New York Police Department to cope with the situation.[49]

The *Globe and Commercial Advertiser* belittled Bingham's charges. "The Irishman, the German, the Italian, and the Jew have successively writhed under the whip of this kind of general indictment," it said. Now Police Commissioner Bingham said that the Jews, one-fourth of the population, committed 50 percent of New York's crimes and that the Italians, one-tenth of the population, committed 20 percent. The Liberal Immigration League, the *Globe* noted, had made a careful study of crime convictions in New York County during the past four years and found that 65 percent of the convictions were of native-born persons. There probably was a tendency toward delinquency in the second generation, it admitted, but this was temporary, "and there is nothing in the situation justifying the highly colored exaggerations of the police commissioner."

Bingham's injudicious article went a long way toward destroying his usefulness. There was resentment among the Italians, of course, but such charges against them were an old story. The reaction among the Jews was much more powerful. The Jews were used to hostility on religious grounds and to being denounced as Shylocks, but they were not accustomed to wholesale denunciation as criminals. Old differences that had kept German and Russian Jews apart were beginning to ease, and a new united front was developing. Bingham's charges acted as a catalyst. The storm of indignation was such that Bingham issued a formal apology. His main purpose in the article, he said, had been to make a plea for a secret service branch in his detective force; the statistics were only incidental. They had been compiled by others and it now appeared that they were unreliable. "Hence it becomes my duty to say so and repudiate them." Prominent Jews were quoted as satisfied with this performance; little was said of what the Italians thought about it.[50]

Whatever the figures on immigrant crime may have been for the few months during which the new file had been accumulating, and however much or little Bingham may have relied on them for the generalizations in his article, there are available statistics over a longer period that throw grave doubt on the validity of his charges against the two groups as a whole. The police department had for years published a table of the nativity of those arrested as part of its annual report. This report consistently showed the native-born far in the lead, with the Irish for a long time'second but far behind. For a number of years the natives of Germany were in third place in the table, with the Italians and the Russians (that is, Russian Jews), competing for fourth position. Gradually the Italians and the Russians, as their numbers grew, elbowed the Germans out of third place, running almost neck and neck. Eventually both overtook the Irish, but neither group had come near achieving first place before the table was discontinued in 1906. The native-born were still far in the lead. Many of these were no doubt second-generation immigrants, but the tables did not take this into account. The Board of City Magistrates also sporadically published figures on the nativity of those held for trial or summarily tried and convicted. They showed much the same pattern as the police reports between 1900 and 1906.[51]

The report of the Board of City Magistrates for 1905 had some interesting comment on "the apparent increase in the number of persons convicted and held of Italian, Greek and Russian birth." There had been "an abnormal increase in the serious and higher crimes" during the year, but many of the cases involving these groups were the result of their selling wares in the streets without having the necessary license and of the stricter enforcement of Health Department and

Fire Department orders and regulations. All of these were "given the dignity of penal statutes when violated." In other words, much of the crime charged against the largest of the new immigrant groups consisted in illegal pushcart peddling, obstructing hallways and fire escapes, and indiscriminately dumping garbage.[52] The crime situation among East Side immigrants—Italians, Jews, and others—was bad enough; this sort of material could be used to make it appear very sinister indeed.

CHAPTER III

The Petrosino Mission and Its Aftermath

The Italian government had often been charged, as Great Britain and other European states were charged, with promoting the migration of its ex-convicts to America. In 1891, following the New Orleans lynching, the commissioner of immigration at New York reported that thirty-one Italian criminals with passports had been turned back at the Barge Office. Former Commissioner of Immigration Joseph H. Senner, testifying before the U.S. Industrial Commission in 1899, referred to "that undesirable immigration—ticket-of-leave men who are brought to this country." This had been a practice in the past, he said, but he was sure that it had been stopped all over Europe by the tight administrative measures embodied in the immigration law of 1893. A representative of the Italian government, testifying before the same body, denied that criminals were exported by his government. He said he knew of only one case of a criminal who had been issued a passport to the United States and that that was by administrative error. Gino Speranza, making a report to the American Institute of Criminal Law and Criminology years later, referred to the belief that there were governments "which are most happy to dump their criminals upon us." He thought that had probably once been true and had "even heard it vouched that at a certain port of Southern Europe officials used to actually take criminals on ship board to make sure that they would come to the land of the free." But conditions had changed, and he was sure this

was no longer done. There still existed, he admitted, conni-
vance among lower officials "at getting criminals out of
Europe."[1]

However general the practice may once have been, the
Italian government in 1901 adopted a strict policy of controlling emigration that visualized protection to honest emigrants
and the screening out of undesirables. A royal decree of that
year restricted emigration to three designated ports and,
among other provisions, forbade the issuance of a passport
to anyone likely to be refused admittance to the country of
destination. This prohibition, of course, included ex-convicts
heading for the United States. The government was further
much concerned about the welfare of its emigrants after they
had passed Ellis Island and subsidized the New York Society for the Protection of Italian Immigrants, of which
Speranza was secretary. An Emigration Department was
created in the government at Rome, and in 1904, Adolfo
Rossi, its inspector, traveled extensively in the United
States, in company with Speranza. He studied working conditions affecting Italians (they were often very bad), tried to
promote colonization in the South, away from the big cities,
and conferred at length with American immigration officials.
The policy of the Italian government looked not only toward
compliance with the American immigration laws but also to
the return of criminals wanted at home. The *Nation*, praising
the measures taken by Italy, thought that international cooperation was better than "sending secret-service men to discover dark and fearful plots on the part of European governments to dump their criminals here." Watchorn, on his
trip to Italy, became convinced that the Italian government
was making every effort to stop the traffic.[2]

There was reason to suspect, however, that enforcement
of the Italian passport regulations left something to be desired. When Congressman Bennet was in Italy in 1907, he
talked with the mayor of a city from which many immigrants
came. The passport procedure called for the mayor to sign a
nulla osta, indicating that there was nothing against a man.
The mayor told him frankly that "if the prefect of police has
no objection, I don't object." A government official who had
been escorting Bennet, telling him how well the Italian gov-

ernment enforced the passport law, thereupon remarked, "Of course we enforce the American law, but if you were a chief of police and there was a man who was making you a lot of trouble, and you had a chance to get him away and not come back, what would you do?" While most criminals got out of the country illegally, Bennet believed, some left Italy with the blessing of the local officials.

Commissioner Bingham now sought more active Italian cooperation in curbing the Black Hand menace. This called for action at the diplomatic level. Arthur Woods, a young man of independent means and with the highest connections in the Republican administration, had been brought into the police department as a deputy commissioner in charge of the detective force. Woods was trying to make it a professional organization something like Scotland Yard, which he had gone abroad to study at his own expense before taking office. Bingham, in the fall of 1908, sent him to Washington, where he conferred with President Roosevelt, who referred him with approval to the State Department. The matter was taken up with Ambassador Lloyd C. Griscom in Rome, and the Italian government obligingly tightened up its passport regulations. Local officials were now required "to make certain that the applicant for a passport is not a person likely to become a public charge, and that he has not been convicted of a crime involving moral turpitude and that he does not emigrate under a labor contract. In all these cases the passport must be refused." As far as Italian law could go, criminals and other unwanted immigrants were barred from leaving home for the United States.[3]

In practice, this was not much more than a friendly gesture, since until years later the American immigration laws did not require the presentation of a passport to the examining officials. If an ex-convict could slip aboard a liner without a passport or with a forged passport, there was no way of identifying him at Ellis Island except through questioning him. The criminal, who as like as not had already been back and forth, usually knew all the right answers. He was likely to be caught only when a tip had come from the Italian consul general or an enemy that he was on his way. Most criminals, however, probably slipped across the border and took ship, usually as members of the crew, from France or some other country where exit passports were not required. The Italian Emigration Department estimated clandestine emigration at several thousand a year.

The U.S. Immigration Commission had employed confidential agents in the collection of data on foreign criminals. The study had been concentrated on the Italian element, "because of the popular opinion, voiced in the press, that large numbers of Italians having criminal records in Italy came to the United States" and that Italian crimes of violence in this country were in large measure due to them. It had been centered on New York City and its vicinity, "because of the large proportion of the Italian population of the country gathered there," and because of the assistance that the New York Police Department could render. Requests were sent to Italian courts for copies of the penal records of a number of persons reported on. A considerable number of penal certificates were secured and turned over to the police and the immigration authorities.[4] Petrosino and his squad had sifted this list with mixed results.

Bingham had been unable to get an appropriation for a secret service, but he had gotten substantial funds from private sources, presumably wealthy Italians of Frugone's committee. Secret agents had been employed and considerable progress had been made in coping with the Black Hand. Much more needed doing, he reported at the end of the year. An Italian criminologist employed by the commission who had also done investigative work for the police, had prepared a plan for the collection at the sources of penal certificates and other data on a systematic and continuing basis. He pointed out that this could not be done efficiently by mail. This plan was commissioned by and presented to Professor Jeremiah W. Jenks of Cornell, a member of the commission, who turned it over to Bingham.

The plan called for sending a trustworthy man to Italy to set it in motion. He was to check the judicial records in certain areas for lists of criminals who had completed their terms in recent years, to determine through the police or private sources who among them had gone to the United States, and to collect statistics on criminals who were to complete their terms within the next few years. He was to set up a network of agents, preferably lawyers, to follow up the work and forward the data, so that the men could be picked up on arrival and deported. Bingham and Woods decided to launch the plan.[5]

This was probably the most ambitious intelligence operation that the New York Police Department had ever undertaken. Certainly it was one of the most dangerous. Petrosino, as no doubt the best qualified man available, was selected to carry it out. The whole operation was supposed to be secret, but there were devastating leaks. Frugone, the *Bollettino* editor, evidently knew much about it; but he confined his comment to local aspects of the plan, which included an intensified campaign in New York. Early in the new year, he printed a formal notice "Against the Black Hand," urging all honest Italians to aid Bingham by sending him, marked "Personal," all threatening letters and information about Black Handers, with descriptions of individuals. At the end of January the *Times* announced "Secret Service for Bingham," telling of the detectives he had who were not on the police force, in spite of the fact that the Board of Aldermen had refused to make an appropriation for a secret service. These men were "gathering evidence about the Black Hand and other secret societies." Petrosino had been transferred from the Italian Squad to head this new secret branch. Lieutenant Arthur Gloster of Brooklyn had taken over the Italian Squad.

On February 20 the *Times* reported that Petrosino had a roving commission to act as he saw fit in breaking up the Black Hand gangs and that he had disappeared from headquarters. It had been given out that he was on vacation, but this was not to be taken seriously. He had been seen in Washington, where he was believed to be in communication with Secret Service officials. He had returned to New York, conferred with Woods and Bingham, and disappeared again. "He may be on his way to Europe." The same day the *Herald* described the new secret service in some detail and stated openly that Petrosino had gone to Italy and Sicily, "where he will procure important information about Italian criminals who have come to this country."[6]

Petrosino had left New York secretly and under an assumed name on February 9, 1909, with letters of introduction from the State Department to Ambassador Griscom and a formidable list of Italian criminals then in the United States. Arrigo Petacco, his biographer, has traced his movements minutely from the time he embarked for Italy. The purser on the ship, the Italian liner *Duca di Genova*, recognized him. Landing at Genoa on February 21, Petrosino hurried to Rome where the next day he found the American embassy closed for Washington's Birthday. Roaming the city, he was recognized by the editor of *L'Araldo*, a New York Italian newspaper, who was covering the recent Messina earthquake. Together they went to a restaurant where they ran into Giovanni Branchi, former Italian consul general in New York, who knew Petrosino well.

The next day Petrosino called on Ambassador Griscom, who arranged for him to see the Italian minister of the interior and the head of the national police. Petrosino did not actually see Giovanni Giolitti, the minister, but his secretary and explained his "study trip" on international crime. He was sent to Francesco Leonardi, the police chief, who gave him a letter of introduction to subordinates directing them to give him "all possible facilities" on what he had explained was his mission to study crime. He did not, apparently, disclose that part of the mission was to set up what amounted to a spy network. Petrosino made a short trip to Padula, his home town, where his brother showed him an Italian paper with a reprint of the *Herald* story. This was alarming, but he went ahead. On the train to Naples he was recognized by a former captain of the *carabinieri*. From Naples he took a coastal steamer at once to Palermo, landing there on the morning of February 28.[7]

He registered at a hotel under a false name and then called on the American consul, William H. Bishop. He told Bishop, and Bishop only, of his plans and said he had informers in Palermo. He went to a bank and opened an account in his own name, asking to have his mail sent there. The same day he began collecting penal certificates of men on his list at the local courthouse. For nearly a week he avoided the Italian police, roaming Palermo and nearby towns without leaving a trace. When he did call on Police Commissioner Baldassare Ceola with letters of introduction from Bishop, he said he was trying to find out whether passports conformed to the laws and made it evident that he did not trust the local authorities. Ceola offered him a bodyguard, which he refused, and turned him over to a subordinate. On March 11 he told Bishop he was going to the town of Caltanisetta to check records in the courthouse. He said he would be back in Palermo the next day as he had appointments there, including an important one at nine in the evening. The same day he was recognized on the street by a man whom he had recently caused to be deported. "Have already met criminals who recognized me from New York. I am on dangerous ground," he recorded in his notebook. Returning the next afternoon, he made copies of material he had collected, adding to his list a fresh note with the name of "Vito Cascio Ferro, born in Sambuca Zabut, resident of Bisaquino, Province of Palermo, dreaded criminal." After dinner at a cafe, where he was seen talking briefly with two men, he went into the Piazza Marina. A few minutes later shots were heard, and his body was found near the Garibaldi Garden at the center of the piazza.[8]

There was a great sensation in the New York press. The *Herald*, which had excellent cable service, first picked up the story. "Police Lieutenant Joseph Petrosino Is Assassinated in Sicily, Where He Had Gone in War on Black Hand," it proclaimed in flaring headlines. Other journals followed suit the next day. Petrosino had gone to Palermo to confer with local police officials in the effort to stop the immigration of criminals, the *Herald* said. Reporters from other papers, less well informed, besieged police headquarters for information on Petrosino's mission, but Bingham and Deputy Commissioner Woods were at first close-mouthed. Under his silence, Italian newspapers began charging Bingham with being in league with the Black Hand and having knowingly sent Petrosino into a trap. Bingham's secretary, a former newspaperman, talked more freely. Commissioner Bingham, he let reporters understand, did not believe that the police authorities in some of the smaller cities of Italy and Sicily were sufficiently vigilant in preventing ex-convicts from coming to America as soon as their terms of imprisonment had been served. He wanted to establish close relations between Italian and New York police authorities so that headquarters would be kept posted on the movements of all the ex-convicts, especially of Sicily, "because from this island come the worst of the criminals with whom Petrosino's special squad has had to deal."[9]

Petrosino was a legendary figure in Italy, where he was called the "Italian Sherlock Holmes." Rumors from Italian cities on his mission and murder were rife. From Naples came a report that they had caused "an enormous sensation among the members of the Neapolitan Camorra." They said that "the Black Hand condemned Petrosino to death" after he had arrested Erricone, the "Generalissimo of the Camorra," in 1907. The *Sun* carried to police headquarters a story from Rome that Petrosino had gone to Italy to prepare security for a forthcoming visit by ex-President Roosevelt, against whose life there was a plot. An official of the police department "who helped plan the work that Petrosino was sent to Italy to carry out," presumably Woods, thereupon gave out an official version of his mission:

> We sent Petrosnio over there to get at the root of the Black Hand business. He had a number of things to do. He was to get certificates and records from the Italian Government and police, to arrange reciprocal methods of work between the Italian police and our department in keeping tab on criminal immigrants, to see if some method couldn't be arranged to keep known criminals from coming to this country, and to do secret service work.
>
> Petrosino was to have stayed in Italy six or eight months and a man was to have been sent from this department to assist him. The man had not been selected when Petrosino was killed. It is simply nonsense to say that he was there in connection with a "plot." He was doing police work, lots of it, and he wasn't much more than started.[10]

The Italian community of New York was deeply stirred by the news of Petrosino's death. He was perhaps better known by sight and reputation than any other Italian in the city. His passing shocked and saddened most citizens, but there must have been more than a few who secretly exulted. Italian newspapers generally praised him and deplored his loss to the community. The *Bollettino*, which was inclined to lay the blame on Bingham for revealing Petrosino's movements, foresaw damaging repercussions. "It will certainly rebound on the American people themselves and may have serious consequences." Italians would feel humiliated. What would be thought and said of Italians in the face of such a crime? "We will answer to the attack that the Black Hand are not all Italians and that the assassins are not all Sicilians, among whom are many honorable people deserving of respect and esteem. The assassins of Petrosino are wild beasts capable of the most terrible crimes. They have no country, no religion, no family, and no civilization."

Il Telegrafo was quoted as saying that "The assassination of Petrosino is an evil day for the Italians of America, and none of us can any longer deny that there is an organized Black Hand Society in the United States. The agents of the Society in Sicily were evidently aware of Petrosino's coming, and they prepared to kill him accordingly." *L'Araldo* pointed out that now was the time for Italians to take action "to prevent the spreading of that criminality which has brought so much unjust discredit on the name of the Italians in the United States."[11]

Il Progresso refrained from editorial comment but carried front-page stories on the Petrosino case for several days. When Hearst's *New York Journal* ran an editorial belittling the Black Hand menace and calling for greater police protection for the Italian community, *Il Progresso* reprinted it in English and Italian on its front page, urging readers to circulate it. "The Black Hand is a good bit of a myth," the *Journal* editorial said. It was the work of small groups of young rowdies who used the picturesque name for the old, familiar blackmail. "The fact is that the Italian, as a rule, is a very peaceful, law-abiding citizen. At his blackhandest, he cannot compare with our American Night Riders, that whip and murder men in a quarrel about tobacco or cotton, and cannot compare with our mob murderers, that burn and hang negroes—often getting the wrong man." New York, it should be recognized, was—next to Naples, Milan, and Rome—the largest Italian city in the world. "The Italians pay their taxes, and pay their rent, and do a great deal of hard work. They are entitled to police protection, AND THEY HAVE NOT HAD IT." The average citizen, and newspaper writers, "should stop the everlasting Black Hand talk."[12]

Hearst was a perennial candidate for public office and consistently made a special play for the immigrant vote. The views expressed in the *Journal* were hardly representative of the general reaction to Petrosino's murder. Students of the Italian experience in America see that event as marking "a significant turning point in nativist thought" and signaling the end of progressivism. It proved to many Americans, not already prejudiced, that the South Italians were an especially violent people and "convinced them that crime in America could be reduced by restricting immigration from Italy." Certainly the immediate effect was powerfully in this direction. The *Outlook*, an influential, progressive periodical, stated flatly that Petrosino's assassination in Palermo was "the outcome of a system of blackmail, terrorizing, and crime transplanted from Sicily and southern Italy to America." The *Independent*, a religious publication of liberal views, pointed out that of all undesirable citizens, murderers were the worst, "and of all murderers the most hateful, the most to be repelled, are the banded, cowardly professional murderers represented by the Camorra, the Mafia and the Black Hand oath-bound societies." "It would seem," said the *Review of Reviews*, "to be an open question whether, if some check cannot be placed upon the emigration of Black Handers, immigrants from Italy and Sicily should not be excluded altogether from the United States." Even Gino Speranza, staunch defender of the Italian immigrant, writing in the *Survey*, spokesman of the social service profession, admitted that "something must be done to check the most cowardly and sinister of crimes—blackmail and extortion." Our social defenses must be strengthened against "the *mala vita* from abroad that has been added to the problems of our native criminal element."[13]

The Petrosino affair was never forgotten by the press. Prejudice against Italians, particularly the South Italians, continued to mount. On the eve of World War I, Edward A. Ross, a leading American sociologist, drawing distinctions between northern and southern Italians, could say, "In nothing are the two peoples so unlike as in their crimes. While northern Italy leads in fraud and chicane, southern Italy reveals a rank growth of the ferocious crimes that go with a primitive stage of civilization." George E. Pozzetta, who recently has made a study of the Petrosino assassination in the light of new evidence, says that "the incident proved to be an important factor in establishing the specter of Italian criminality in the American mind and reinforcing the supposed undesirability of Italian immigrants. . . . The final success of the restrictionist movement owed no small debt to the death of Joseph Petrosino."[14]

Petrosino's body was shipped home to New York and he was given an impressive funeral. The immense procession was headed by Mayor McClellan and Police Commissioner Bingham but was made up largely, the *Sun* reported, of "men of Italian birth, who testified by their presence to their esteem for this valuable peace officer and their approval of the work he did." A few weeks later, however, Petrosino's friend, Pioggio Puccio, who had helped to arrange the funeral and a benefit for the widow, was shot and killed at his door on East 75th Street in Manhattan. The benefit performance at the Academy of Music had not been a great success, "for the majority of those who promised to take part at the last moment sent excuses." Nearly everyone connected with the benefit, including Puccio, had received threatening letters. Petrosino's enemies were carrying on the vendetta even after his death. An Italian grocer on Spring Street soon received a letter demanding money and boasting that "Petrosino is dead, but the Black Hand still lives." He took the letter to the police and a few days later the tenement house in which he lived was set on fire with a loss of nine lives.[15]

There had been a roundup of Black Hand suspects in New York and, at the request of the New York police, in other cities immediately after the news of Petrosino's murder was received. In New York "there was no concealment of the fact that the police were resentful and revengeful in the arrests," especially the members of the Italian Squad who did most of the work. Nothing came of these arrests in the way of clues to Petrosino's murder, though it was generally believed that it had been planned in New York. Ignazio Lupo, known as a bitter enemy, had disappeared from his usual haunts some months before, though it was not believed that he had returned to Italy where he was wanted for crimes committed many years before. He had been heard to make threats against Petrosino, it was said, and Petrosino had gone to his place of business and given him a severe beating.

Assistant District Attorney Francis L. Corrao of Brooklyn had recently spent several months in Italy on an unpublicized criminal investigation of his own. He was inclined to blame the Italian government for Petrosino's death, through its failure to give him better protection. "From what I saw and heard on my recent trip," he told a *Times* reporter, "I have no doubt that the public officials in Sicily are in league with the Mafia." It seemed to him that the government assisted in maintaining the spirit of the Mafia. Until it destroyed "the community of interest existing between the leaders of the assassins and the police and soldiery, the reign of the Mafia in Sicily will not cease."

An article in the Sunday *Times* by "A Veteran Diplomat" prophesied that "Petrosino's murderers will never be brought to justice. It is just as well that the people of New York should resign themselves to the fact." Neither the police nor the magistrates of Palermo would lift a finger in the case. "Italian officials abroad deny the existence of the Mafia or the Camorra under instruction." But Raffaele Palizzolo, a Mafia chief and long-time deputy for the city of Palermo in the Italian parliament, who had been tried three times for murder, was "the political boss of Palermo; indeed, the uncrowned king of Sicily." Palizzolo had visited New York in the summer of 1908 and had been treated as a "distinguished citizen" by the Italian community. Commissioner Bingham had had Lieutenant Petrosino shadow him. "This should be kept in mind."

Palizzolo, apparently, had actually been slipping from power and had come to the United States to recoup his fortunes by raising money among his fellow Sicilians and making political capital at home toward a forthcoming election by the publicity of the tour. In New York, where he was at first enthusiastically welcomed by both Italian officials and the Italian community, he posed as an enemy of the Black Hand and the Mafia. Both the *Times* and Petrosino himself had at first been taken in; but stories of Palizzolo's being "the king of the Mafia" soon began to circulate, and Petrosino followed him wherever he went. These close attentions hampered his efforts greatly and seem to have caused his departure long before he had planned to leave. According to Mayor McClellan, on leaving, Palizzolo had shaken his fist at Petrosino, who had followed him to the pier, and shouted, "If you ever come to Palermo, God help you."[16]

There were certainly many criminals in both countries who feared and hated Petrosino; suspicion pointed in many directions. It had been prophesied that the police in Palermo would do nothing to solve the murder, and Bishop, the American consul, felt that he was "delayed and hindered" by local authorities in his own efforts to investigate it. Nevertheless, Commissioner Ceola, under harassment by both his own superiors and American officials, conducted an intelligent and methodical investigation, Petacco, who has sifted all the surviving records on the case, calls him "an honest, capable official," who had been purging the local police of Mafia infiltrations. His report, submitted in April, called for the indictment of fifteen men, including Vito Cascio Ferro, who had been in America from 1901 to 1904 and who now was rapidly becoming a power in the "upper Mafia." Also listed were Carlo Costantino and Antonio Passananti, two men who had been involved in the barrel murder case in New York and who had returned unexpectedly to Sicily only a few days before Petrosino's arrival. Most of the men already had been picked up, and Cascio Ferro was arrested a little later.

Cascio Ferro had a very convincing alibi for a period of several days including the day of the murder, backed by his political associate and host, De Michele Ferrantelli. Ferrantelli had been elected to the chamber of deputies in the general election that was held only a few days before the murder. Palizzolo, running in another district, had been soundly defeated. He had tied his fortunes to Francesco Nitti, Giolitti's rival. The election as a whole was a landslide victory for Giolitti, minister of the interior and premier, whose administration was called by the historian Gaetano Salvemini "The Prime Ministry of the Underworld." Ceola, after submitting his report, continued his investigation but was suddenly relieved of his duties in July and recalled to Rome; he then retired. All the suspects then were set free, on probation of bail. Two years later, when popular attention was focused on the forthcoming war in Libya, the charges against all the suspects were dismissed.[17]

For years tips on the murder of Petrosino continued to flow into the police files in New York and Palermo. Cascio Ferro, known as Don Vito, already had great influence in Palermo and western Sicily. He was soon practically supreme. Luigi Barzini, in his authoritative study, *The Italians*, says that he was "perhaps the greatest head the Mafia ever had." It was not until the 1920s, when Mussolini ordered the ruthless suppression of the Mafia, that his rule came to an end. In his old age, when he was in prison, he admitted to having killed only one man, and that one man was Petrosino. This was done for the honor and prestige of the *società*. Petrosino had challenged the Mafia on its home ground "and had to be killed personally by Don Vito and nobody else." Petacco accepts Cascio Ferro's confession as factual and evidently believes that a number of returned Black Handers then in Palermo, including Costantino and Passananti, old associates of Lupo and Morello, helped to set the victim up for killing. Some recent students of the Mafia are inclined to accept this version of the murder, which for generations had been an unsolved mystery.[18]

Shortly after the tragic outcome of Petrosino's mission was known, Deputy Police Commissioner Woods sent to *McClure's Magazine*, the first of the muckraking periodicals, a detailed and thoughtful article on the Black Hand problem. Along with the masses of Italian immigrants who had been passing through Ellis Island in the past ten years, respectable, industrious, and self-supporting as a whole, he said, there had come a thin stream of immigrants of a very different character. These were men who had left criminal records behind them in Italy; these were the Black Handers. "In New York it has been found in almost every case that a man arrested for a Black Hand crime has been convicted of crime in Italy." They were parasites "fattening off the main body of their fellow-countrymen." They came because the Italian police, with the detailed national registry system at their disposal and their powers of close surveillance of ex-convicts, made their lives difficult at home. In America they could go practically unnoticed by the government; there was no national police force here, and if a criminal became known in one city, he could easily move to another almost without trace. Our immigration laws, no matter how conscientiously enforced, were inadequate to keep him out. If he should be arrested, the American legal system, with its emphasis on the protection of the innocent, gave him a very good chance of going free:

> From this it will readily be seen that the Black Hand is not a cohesive, comprehensive society, working with mysterious signs and passwords. Given a number of Italians with money, and two or three ex-convicts, you have all the elements necessary for a first-rate Black Hand campaign. In New York City, however, there are so many groups of these Black Handers that they have to come in more or less close contact with each other. Investigation seems to show that the leaders, at any rate, of the different groups are acquainted, and that they work their schemes in harmony, especially when their extortion takes the form of commercial swindling. In other words, the situation seems ripe for the creation in the city of one fairly powerful society. A little police laxity, coupled with the appearance of a leader of magnetism and force, would very likely bring about the formation of a Black Hand trust.

The New York Police Department, Woods said, had reports of about five hundred Italian aliens with official police records in Italy or who were convicted criminals. There were probably a great many more than the police knew about, and they continued to come in. Their victims, by their passivity, were practically in league with them. The department had only about fifty policemen who spoke Italian, and few of these spoke the Sicilian dialects. All of them became well known in the Italian colonies. "Lieutenant Petrosino, in spite of his devotion to duty, his long experience, and his great detective skill, was unable to overcome the handicap.'' The same difficulty, to a lesser degree, confronted his men:

> In casting about for remedies for the Black Hand situation, it is, of course, assumed that no change will be made in our method of legal procedure. Even a police official would not urge this. It would involve questions so far-reaching that, compared with them, the mere Black Hand problem would become insignificant. It must also be granted that improvement, however great, in police and detective work in the big cities of the United States would not get at the roots of the situation. The problem will not be solved by catching the Black Handers who are here to-day and seeing to it that they get their deserts. This would help; it would relieve the immediate tension. In fact the prosecution in New York of some of these individuals during the past year has largely reduced Black Hand crimes in the city. To solve the problem, however, we must not only put in jail or ship away those that are with us now; we must see to it that no more come to take their places.

Woods urged not only the creation of a secret detective service, as Commissioner Bingham long had been campaigning for, to cope with this type of crime but also the tightening of the immigration laws on both the admission and the deportation of criminals. All immigrants, he thought, should be required to bring with them full passports, with photographs, description, and any criminal record. To deport those who did sift through, the first thing necessary would be to extend the causes for which a person could be deported and to lengthen the time during which they could be deported. ''From the police point of view, certainly, it would seem wise to specify that any person could be deported if he had been convicted of any crime or if he had had a bad official police reputation abroad, and that he could be deported, not merely within the three-year limit, but at any time until he becomes a citizen of the United States.''[19]

Bingham and Woods decided to salvage what they could from the wreck of Petrosino's mission. Lieutenant Vachris, who had led the Italian Squad raids in Brooklyn on the news of Petrosino's death—raids that resulted in nothing but the holding of a few suspected Black Handers on weapons-carrying charges—volunteered to go to Italy and Sicily, though he believed that Petrosino had been betrayed by the Palermo police and lured to his death. Palermo, he said, was "the worst hole in Southern Italy for the Mafia," and there were at least a hundred criminals of the worst type there who knew Petrosino. He was eager to go and try to bring the assassins to justice. Bingham soon after ordered him to Italy with the same instructions that had been issued to Petrosino. He was accompanied by Detective Sergeant John R. Crowley, who had learned Italian to increase his usefulness in the police department and bore the temporary rank of lieutenant.[20]

While Vachris was gone, reverberations from Petrosino's assassination continued in the periodical press. The *Survey* declared that the police force of our cities, as then constituted, was incapable of meeting the problem of Black Hand crime. In New York, for instance, there were about four and a half million people, of whom from half to three-quarters of a million were Italian. The police force numbered ten thousand men, but only about fifty of them were Italian. "The consequence is that New York has become a paradise for the Italian criminal. The average policeman of Irish or German descent is as helpless to deal with conditions as an American traveller set down for the first time in Naples or Milan. A Black Hand plot may be hatched out under his very face and he be none the wiser." An adequate Italian police force probably could not be recruited in New York alone. "We should send to Italy for at least the nucleus— men from the *carabinieri* might be obtained." This would, of course, call for amending the city's charter, as the men would have to be excepted from civil service examinations. "The attempt, of course, should be to secure authority for a foreign rather than an exclusively Italian squad," for incipient Black Hand methods had appeared "among the Greeks, Magyars, and Slavs." The Black Handers, as the *Bollettino* had already pointed out, were by no means all Italians.[21]

The Black Hand was not a great criminal organization, *Cosmopolitan* insisted a little later. The facts, it said, were "furnished by the man who, now that Petrosino is dead, probably knows more about this 'society' and its methods than anyone living." This man had worked with Petrosino for years and took up his work where the assassin's bullet stopped it. He was now in Italy, searching for the murderers. It was a squalid story, divested of all the glamor that imaginative writers had woven about it. There was no central organization. There were no blood-stained oaths. "The Black Hand is the generic name of innumerable small groups of criminals operating under its flag to blackmail and murder."

A typical Black Hand gang was organized by an ex-convict from Italy, "who plundered there in the name of the Mafia or the Camorra," or a criminal who had not been caught and given the convict brand. Such men had "skill, daring, and brains." "One of these skilled laborers of crime—or perhaps a pair of them—will gather about him four or five dull, unimaginative, lazy fellows—preferably 'black sheep' of the town or section in Sicily from which the leader came—and there you have as near an organization as the Black Hand has yet perfected." The leader was known as a bad man and ruled the gang by fear, not even bothering to extract oaths from them.

The Black Hand had been invented by a newspaper reporter as "the American edition of the much-feared Mafia, a reincarnation of the deadly Camorra," and the name was an instantaneous hit. The crimes committed in its name numbered in the tens of thousands and had sent many a criminal back to Italy with a fortune, according to Sicilian standards. "In many quarters," *Cosmopolitan* concluded, "there is a demand for severer penalties for Black Hand crimes. An Italian official who recently visited New York was amazed at the small number of convictions the authorities were able to secure. He suggested that every man suspected of Black Hand work and arrested be kept in jail a couple of years before trial." This was a typically Italian suggestion and one not likely to be adopted. "One thing stands forth absolutely certain, however—something must be done or the Black Hand in time will fester and grow until its blackmailing is no longer confined to Italian-Americans."[22]

Commissioner Watchorn, who had recently left the Immigration Service, now placed an article in the *Outlook* taking a rather more optimistic view of the Black Hand problem. "Of all the arguments against immigration in general, and against certain classes of immigrants in particular," he noted, "none has touched a more popular chord than that which has singled out the 'Blackhanders' as examples of undesirability." They were undesirable, and their exclusion was greatly to be desired. But was it either wise or just to use the term "Black Hand" as a prejudgment against all immigrants of a nationality, "and thus punish the industrious, the thrifty, and the eminently desirable?" We had had in their turn, he pointed out, "cliques of Russian Nihilists, the society of Anarchists, the Molly Maguires, Armenian Hunchakists, and Italian Blackhanders." During each period in which one or the other had been much in the public eye, "the race or nationality with which they were identified was made to bear the brunt of popular disapproval of their admission to these shores."

The Molly Maguires had been condemned by all law-abiding Irishmen, Watchorn declared, and most immigrants from Russia had disowned the anarchists. "The Legislature will undoubtedly act on its patient inquiry of the facts; and the police, with their ever-increasing efficiency, may be depended on in due time to render the Blackhander of today as innocuous as are the Anarchists and Molly Maguires of former days."[23] Watchorn was evidently counting on more effective legislation to come from the reports of the U.S. Immigration Commission, then still in the midst of its investigations. He had never been a nativist and had defended the Jews as he now defended the Italians.

Frank M. White, a writer who for years made the Black Hand his specialty, blamed the federal government for the problem. The frequency of Italian names in our criminal news, he charged, was "not so much a proof of unfitness in the immigrant as of the failure of the machinery of American justice to give him protection." The only legislation on the subject of alien crime that had been passed in recent years, he pointed out, had been a part of the immigration law of 1907 permitting the deportation of a criminal within three years of his arrival. Even this limited measure was vitiated by the interpretation given to it by the Department of Commerce and Labor, of which the Immigration Service was a part. It had "dealt leniently with the mediaeval desperadoes of the Black Hand, criminals by heredity and environment, who are entirely beyond reform." Its regulations placed the burden of proof of status on the police instead of on the suspect. Many of the criminals that Lieutenant Petrosino had taken to Ellis Island had been set at liberty. The new immigration commission had not yet published its report, and meanwhile Italian criminals had been flocking into the country. Petrosino's murder was unavenged, the morale of the New York Police Department was low, and the Italian Squad, "which lost fifty percent of its potency with the death of its former chief," could not fail to decrease in efficiency. Only a law "providing for the deportation of *all* criminals from other countries who cannot show that they are living honest lives, whether they have been in the country three years or thirty," would rid the United States of alien malefactors.[24]

Vachris and Crowley returned to New York in August, having spent several months in Italy. They went at once to police headquarters and reported. There was great relief at their safe arrival. Stories circulated to the effect that they had spent much time in dangerous Sicilian dives and that they had had their photographs taken on the spot in Palermo where Petrosino had been killed. Although their mission had been curtailed, they brought the criminal certificates and photographs of hundreds of Italian ex-convicts who recently had gone to America, with several hundred more to follow as the Italian authorities transcribed the records. "Lieuts. Vachris and Crowley report as the result of their visit that they have brought back much valuable information in regard to Italian criminals now in America," the press was informed, "and that we will be enabled to establish a working agreement between Italy and this department, which will be of great benefit in connection with Italian criminals who may in the future sail for this country." They also had information on Petrosino's assassination, which it was hoped would lead to those who had planned his death. Arrests and many deportations of immigrants with criminal records were expected, according to the impression that the *Times* got at headquarters, "as well as the capture of the assassins of Petrosino."[25]

Actually, they had never gotten to Sicily at all. According to Mayor McClellan's manuscript autobiography, Vachris and Crowley got as far south as Naples and remained there. "After a week I called the Ambassador for information and he replied 'Giolitti (the Minister of the Interior) declines to guarantee their safety south of Naples.' I took the hint and recalled them." McClellan does not mention their bringing records with them. Vachris himself, testifying much later to an investigating committee, indicated that they had spent most of their time in Rome. "The Italian Government was not willing to risk that we should go to Sicily and told us that any record we wanted they could supply; so they did. . . . They did not care to assume the risk of having us killed or something to that effect." He testified also that he and Crowley had been ordered home by cable on or about July 1 but had asked for more time.[26]

Much had happened at police headquarters while they were gone. Bingham's tactless attack on the Jews and the Italians the year before had not been forgotten; his persistent raids on illegal establishments under powerful political protection made him more and deadlier enemies. Having, by trial and error, found a group of inspectors and captains who would take orders from him rather than from Tammany leaders, Bingham had dared at last to raid premises under the known protection of the Sullivan clan, pillars of Tammany Hall in Manhattan, and of Boss Patrick H. McCarren in Brooklyn. Supreme Court Justice William J. Gaynor of Brooklyn, personally incorruptible and a stickler for civil rights but ambitious and cantankerous, was being mentioned as McClellan's successor in the mayor's office. At the beginning of June, Gaynor made a ferocious attack on Bingham and the police department for the arrest and rogues' gallery photographing of the young man who delivered his milk. This business of "the Duffy boy" was blown up into a major issue, as a prime case of police arrogance. Mayor McClellan, seeking to make a truce with Tammany in the hope that Boss Murphy would send him back to Congress, acted as magistrate and upheld Gaynor's charges, demanding that

Bingham dismiss key members of his staff. Bingham refused and the mayor dismissed him. With him went his personal secretary and two of his deputy commissioners, including Woods, who resigned rather than receive a promotion under the new commissioner. The smell of politics was rank. A close friend of Boss Murphy's told a *Times* reporter that he was sure Bingham's departure would please Tammany Hall and that his successor would be "a man much more friendly to the organization."[27]

First Deputy Commissioner William F. Baker became police commissioner. "For the rest of my term of office," McClellan recorded later in his autobiography, "the Police Department ran smoothly and well and gave me less trouble than it had at any time that I was mayor." He added, however, that "During my last six months I was practically my own police commissioner." What this meant was that the powerful personality of Bingham, who long had irked McClellan and infuriated the Tammany organization, was gone and that Baker took orders respectfully. One of these orders apparently had to do with the penal certificates that Vachris and Crowley brought back from Italy and that followed them in a steady stream. When they first arrived it was fully expected that many arrests and deportations would follow and quite likely the capture of the assassins of Petrosino. But nothing happened along this line. Commissioner Baker at first assured newspaper reporters that the work would begin at once, but "Something happened over night to interfere with the project." Vachris and Crowley were ordered not to talk with reporters or anyone else about their visit to Italy. Crowley was sent out to partol a distant beat far from any Italian settlement. Vachris was set to translating the penal certificates. When he had finished this and made a card index file of the material, he was sent back to duty in Brooklyn. There was no roundup of the Italian malefactors. "The machinery that, with the assistance of high officials of Italy and the United States, and at the cost of human life, General Bingham had constructed for the suppression of the Black Hand, was allowed by Mayor McClellan to fall into decay before a wheel was turned," a well-informed writer said later.[28]

Judge Gaynor became the Democratic candidate for mayor in the city election in the fall of 1909. McClellan found himself in the embarrassing position of having to support a man who attacked his administration in vitriolic terms. Gaynor made many insulting speeches, attacking former Police Commissioner Bingham in particular as a "foreign buffoon," "scatterbrain," "strut-about," and "White House butler." With the support of Tammany Hall and a superficially united Democratic front, he was duly elected, though the Fusion forces captured most of the minor offices in a three-way race. The old issue of Tammany protection to vice, or "white slavery" as it now was called, had been unexpectedly and dramatically injected into the campaign in its closing days and probably damaged the Democratic ticket considerably. It did not affect Gaynor personally, as he had never been an organization man. Gaynor had promised "to .return the city to its citizens, govern efficiently and progressively, destroy corruption." To the disgust of the Tammany organization, he seemed to have meant it. Only one of his new appointments as heads of departments was a Tammany district leader. "They were all men who had some special fitness for the work and who stood high in the community," according to Gaynor's biographer.

For the time being he retained Baker as his police commissioner, but he treated Baker like an office boy and tried to run the police department from City Hall. Gaynor was determined to keep the force under strict control in the matter of civil rights. "Let the whole force know once and for all," he ordered Baker early in his administration, "that it will be deemed a greater offense to commit an unlawful battery on a citizen, or to unlawfully enter a house, than to let a criminal escape." Gaynor's hostility to traditional police methods was such that he even ordered the detective force out of plain clothes for a time and put them on patrol in uniform. The results seem to have been disastrous.[29]

The implication of the available evidence is strong that McClellan had sabotaged the mission of Vachris and Crowley, as he had dismissed Commissioner Bingham, at the behest of Tammany politicians. There were certainly Black Handers among some of the gangs that were active in Tammany's behalf on election day; a major drive against them just at this time might have had an unhappy effect on the Italian community, still smarting from Bingham's charges of criminality. It is clear that the criminal records brought from Italy and that continued for a time to come in from Rome were not used. What is puzzling is that Mayor Gaynor, no friend of criminals and little subservient to Tammany in general, continued this policy of neglect. The election was over and the possible alienation of Italian voters was no longer a problem. Probably Gaynor's hostility to Bingham was such that it extended to all his works.

In any event, Police Commissioner Baker under Mayor Gaynor, as under Mayor McClellan, failed to make use of this priceless material in dealing with the Black Hand problem. He did not go after the criminals on the long list provided by the Italian government and obviously had no instructions to do so. A writer for the *Independent* declared later that he had "made many efforts to interview Police Commissioner Baker on the subject, and the Commissioner, knowing what was wanted, persistently avoided the interview." More and more of the ex-convicts on the list became immune from deportation as they established three-year residences in the United States.[30]

While the police drive against the Black Hand faltered, the Secret Service, with some help from the Italian Squad, was preparing the most effective coup yet accomplished against criminals of the Black Hand type in New York. The gang of counterfeiters and extortionists suspected of the barrel murder, who had escaped him in 1903, was rounded up after long and painstaking investigation by William J. Flynn and his men. "That will help some," Flynn remarked as he left the heavily guarded U.S. Circuit Court in Manhattan after hearing a federal judge pronounce sentences aggregating 150 years against eight Italian counterfeiters who had been on trial. Guards were felt to be necessary, as Flynn's star witness had been denounced and threatened in the Italian press. No one old enough to remember when the ballad of Jesse James was popularly sung in the United States, no one young enough to have thrilled at the movie adventures of the bandits Bonnie and Clyde, should be surprised that these gangsters were regarded as heroes in part of the Italian community. Italians were driven from the courtroom before the sentencing. The leaders of the gang, Ignazio Lupo (whose real name seems to have been Saietta), known as Lupo the Wolf, and Giuseppe Morello, sometimes called "the gray fox," were sentenced to thirty and twenty-five years, respectively, to be served in the new federal penitentiary at Atlanta. Detectives and Secret Service agents, the *Tribune* understood, looked upon these two "as the most dangerous men in this country." As these sentences were pronounced in February 1910, eight more of the gang were coming up for trial. Twelve smaller fry, convicted of passing the bad bills manufactured by the gang in a hideaway at Highland, New York, already had been sentenced to lesser terms.

This cleanup, the *Times* remarked with satisfaction, was "pretty likely to make both the counterfeiting and 'Black Hand' professions unpopular in this vicinity for some time." The gang was believed to have been the source of most of the serious Black Hand work that had been done in the city for the past half-dozen years and was strongly suspected of having planned Petrosino's assassination. According to Flynn, the gang had gone into legitimate businesses of varied types with the profits from Black Hand extortion but could not refrain from operating them as rackets and had run into financial difficulties. They were perhaps merely trying to climb "one of the queer ladders of social mobility in American life," as the sociologist Daniel Bell calls the recurring efforts of gangsters to achieve respectability and social acceptance. If so, they did not make the grade as some of their predecessors and successors have done. They then returned to counterfeiting on a large scale, and their bad money appeared in 1909 in a number of large cities as far apart as Boston, Chicago, and New Orleans. The source was traced to the vicinity of New York, and enough hard evidence finally was obtained to assure convictions.

This major counterfeiting operation was not completely eradicated by the arrest and conviction of the leaders and a considerable number of underlings. Although it was believed that the gang had been broken up, the Secret Service and members of the Italian Squad toward the end of the year

found in a wine cellar on Chrystie Street a package containing $1,000 in counterfeit two-dollar bills. They promptly
raided the homes of thirteen men, a number of whom they
said were "disciples of the notorious Lupo the Wolf-Morello
gang." Many counterfeiting plates had been seized at the
time the leaders were captured, but more bills apparently
from the same plates had been circulating. It was decided
that some younger branch of the gang had escaped and a
secret "plant" of the old gang left in their hands. Nine of
the men were held on charges of possessing counterfeit
money; the others were released. At least one of this group,
Giuseppe Boscarino, was convicted shortly in federal court
of passing counterfeit money. He was described as a
member of the Lupo-Morello gang and "the organizer of the
Italians who undertook to carry on the work of that combination after the United States had arrested most of its members." Lupo and Morello had been put away, but their
influence lingered.[31]

The annual report of the secretary of the treasury for 1910,
recounting the activities of the Secret Service, laid particular
stress on this case. "The greatest public service rendered by
the division," the secretary said, "was doubtless the suppression of a dangerous and exceedingly active organization
among the desperate class of Italians in New York." The
leaders of this group were responsible for most of the counterfeiting among Italians, and they had also "directed an active blackmailing campaign among their own people." Reports from New York were to the effect that "there has
been a decrease of fully 75 per cent in the so-called 'black-
hand' outrages since the arrest and conviction of nearly
two score of these men in connection with a very extensive
note-counterfeiting conspiracy." In the following year the
secretary reported with considerable satisfaction "the final
disposition of the cases of the Lupo-Morello black-hand
counterfeiting conspirators." The circuit court of appeals
had refused a new trial, "and society is rid of these dangerous criminals for many years to come."[32]

Morello had been arrested late in 1909. When his apartment was searched, Secret Service men found correspondence linking him with Don Vito Cascio Ferro, then becoming

dominant among the Mafia of Sicily and since credited with
having killed Petrosino. Some of the correspondence concerned the admittance into the Chicago branch of the society
of a man questioned by the leaders in New York, who put
the responsibility for his admittance up to the Chicago gang.
They questioned Cascio Ferro's judgment in "not asking information of the townsmen" before admitting a member.
Evidently Cascio Ferro was seeking to direct policy from
Palermo.

Another letter to one Vincenzo Moreci in New Orleans referred to good news from Palermo. The letter, signed, "G.
La Bella," which Flynn says was an alias that Morello used,
extended greetings to "all the friends of New Orleans." As
students of the Mafia assure us, the word *friend* to a member
means another mafioso. In spite of repeated protestations
then, and since, that nothing of the sort existed in America,
Lupo and Morello seem to have headed an affiliate of the
Mafia with wide ramifications. Flynn traced Morello's record
back as far as 1889, when he was charged with murder in
Corleone but escaped punishment through "powerful
influences of the Mafia." He seems to have come to the United States later to escape police surveillance. Flynn came to
consider Black Hand and Mafia as synonymous.[33] This simple definition of "Black Hand" has had wide currency since.

Petacco regards Lupo and Morello as unquestionably having been important members of the Mafia and evidently believes that after a long and at times quite lucrative career in
crime they were betrayed in court by younger rivals. He
stresses their connection with Don Vito Cascio Ferro. Don
Vito, to escape police surveillance in Sicily, had come to
New York in 1901 and had influenced the Lupo-Morello
combine greatly, Petacco says, coaching them on the latest
techniques in vogue in the urban Mafia of Palermo and re-
fining their extortion methods. Instead of the brutal demand
of an excessive sum that might bankrupt a victim and then
bargaining for lesser payment, they were instructed to levy
regular assessments tailored to actual ability to pay. This
method was called "wetting the whistle" and turned the
Black Hand bomb-thrower into a fatherly "protector."
Petacco calls Don Vito "the grey eminence of the Black

Hand" during his few years in the United States. He helped
the Lupo-Morello gang organize their defense in the barrel
murder case in 1903 but left town before becoming openly
involved in it. After another year in New Orleans, where he
had good contacts, he returned to Sicily and pursued his
own eminently successful career as Mafia chieftain there. He
continued to be held in "unlimited esteem" by the Lupo-
Morello combination.

Michele Pantaleone, Sicilian Socialist writer and lifelong
opponent of the Mafia, seems to share this view. The Mafia,
he explains, essentially a rural phenomenon resulting from
continuing feudal conditions in the interior of Sicily, took to
politics after the unification of Italy and the introduction of
parliamentary democracy. Many of its chiefs moved into the
towns, without losing control of their gangs in the villages.
By 1900 they dominated Palermo. Don Vito Cascio Ferro
perfected the Mafia organization there and controlled the
city's underworld until his downfall in the 1920s. "Men
schooled by Don Vito Cascio Ferro," Pantaleone states,
"founded and organized gangsterism in America fifty years
ago." It has continued to thrive there, he notes, "and it is
noticeable that the period of Don Vito's maximum power in
Sicily coincided exactly with the appearance of the 'Black
Hand' organized in St. Louis, Chicago, Kansas City, De-
troit, New Orleans, New Jersey and other cities."[34]

These estimates of Cascio Ferro's influence on Italian
crime in the United States seem greatly exaggerated. Both
methods of the Black Hand shakedown continued to be used
throughout the period, no matter how much the Lupo-
Morello gang may have taken his teachings to heart. Lupo
and Morello never rose to any such commanding position in
the field as Cascio Ferro did in his native Sicily. Conditions
were not ripe for it, competition was always keen, and they
were cut down in mid-career. As for Don Vito's founding
gangsterism in America, this was beyond the powers of any
man. Gangsterism was a well-known phenomenon here, both
along the frontier and in the big cities, long before he visited
the United States, even before more than a handful of Italians had reached these shores. It is interesting to notice that
Joseph Petrosino, who was supposed to know all the leading

criminals among the Italians in New York, seems to have had no knowledge of Don Vito until he reached Palermo. If Cascio Ferro had been so influential among the nascent Black Handers as has been affirmed, Petrosino would surely have spotted him while he was in New York. By all accounts he was a commanding figure, but neither Lupo nor Morello was exactly a neophyte in crime when he landed in New York. At most, he probably suggested some technical refinements to their growing gang, for which they were duly grateful.

Francis Ianni, Columbia anthropologist, who has made a careful study of the Mafia and its structure, argues that the Mafia could not have existed here during this period. It was the product of slow growth on its home ground and had never thrived even in the eastern part of Sicily; how could it have made the great leap to the United States? All Mafia chiefs in Sicily at the time were men of some wealth, power, and prestige. There was no reason for them to leave until Mussolini cracked down on them in the 1920s. While minor Mafiosi and Camorristi were probably present in the mass migration of these years, "they were few in number and did not represent any potential leadership or they would have remained in Italy." He makes no mention of Morello or Lupo or Cascio Ferro or for that matter of the Pelletieri brothers and others who did come to the United States, temporarily or permanently, and did display some qualities of leadership. Italian immigrants did bring public notice to crime in the ghetto through the Black Hand, Ianni concedes, but its activities were unorganized, the work of individuals or small groups of extortionists; "and there is no evidence which suggests that there was any higher level of organization or any tie with the Mafia in Sicily or Camorra in Naples." He does not mention the evidence uncovered by the Secret Service. The Black Hand, as Ianni sees it, "was a cultural but not an organizational offshoot of *Mafia*," completely Italian in origin and character.[35]

As between Morello and Lupo, the two leaders of the gang broken up by the Secret Service in 1910, Lupo (or Saietta) occupies a special place of horror in the popular literature on crime. Herbert Asbury, in his study of the gangs of New York, says that "The most celebrated of the Italian gangs was that captained by Ignazio Lupo, who was one of the most desperate and blood-thirsty criminals this country has ever seen." He and his followers were greatly feared by their countrymen not only because of their proficiency with bomb, revolver, and stiletto but also because "they were reputed to be able to cast the evil eye, and to possess other magical powers." In addition to "participating in the vendettas of the Mafia and the Black Hand, Lupo the Wolf hired his killers and thugs out to other Italian secret orders, and was also an expert counterfeiter." John Kobler, in his biography of Al Capone, says that the Unione Siciliana, founded by Sicilian immigrants as a lawful fraternal order in the late nineteenth century, was infiltrated and perverted by New York hoodlums led by "Ignazio Saietta, known as Lupo the Wolf, a pathological killer," who linked it to the Mafia. Saietta himself, who evidently had more than one base of operations, "maintained a 'murder stable' in Harlem, with meat hooks from which to hang his victims and a furnace in which to burn them alive." Flynn had traced sixty murders to his gang.[36]

A former chief of the Homicide Bureau of the New York City police, reviewing in 1930 the evolution of criminal gangs from the turn of the century, recalled that "The most villainous Italian gang that ever supplied cases for the Homicide Bureau while I was connected with it was the Morello and Lupo outfit of counterfeiters and blackmailers." The police department, in trying to cope with it, "stacked up the most imposing number of criminal charges ever recorded against a single gang—548 major felonies ranging from stiletto assaults, bomb-planting and murder to kidnapping." Petrosino, "the great detective," whom he had known, had lost his life as an indirect result of his work against this gang.[37]

When Black Hand extortion was practiced by professional criminals such as Lupo and Morello, it was usually only one of a number of activities. Amateurs, on the other hand, seem to have relied on it alone, often in a one-shot operation. Although some fairly large groups practiced it and extended their operations widely, most Black Hand work was loosely organized at best. Many lone operators, not affiliated with any gang at all, practiced it. Much of it was distinctively imitative, a cashing-in on a national phobia. No Black Hand group, even such a powerful gang as the Lupo-Morello outfit with contacts extending from Palermo to Chicago and New Orleans, ever had anything approaching a monopoly, even in New York City.

The basic Black Hand technique was simple and was widely used by amateurs as well as professional criminals as long as the myth was viable. Practitioners were by no means confined to the Italian population. Black Hand letters were used for such diverse purposes as driving a lone Negro out of a Westchester village and a minister from his pulpit on Long Island. A young man of undoubted WASP antecedents tried systematically shaking down wealthy summer residents of Huntington, Long Island, with Black Hand letters. He was caught by post office inspectors. A German widow in Brooklyn, owner of a brewery, received three Black Hand letters demanding $10,000 on pain of having the brewery blown up and her entire family murdered. Black Hand letters threatened witnesses in a murder case in Flushing, New York, involving Germans.

A young Jewish boy in Brooklyn terrified a neighboring family and kept the police busy for a time writing Black Hand letters "just for fun." The New York police encountered Black Hand letters written in Greek and threatening Greeks. A Jewish Black Hand gang was broken up on the East Side in 1913. A year later Ignace Paderewski, the pianist, was forced to call off a concert tour in the West because of persistent threats from a Black Hand group, presumably Polish. Years before, the *Tribune* had reported "A Polish 'Black Hand' " at work in the Polish community of Buffalo. A Polish youth was caught writing Black Hand letters to a Polish priest in New Jersey in 1909. The poison pen probably has been wielded among all literate peoples ever since letter writing began. For a time, in New York and other American cities, and even in the countryside, the Black Hand name or symbol or both often were used to add extra venom and terror. Sociologist R. A. Schermerhorn, writing on the Italians as one of our minority groups, is on safe ground in saying that "There is evidence that not only Sicilians and Italians but members of other groups hid themselves under the Black Hand cloak to carry on illegal activities." But this symbol and name had first come into use among Italians and continued in use most systematically and persistently among them.[38]

CHAPTER IV
The Black Hand in Control

While an uneasy peace descended for a time on the vicinity of Elizabeth Street, where the Lupo-Morello gang had once made its headquarters, and the incidence of Black Hand outrages there seems to have diminished considerably for a time, they continued elsewhere in New York City. Only two weeks after the leaders of the gang were sent to Atlanta, Enrico Caruso, then nearing the height of his fame as the star tenor of the Metropolitan Opera and the idol of the Italian community, received threatening letters demanding $15,000. The police were notified, and a trap was laid at a lonely spot in Brooklyn, employing a number of detectives of the Italian Squad. Two members of the gang were captured.

Only a day or two later Caruso sang at the Academy of Music in Brooklyn. The Italian community turned out in numbers and he was heavily guarded. There had been rumors of vengeance, but nothing untoward happened. Although there were predictions among Italians that he would not prosecute and though he was even criticized severely for giving the Italian community a bad name, Caruso came to court later with a bodyguard and testified against the accused. The two blackmailers, Antonio Cincotto and Antonio Misiani, both of Brooklyn and both with long police records, were sentenced to lengthy terms in Sing Sing. But though he had helped to put them there, Caruso was the first to sign a petition for their pardon only a year later.[1]

Like the hysteria over the White Slave trade, which was running its course at much the same time, the Black Hand alarm produced its own crop of fiction. Like the White Slave fiction, it doubtless added to the growing national prejudice against the new immigration, in this case specifically the Italians. Arthur B. Reeve, a writer of detective fiction, had created the figure of the supersleuth Craig Kennedy. Building on the Caruso case, Reeve produced a story for *Cosmopolitan* in which his hero found himself in conflict with the Black Hand. A gang of these desperadoes kidnaped the daughter of the great Italian tenor Gennaro, who was also the granddaughter of the Italian banker Caesar, and held her for $10,000 ransom. The story involved the use of rare poisons, dynamite bombings, secret signs, Italian mistrust of the police, dangerous dives in Greenwich Village, the counter "White Hand" society, the use of a dictograph, wire tapping, and other features, some of which would no doubt have amazed the typical Black Hander. It all ended happily, of course. The infamous Paoli gang were all captured after a thrilling battle, and Gennaro's little daughter was returned to him unharmed.[2]

In June 1910, three-year-old Michael Scimeca, son of Dr. Mariano Scimeca of 2 Prince Street, was taken from the third floor of his home by a man who promised him candy. Dr. Scimeca had been a personal friend of Lieutenant Petrosino. He had received a number of Black Hand letters over a period of years demanding from $500 to $1,000, each time under threat of having his house blown up and his family killed. When he showed some of the letters to Petrosino, they ceased coming but began to come again after Petrosino's death. After the kidnaping, Dr. Scimeca received a letter signed, "Black Hand," demanding $8,000 as the price of the boy's return. Italian Squad detectives were assigned to the case, but Scimeca told them he preferred to handle the matter himself; and they did not follow him when he went out, apparently to negotiate. The whole Scimeca family joined in what evidently was intended to be a homecoming celebration, but the boy was not returned.

The detectives said that they knew who took the boy but that they did not want to make an arrest, as it would inter-

fere with the child's return. The case hung fire, and the detectives came under a good bit of criticism. A few weeks
later Dr. Scimeca received another Black Hand letter demanding $5,000 within two days, or "his kidnapped child
would be cut to pieces and the dismembered body returned
to him in a box." Scimeca broke down and told the reporters he could not meet the demand; but some time later, an
accommodation evidently having been reached, the boy was
returned through a relative in Brooklyn. There was some
talk of prosecution for the compounding of a felony, but no
action was taken along this line.

The Italian Squad detectives eventually tracked down the
kidnapper. They had, as they said, known who he was all
along, as also had Dr. Scimeca. He was Pietro Pallazpolo,
apparently a lone operator, who had gone to Italy to spend
the ransom money and returned. He was convicted and sentenced to up to fifty years' imprisonment. Although the case
ultimately was solved, however, for the time being the detectives had looked helpless. Frugone of the *Bollettino*
pointed out that they were far too few and were all easily
recognized. He lamented "that ex-Commissioner Bingham's
plea for an appropriation of $100,000 for the Italian branch
fell through."[3]

Frugone's Italian protective association, though it probably had financed Petrosino's and Vachris's trips to Italy and
the temporary employment of a few secret agents, evidently
had become inactive, as had the White Hand Society in
Chicago. Now a relative newcomer in the Italian community
took up the fight against the Black Hand. He was Dr. Alberto Pecorini, a graduate of the University of Rome, who
later had studied in Paris and at Columbia University. He
had become active in settlement work, had taken part in the
political campaign of 1909 on behalf of the Fusion ticket, and
recently had founded the Italian-American Civic League. On
the league's board were some of the most influential Italians
in the city as well as a number of prominent Americans interested in the Italian colony. It prepared a memorial on the
problem of crime to present to Mayor Gaynor but held it up
for a time after he was shot and badly wounded by an assassin (not an Italian) in August. As his return to office seemed

for a time doubtful, the memorial finally was presented to Acting Mayor John Purroy Mitchel, a vigorous young Fusionist, who as the new president of the Board of Aldermen had taken over the mayor's functions.

The purpose of the league, it was stated, was to aim at "transforming a great civically inert mass of half a million Italians of New York into an active and organic part of the city's life." The memorial deplored the sensational treatment of Italian crime in the press and periodicals, which had created an impression among Americans all over the country that the Italians were a criminal race. Crime among Italians admittedly had increased "disastrously" since the death of Lieutenant Petrosino had left the Italian detective bureau weakened. However, "That crimes committed among Italians are due to an exceedingly small minority of criminals is conceded by all intelligent persons acquainted with the situation." What was needed was a thorough reorganization of the Italian Squad, an increase in the number of men attached to it, and the assignment to it of first-class detectives. This would go a long way toward changing existing conditions and "giving the honest mass of Italians in this city the confidence which it ought to have in the authority of the government and the administration of justice." The memorial itself did not mention Black Hand, Mafia, or Camorra.

The *Times* printed the memorial in full in a Sunday feature section, and along with it was an illustrated article by Frank M. White, "Italians Seek Protection Against Black Hand." Boxed within it was a summary of Italian crime in the city for the month of August. Along with bombings, murders, kidnapings, and rapes, there were listed such lesser offenses as wife beatings and ruffianism in the subway. There were thirty-five crimes in all listed. Whether this was really a startling record for a community estimated at half a million people might be debated, but the *Times* evidently thought so. If the journal wanted to promote Pecorini's cause, as presumably it did, this handling of material may have done more harm than good among Italian readers.

The accompanying article called the increase in Italian crime remarkable, "in that several of the principal Black Hand leaders have been sentenced this year to long terms in

Federal prisons, the result of work by the Secret Service of the Treasury Department." Things were much the same in the Italian colonies all over the country, it declared; very seldom did the police find "a Black Hander who is without a criminal record at home. It was to obtain these records that Petrosino went to Italy." Vachris and Crowley had returned from Italy, where they had taken up the work of the slain Petrosino, with the criminal records of some seven hundred of the Italian ex-convicts. But General Bingham meanwhile had fallen victim to the politicians, and Baker, his successor, was making little use of these records. He acted under the orders of Mayor McClellan, whose dismissal of Bingham "had been reprehended by all good citizens." Obviously it would not increase McClellan's reputation to carry out a project that would reflect credit upon Bingham. "Many of these certificates are already useless since they are only of service in the deportation of men who have been in the country less than three years." Most of them had only a year or two to run in the first place. "In a short time the entire lot will be worthless."

"The Italian-American Civic League," said White, "which has brought the matter of police inefficiency as bearing upon Italian criminality before the public, was formed early in the year for the promotion of the civic and social welfare of the Italians in this city. Its managing board contains the names of some of the most influential Italians in New York," as well as those of many other "representative citizens." The moving spirit of the league, however, was its managing director, Dr. Alberto Pecorini, "a young man from whom New York is likely to hear more." White reviewed Pecorini's career since he had come to the United States, stressing stories of his defiance of the Black Hand. White also noted this new effort to curb the Black Hand in a brief article in *Collier's*. "The conditions which inspired it are not confined to New York," he warned. "After Petrosino's death an attempt was made to kill Detective Langbardi, who holds a position in the Chicago Detective Bureau similar to that which was held by Petrosino here." Blackmail and crimes of violence were a menace wherever Italians were found in considerable numbers in America, "and fear on the one side and the lawlessness of the few on the other put peaceable citizens outside the law's protection."[4]

A few months later there was a conference at the City Club, under the joint auspices of that club and the Italian-American Civic League, "the professed purpose being to discuss the cutting down of Italian criminals in this city." Due to the speeches of several Italians, "who declared passionately that the newspapers exaggerated the proportion of crime due to the members of their race as compared with the other races, the resolutions which were adopted related to criminality of all foreign-born residents." In accordance with these resolutions, President Charles H. Strong of the City Club appointed a committee of five men who were to consult with the immigration commissioner, the police commissioner, the United States district attorney, and the district attorneys of the counties embraced in the city, "as to how best to prevent the coming in of alien criminals, how to obtain the deportation of those already here, and how to detect and prevent crime among the alien residents of the city." There was one Italian name on the list.

Pecorini led the discussion, pointing out that when Lieutenants Vachris and Crowley had returned from Italy with over seven hundred ceritficates of criminality, "Commissioner Baker did not seem enthusiastic over them." No action had been taken against the men on the list unless they were arrested for some serious crime here. He wanted foreign criminals made subject to deportation for five years, instead of only three years, and the police department to have a fund to employ skilled men, "even if they have to be employed in Italy, their work to be kept secret from the regular men on the regular force." John Lordi, a Mulberry Street banker, said it was foolish to expect to hold in check over five hundred thousand Italians with forty or fifty Italian detectives. For that many of its citizens, he declared, the Italian government provided "500 policemen and three regiments of soldiers."[5]

Rudolph Vecoli, in his study of the Italians in Chicago, stresses the lack of a philanthropic tradition among the well-to-do and the failure of many such community projects as were developed by other nationalities there. The educated and successful Italians were "more liberal with advice than with good works" and were torn with rivalries and jealousies. "Projects were launched for an Italian hospital, an Italian school, an Italian charity society, an Italian institute to curb the padrone evil, and a White Hand Society to combat the Black Hand, but they all floundered in this morass of discord and disinterest." The record of the prosperous Italians in New York was better than this, but the same forces seem to have been at work. When Lordi, at the City Club conference, remarked in passing, quoting Dumas, "that Sicily was a paradise populated by demons," stating with evident satisfaction that he was from Naples, he was taken up at once. "J. G. Gambalvo, who said that he came from Brooklyn and that he was a Sicilian, said that Sicilians were no worse than Neapolitans." *Il Progresso* was highly critical of the meeting as a whole, even going so far as to suggest that Pecorini ought to be lynched for attempting to bring disgrace on the Italians of New York. Harmony and effective action in the joint committee that was appointed at the conference seemed doubtful.[6]

Pecorini followed up this meeting with an article in the *Forum* on the Italians in the United States, which included not only his own definition of the Black Hand but also sharp criticism of the Italian-American press. "It is to be regretted," he said, without mentioning *Il Progresso*, "that the Italian press, by reason of a mistaken idea of patriotism, is not serving as an interpreter of American life and ideals to its constituency." There were six Italian daily newspapers in New York with circulations varying from ten thousand to thirty thousand copies. Some of them had large circulations outside the city, in the smaller towns, the mining districts, and the labor camps. They were deficient in local news service of their own but imposed on themselves great sacrifice for cable service from Italy. A great part of their advertising came from steamship companies, professional men, importers and merchants, but there was too large a proportion of fake doctors, real estate swindlers, and alleged brokers who sold to the immigrant the stock of companies that did not exist. He implied strongly that most of them were corrupt. "However, there are two Italian dailies that enjoy the distinction of having refused money offered for political support at the last municipal election, and of having helped the Fusion cause without recompense—a startling reform in Italian journalism." It was to be hoped that in the future the Italian press would not confine its benevolent activities to "the providing of the city with monuments to Italian worthies," but would "attempt to instruct the Italian masses with regard to their duties in their new environment." Pecorini was a strong supporter of the movement to Americanize the immigrant, then gathering momentum in the social service profession. He evidently believed that the Italian press, as a whole, had been a great obstacle in the way of this objective.

There was a surplus of the Italian intellectual class in the United States, he noted. These men, who had a hard time making their way into American society at their proper level, often were forced to work for half-illiterate bankers, padrones, real estate men, and the like. There was something of the intellectual snob about Pecorini, judging by his treatment of the Black Hand:

Aside from the professional men, the half-illiterate man of business, and the laborer, there is still another intermediate Italian-American type, somewhat above the others in education, but not sufficiently cultivated to associate with the university graduates. He is the son of the little merchant in Italy who has been through the elementary schools, but could not meet the requirements of the high school; the man who served three years in the army, and went to prison for making fun of his peasant corporal, and who finally landed in America without any trade, and, what is worse, with no inclination or intention to work. A new land, a new environment, often works wonders, and some of these derelicts find fields of honest activity in trade and industry, but a large number of them unite with the few criminals escaped from Italy, and form a class of half-educated malefactors—the "Black Handers," if you care thus to term them. To these outlaws the poor, illiterate laborer and his prosperous half-illiterate boss fall an equally easy prey, and on them they manage to subsist. The laborer they exploit and swindle at every turn, and occasionally succeed in robbing him of all his savings as he is about to take the steamer home. The boss is duped and despoiled in many ways. These predal opportunists flatter him in magnificent articles published in weekly newspapers and magazines that are born and die in the Italian quarters with wonderful rapidity; they get money for subscriptions to and advertisements in newspapers that are never published at all; they take his part in foolish quarrels with equally vain competitors for the presidency of a society, perhaps, or over a decoration expected from the Italian government; and, after all other expedients have been employed, they demand money with threatening letters, kidnap his children, or put a stick of dynamite in his cellar.[7]

Acting Mayor Mitchel had scarcely taken over from the disabled Gaynor when he became greatly concerned over the state of affairs in the police department. He found Commissioner Baker unwilling to take action in the suppression of vice and gambling. Conditions at Coney Island, in particular, were reported as "gross and revolting." Complaints of disorderly houses and gambling places operating openly in various parts of the city flooded Mitchel's office. These were forwarded to Baker, but no action followed; and Baker even questioned Mitchel's authority. In a long conference with the convalescent Gaynor, Mitchel demanded his removal.

Gaynor, far from having recovered from a gunshot wound in his throat, nevertheless returned to City Hall early in October, and Mitchel presented him a written report on Baker's derelictions. Not long after, Frederick H. Bugher, first deputy police commissioner, resigned in terms reflecting not only on Baker but also on Gaynor himself. "Since the first of the year," he said, "I have seen the Department become increasingly demoralized and the violation of law more and more flagrant until I am now convinced that I can no longer retain my position with self-respect." The mayor repeatedly had promised to reorganize the department, he charged, but had not done so. A "complete break-down of police control" was threatened.

There was almost immediately a great upheaval in the police department, and Baker and his two top deputies were replaced. James C. Cropsey, a Brooklyn lawyer who had impressed Gaynor with his courtroom manner, became police commissioner; Clement J. Driscoll, a former newspaperman, became first deputy; and William J. Flynn, of the Secret Service, became second deputy. Flynn, it was announced, was to have "full supervision over the detective

work of the department.'' Gaynor for some time had been
wanting to bring him into the city's service, it was understood, but Flynn did not want to give up his federal government work unless he had a free hand in the reorganization of
the detective system.[8]

Flynn's appointment was praised by Washington officials,
including not only the assistant attorney-general and the secretary of the treasury but also the President himself. A
highly laudatory feature story on him soon appeared in the
Sunday *Times*, based in part on an interview. Flynn had left
the Secret Service ''to provide New York City for the first
time with a real detective force.'' ''Until now the city's so-
called 'detectives' have been only policemen in uniform,''
and a berth as a detective had been regarded as ''soft.''
Flynn was going to change all this. His detective force
would have to be able to do hard and grinding work, and he
would be one of his own detectives. New Yorkers were accustomed to changes in the police department; to them it
was the same old story of new names. But this time it was
different, it was declared, and Mayor Gaynor was responsible. Gaynor's idea was not just to change commissioners but
to reorganize the system. ''What he wants is a
Commissioner—like Cropsey—who is downright honest, to
begin with; a First Deputy Commissioner—like Driscoll—
who can cope with the vice situation without making New
York odious; a Second Deputy—like Flynn—who can create
for the first time a force of real detectives . . . . They are to
put an end to New York's reputation as the City of Unde-
tected Crimes.''[9]

There had been a good bit of criticism of the Italian Squad
since Petrosino's death. The inspector in charge of detectives, John Russell, of whom Commissioner Bingham had
thought highly, now made a report on the subject to Flynn,
returning a letter of complaint to Mayor Gaynor that had
been referred to him. The letter, by a reporter on an Italian
paper, had charged that after Petrosino's leadership had
been withdrawn, ''jealousy became general amongst them
and consequently some of the best men were removed there-
from unjustly.'' The squad had become ''so demoralized as
to cause the disgust of the entire Italian colony.'' Most of

them, he charged, had agents who collected from crooks, Black Handers, houses of prostitution, and so forth, "offering protection in return." There was a band of Italian criminals who made a specialty of stealing horses and wagons. "This dangerous gang is the same one who does all the kidnapping, bomb-throwing, extortion, murders, and crimes of the worst kind." The Italian detectives knew this but made no effort to arrest them. The writer said that his specialty was court reporting and therefore he knew what he was talking about. The squad should be reorganized, and a competent man put at the head of it. He named his own candidate, a former associate of Petrosino by the name of Frank Bonanno. "I refrain from signing my name," he said in a postscript, "because like everyone else I fear this band of lawbreakers."

Inspector Russell, in reporting on this complaint, said that when he had been placed in charge of the detective force the Italian Branch in Manhattan had been under the command of Lieutenant Gloster, and that Lieutenant Vachris had charge of a smaller unit in Brooklyn. He had no complaint to make of Gloster, but thought "that a man born in Italy who could speak the different dialects could accomplish better results." On his recommendation Vachris had been brought back from Brooklyn and placed in charge of the Manhattan squad. Since then, he believed that "the entire squad under him are doing better work than they have ever done before." The number of arrests and convictions was increasing every month. He had heard from time to time complaints that some of the men were not honest. He was looking into these charges and would take proper action as soon as he could get anything definite.[10]

Flynn, who had worked intimately with Petrosino in the past and also must have known Vachris well, apparently did not take these charges too seriously or else regarded them as pretty much out of date. In any event, when he reorganized the detective force he left Vachris in command of the Italian Squad in Manhattan. He spent about a month studying his problem and then announced his new plan. All branch detective bureaus except the one in Brooklyn were to be abolished. Detectives in the future were not to be under the command of precinct captains or district inspectors, but "they will be under the direct personal command of Commissioner Flynn." They were to take their orders from detective lieutenants in their districts. "The Italian Squad," it was announced, "will retain its old headquarters in Centre Street, but its numerical strength will be reduced. Many of the Italian detectives will be assigned permanently to Italian settlements, and Hebrew detectives will be among those assigned to the east side." Flynn's intention was to have the detectives remain incognito as much as possible. Like the Secret Service, they were to detect criminals and then call in uniformed officers to make the arrests whenever possible. There would be about five hundred men in the whole force, but only sixty of them would be kept at headquarters.[11]

Flynn's assignment of Hebrew detectives to the East Side was certainly called for. Jewish gangsters were steadily becoming more prominent, and alarm at Jewish crime was voiced in the Yiddish press. "It is almost impossible to comprehend the indifference with which the large New York Jewish population hears and reads, day after day, about the thefts and murders that are perpetrated every day by Jewish 'gangs,' " said the *Jewish Daily News* a little later. These were real bands of robbers and none raised a voice of protest, it lamented; no demand was made for the protection of the reputation of the Jews of America and for the life and property of the Jewish citizen. "A few years ago, when Commissioner Bingham came out with a statement about Jewish thieves, the Jews raised a cry of protest that 'reached the heavens.' The main cry was that Bingham exaggerated and gave too large the number of Jewish criminals. But when we hear of the murders, holdups and burglaries committed in the Jewish section and by Jewish criminals, we must, with heartache, justify Mr. Bingham."

Among other nefarious operations, Jewish blackmail, as well as Italian, was practiced on the East Side. At least one Jew used dynamite to frighten his victim, another Jew, apparently assuming that it would be blamed on the Italians. He was caught. The police were interested; it was "the first time in their knowledge," they said, "that Jewish blackmailers of the east side have ever used explosives as a means of intimidation."

The group that had founded the Kehillah, or "Community," that was formed between German and Russian Jewish elements in the wake of Commissioner Bingham's charges of criminality in 1908 came to take the situation seriously. At a later date the Kehillah came to Mayor Gaynor's assistance when he was sorely beset in other quarters. It formed a Bureau of Social Morals that fought extortion, prostitution, gambling, and other crimes in the Jewish quarter during his last year in office. Gaynor was glad of its help. Perhaps its greatest single achievement was the breakup of the so-called Yiddish Blackhand Association, which had long terrorized East Side stablemen by poisoning horses.[12]

Flynn's new plan, as far as the Italian Squad was concerned, was put to an immediate test. Two young Italian boys in South Brooklyn, Giuseppe Longo and Michael Rizzo, cousins and the sons of prosperous parents, were lured to a moving picture show and disappeared. Black Hand letters demanding $15,000 for one of the boys and $5,000 for the other, on pain of having their heads returned, were turned over to the police. While Flynn had left Vachris in command in Manhattan, Lieutenant Charles Corrao, another former associate of Petrosino, now in command in Brooklyn, was put in immediate charge of the case. The kidnappers were traced to a group of houses on East 63rd Street in Manhattan, "a centre noted for years as the haunt of kidnappers and blackmailers." The houses were put under constant surveillance by disguised Brooklyn detectives, supplemented by men from Vachris's force and under the personal direction of Flynn himself. Flynn insisted that they get the boys with their abductors and establish an ironclad case. "There was to be no unprovable case in which the Italians concerned refused to talk. The evidence Flynn demanded was the child itself."

When all was ready, a large force of detectives closed in, searched all the houses, found the Longo boy alive, and picked up a number of inmates. These all were taken to Brooklyn and put under heavy bail. They were strongly guarded from the angry crowd that gathered at the police court there. Other members of the gang, obviously alarmed, turned the Rizzo boy loose in Harlem. Accompanied by detectives, he was able to identify the house on East 63rd

Street where he had been held. Only two of the gang, a man and a woman, Stanislao Pattenza and Maria Rappa, were indicted on positive identification by the boys. They were quickly tried in Kings County Court and convicted on kidnaping charges; the Longo boy was the star witness in both trials. Judge Fawcett gave them the limit of the law—twenty-five to fifty years' imprisonment. He had barred all Italians except witnesses from the court. He congratulated the jury, which had deliberated only fifteen minutes in finding Pattenza guilty. The Rappa woman, he said, had admitted that Pattenza was a leader in the so-called Black Hand. "These," he said, "in my opinion, are the worst blows which have been struck at the so-called Black Hand since that element began operations in this country." The committing magistrate had already congratulated the detectives. "It proves that the Italian Bureau is all right, and that the Detective Bureau is in splendid hands," he had said, announcing rather prematurely that "under Commissioner Flynn the reign of intimidation among the Italians is at an end." Flynn's achievement was hailed in the press and by private congratulations.[13]

During the investigation, which brought a fresh wave of excitement over the Black Hand, Lieutenant Corrao had been asked by an *Eagle* reporter: "Is there such a thing as a Black Hand organization—an organization with ramifications abroad, or is the Black Hand merely a fiction?" Corrao had replied that "The Black Hand as an organization is a fiction." The New York *Sun* was not so sure. Just after the conviction of the kidnapers it published a strange document purporting to be the constitution of a Black Hand society, or "family," as it was called. It had been brought to Rome by an Italian woman living in the United States and was first published in the *Giornale d'Italia* there. There were thirty-nine articles, written in bad Italian with many Sicilian and Calabrian dialect words and much slang and jargon. It prescribed the duties of members and the penalties for infraction of rules, ranging from death down to disfigurement by knife and mere fining and boycotting. Regular meetings were prescribed, which all must attend, and ceremonies were implied but not described. There were regular tours of duty, at the end of which all money collected must be turned in. There were senior and junior grades of membership. The officers were a chief and a treasurer, who were elected by the members. Once he was elected, the chief commanded absolute obedience. There were provisions for the entertainment of "foreign society" members.

"It is a well known fact," the *Sun*'s correspondent in Rome said, "that the Black Hand, like the Camorra and the Mafia, owes its perfect organization and discipline to a sort of code or statute founded on custom and handed down by tradition which as a rule is kept secret." While the main features of practically all the criminal associations in Naples, Calabria, and Sicily, "and of their ramifications in America," were no longer kept from public knowledge, "the details connected with their organization, such, for instance, as the rules followed by their members, the punishments inflicted and the partition of the spoils, have remained unknown." He had no doubt that this was "an authentic statute of the Black Hand."[14]

The debate over the existence of a Black Hand organization continued all through the period, as the debate over the existence of a Mafia organization has raged in our own time. Most Italians insisted that the Black Hand, organized or not, was unknown in Italy and was purely an American phenomenon. But Black Handers based in Italy at a later date wrote to Marc Klaw, American theatrical producer in New York, threatening him with death at the hands of gang members in the city if he failed to send them the equivalent in Italian money of $5,000. He reported the letter to the police. They took the matter up with the Italian consul general, who caused the arrest of the gang at Avellina in South Italy. The *Herald*, which got the story from the consul general, reported that "It is said that Avellina is a hotbed of Black Hand Societies." Possibly these were returned immigrants who had learned their trade in America. But when Pattenza was on trial the district attorney asked him if he knew the Black Hand, and he said he knew about it before he could talk. "Everybody knows the Black Hand in Italy." It was everywhere. He came to America to get away from it. "It is a society of bad men, who make their living without working." Pattenza was asked to show his hands. They were the soft hands of a man who did not work with them.[15] Pattenza's remarks cannot be taken at face value, of course. Obviously he did not come to America to get away from the Black Hand. But they do suggest that the name and the symbol were not unknown in Italy.

Pattenza and his associates were Sicilians, but from time to time stories cropped up indicating that the Black Hand was another name for the Neapolitan Camorra. This had been suggested in the American press at the time of the Cappiello case in 1903. Two years later there appeared from the press of the *Bollettino della Sera* an Italian novel, *La "Mano Nera."* It told of one Salvatore Esposito, a noted Camorra leader who had fled from justice in Naples and established his reputation in the Neapolitan district on New York's lower East Side by overcoming a noted gangster named Don Ciccio. He had thereupon founded his own criminal organization, a copy of the Camorra in all essentials except its name, which was La Mano Nera, the Black Hand. Its first major exploit was to extort a large sum from a banker, then to kill him and leave his head in the street, to the utter bafflement of the American police.

Although the author had cast his material in the form of a novel, he meant to be taken seriously about the origin of the Black Hand. He was a scholar and a writer with an established reputation in Italy, he stated in his preface. On coming to the United States he had undertaken a sociological study of the immigrant colonies, beginning with the Italian. This novel was the first of a projected series. While still in Italy he had heard of "that terrible criminal society known as 'the Black Hand,' " whose frightful crimes in America, and especially in New York, were reported daily. He had "sought to investigate, with every care (as thoroughly as possible), the origins of this 'society,' its practices and its deeds." Some might observe, he said, that the author had given too much space to the Camorra in the volume. "To this the author responds that this was necessary, since faithfully enquiring into the history of the origin of the 'Black Hand' . . . it is eminently clear, on reading the volume, that the author believes (and it is so) that the 'Black Hand' derives from the Camorra":

It developed that Southern Italians brought here their terrible criminal societies, much as they existed in their villages: Sicilians perpetuated the "Mafia", and Neapolitans, unable to perpetuate the "Camorra," changed both its name and style of operation, calling it the "Black Hand," a name more appropriate and Italian, since "Camorra" was Spanish and without contemporary reference, deriving from the name of a mountain where (in strict origin of the word's derivation) criminals gathered.[16]

There is much evidence of friction between Sicilians and peninsular Italians in New York and elsewhere. Iorizzo and Mondello, in their study of the Italian-Americans, point out that earlier Italian immigration to New York and most other American cities had been largely from the northern provinces. The North Italians had met their share of prejudice but were making a fair adjustment when the huge South Italian and Sicilian influx began, disturbing them as the Russian Jewish immigration alarmed the established German Jews. Mutual suspicion and hostility were likely to show up when, as seems often to have happened, the northern Italian, long established and prosperous, became a landlord and South Italians or Sicilians became his tenants. Mario Puzo makes the point in *The Godfather*, and a reverberation from the Longo-Rizzo kidnaping illustrates it.

John (Giovanni) Bozzuffi was a prosperous, second-generation North Italian who owned considerable property and operated a bank at 63rd Street and First Avenue. He defied Black Handers and urged his business neighbors to stick it out "for the sake of the decent Italians in New York who are making their way in the world, and who will be easy victims of the banditti if you or I give tribute to such cattle." In 1906 his son was kidnaped and there was a run on his bank. He refused to deal with the kidnapers, it was said, and they became alarmed and let the boy escape. The run on the bank stopped, more depositors came, and, as a flattering story in the Sunday *Times* related shortly afterward, "to-day the banker stands higher in the regard of the people in his colony than ever before."

A year later there was a report from Palermo of incriminating letters thrown out of a window and picked up by the police, as a murder case was about to be tried. These letters indicated "direct connection of the Sicilian Mafia with the Black Hand of New York in the kidnapping of Tony Bozzuffi, son of the Italian banker of New York." This story, which the *World* evidently gleaned at police headquarters, put a slightly different slant on the kidnaping. It now was said that the boy had escaped while negotiations for a $5,000 ransom were going on and that his guard was later stabbed to death for negligence. The seized correspondence had been communicated to the New York police.

Bozzuffi's affairs became a matter of police concern again four years later, when he complained in a letter to the mayor of Black Hand operations, including bombing and shooting, in his neighborhood. Vachris, a Genoese, was then acting captain in charge of the Italian Squad at headquarters. He made a careful investigation. He reported that Bozzuffi's neighborhood had had its share of Black Hand letters and bombings, but no more than in other Italian districts. A number of suspects had been picked up there. It was there, however, that the kidnapers of the Longo and Rizzo boys had been rounded up a few months before. There had been no more complaints from the neighborhood until Bozzuffi wrote to the mayor. The real cause of his complaining, Vachris said, was that one Pietro Salamone, to whom he had subleased a number of tenement houses, had severed his connections with the property and leased several houses a few blocks away, drawing many of Bozzuffi's tenants from him.

The tenants told Bozzuffi that they were afraid to stay any longer in the area where the kidnapers had been captured, "but the real reason," Vachris reported, "is that Salamone being a Sicilian and a townsman of these tenants, they have simply followed their clannish customs and gone with Salamone." Bozzuffi knew well that "these very tenants are the ones who have caused all the trouble in this neighborhood, and as the kidnapped children were found among them, they know that they are more or less watched by the Police, and therefore have shifted, but have lied to Mr. Bozzuffi as to the real motive." Vachris had assigned three Italian detectives to the neighborhood, and they called on Bozzuffi as often as possible. As to the shooting, Bozzuffi knew that it had also taken place among his own tenants but that neither of the two victims would identify his assailant when the police had rounded him up. The tone of Vachris's report suggested that, though he and his squad were doing their duty conscientiously in protecting the peace and property of a substantial citizen, Bozzuffi's sorrows left them cold. He should have known better than to lease his houses to a Sicilian in the first place.[17]

Flynn and Vachris followed up their success in the Brooklyn kidnaping case by raids on Italian saloons and restaurants on Prince Street in Manhattan, in what the *Times* called the "Black Hand Block." The saloon and spaghetti kitchen at 8 Prince Street, it said, "was the favorite rendezvous of the Lupo and Morello counterfeiting gang." Dr. Scimeca, whose boy had been kidnaped the year before, lived only a few doors away. He had said to detectives at the time, it was recalled, that "This block is full of Black Handers; they are in nearly every house." The raiding parties now picked up a number of men whose Italian criminal records were on file, "but all of these had been in the country more than three years and could not now be deported." The Longo and Rizzo boys could not identify any of them as part of the kidnap gang, and they were all turned loose. But meanwhile Italians in Brooklyn had been greatly encouraged by the successful outcome of the kidnaping case. Police were "receiving information regarding threats which a few months ago never would have been mentioned." It was believed at the detective bureau there that "almost every time an Italian receives a threat now he reports it." The myth that most Italians felt themselves bound by the *omertà*, or conspiracy of silence assiduously cultivated by the American press, tended to break down whenever they gained a little confidence in the police.

Even before the convictions in the kidnaping case, Flynn had been directed to take charge of vice and gambling raids. First Deputy Commissioner Driscoll had been assigned to this field and had begun with energy, borrowing detectives from Flynn. But he had been injured in an auto accident, and it now was said that he had not yet recovered. More and more of Flynn's time and energy were taken up with this activity. There had been bomb explosions in Harlem and downtown that were believed to be part of warfare among gamblers, "similar to what happened in Chicago for two years." Two syndicates were supposed to be competing for the business that had been cut down "since the Driscoll raids." It was later suggested that "influential politicians had the welfare of the Black Hand at heart at that time" and that Flynn's successes against it had alarmed them. This is plausible and might be convincing as to the cause of Flynn's transfer, if it were not also true that gambling operations were notoriously protected by top Tammany men.[18]

In the spring, Police Magistrate Joseph H. Corrigan charged that the city was "wide open" and that Mayor Gaynor by his police policies had allowed a crime wave to develop. A special grand jury was called to investigate. Gaynor replied to Corrigan's charges in an open letter to the City Club, and Corrigan repeated the charges at a crowded open meeting there. Corrigan stressed widespread gambling operations, unlicensed liquor sales, opium joints, streetwalkers, burglaries, and an influx of known criminals from out of town. He seems to have made no mention of Black Hand activities. Apparently they had dropped off for a time. Flynn made two spectacular raids on big gambling houses at almost the same time. Not long after, he raided the Hesper Club at 111 Second Avenue, "generally believed to have the support of political interests allied to those of 'Big Tim' and 'Christie' Sullivan, and known as the gamblers' own club." Gamblers were amazed that he had dared to do this, knowing the influence that the club was supposed to have.

A week later Flynn resigned, returning at once to the Secret Service. He declined absolutely to give his reasons to a *Times* reporter, but gossip at police headquarters was that he did not have the authority he desired and felt that his work was being interfered with. It was said also that he and Commissioner Cropsey did not get along well, and that "Such work as spying out pool rooms and gambling houses, then raiding them, was not what he especially wanted to do." Flynn had "demonstrated his ability to cope successfully with the Italian criminals of the city," the *Times* observed.

Flynn also refused to talk to a *World* reporter, but that newspaper got some information from friends of his at the

Federal Building. They said that Flynn felt there was crooked work going on around him and that he had not been given the support he had been promised. A day or two later the *World* got a statement from Flynn himself. In it he made general charges of crookedness among his superiors but named no names. His friends, however, had said that Driscoll, though no longer more than a figurehead, stood in his way and refused to quit. More and more work that was distasteful to him was shouldered on him, Flynn explained, while the work that he wanted to do, and was fitted to do, was interfered with in every possible way. "I either had to submit to the conditions as they exist or get out, and I am getting out."

Not long before Flynn's resignation was announced, an article appeared in the *Independent* reviewing Italian crime in the United States and holding that the Black Handers were numerous, well organized, and until recently generally covered by their fellow countrymen through the terror of reprisal. In New York, after the death of Petrosino, they had received protection from the police department itself, "and the situation in regard to Black Hand crime seemed utterly hopeless":

> That was four months ago and since then there has been a great change. Mayor Gaynor secured and installed as head of the New York police Commissioner Cropsey, a man of high ideals, keen mind, legal training and great activity. The Mayor also secured W. J. Flynn and put him in charge of the detective force. Flynn was for many years chief of the United States Secret Service in New York. He knows all about Black Handers, and has for years been capturing and breaking up their bands of counterfeiters. He is a big man and a great detective. Since his appointment he has done many things to make Black Handers unhappy.

There was another good sign, the writer said, "perhaps best of all." Italians themselves were coming to the aid of American authorities. They had organized in the city the Italian-American Civic League, led by bankers, merchants, and professional men, who now joined hands with other good citizens to stamp out criminality. "Strong differences of opinion as to which particular sort of Italian is responsible for the crimes have developed at the conferences of this body," it was admitted—Sicilians being hotly assailed and as hotly defending themselves—"but there has been no difference of opinion in regard to the main point—that the crimes should cease and the criminals be deported":

> Flynn is a worker. He already has his fine force in good shape and there is little doubt that he will solve New York's Black Hand difficulty. The thousand Italian criminals whose records are at police headquarters will be captured and sent back to Italy, and steps will be taken to see that other criminals do not come here.[19]

Flynn immediately resumed his old position as head of the Secret Service office in New York. Not long after, headlines announced "Death to Escape Secret Service Men." Francesco Martino, "a middle-aged Sicilian with a bad record in his native land," had jumped to his death from a North River ferryboat, as Secret Service men were taking him to the custom house in Manhattan for interrogation. Chief Wilkie of the Secret Service in Washington had received information from Sicily that criminals there were making plates to counterfeit American one-dollar silver certificates, to be brought over by Martino and an accomplice. Flynn had shadowed Martino from the time he landed. Martino had bought a printing press and rented an isolated house in Coytesville, New Jersey. Flynn's men captured him there. When he jumped from the ferryboat he refused a life preserver thrown to him. His confederate, Carmelo Coudero, was picked up on the East Side. "This is the first big capture that Chief Flynn has made since he returned to the Secret Service Bureau, after his experience in the New York Police Department," the *Times* noted approvingly.[20] Martino obviously preferred death to the sort of sentence that had been pronounced on Lupo and Morello the year before. Whatever the failings of the municipal authorities in New York, Chicago, and elsewhere, federal crime control agencies seemed to be functioning well.

A month after Flynn left the police department, Commissioner Cropsey resigned. He and Mayor Gaynor had fallen out over an interpretation of the civil service law in the matter of police appointments, and this was stressed at the time. Cropsey insisted on high standards, regardless of the civil service rating of the candidate. The head of the municipal Civil Service Commission accused him of violating the law and was backed up by the mayor. Gaynor's biographer, however, indicates that it was a personality clash that went much deeper. Gaynor had thought that he wanted a stronger man than Baker as police commissioner but found Cropsey too independent. "With a man like Cropsey in the office no one else could be Commissioner." He was loyal to the mayor but "constitutionally unable to subordinate his ideas or take dictation from anyone." If Gaynor, his biographer thinks, had let him alone, Cropsey would have escaped much annoyance and criticism. "No one man can be both Mayor and Police Commissioner of New York and long survive." There seem to have been too many strong personalities altogether in the city administration at the time; Flynn could not take orders from Cropsey, and Cropsey could not take orders from Gaynor. But crime and corruption grew much worse after Flynn and Cropsey resigned.

As Cropsey's successor, Gaynor brought in Rhinelander Waldo, who had some police experience but was then serving as fire commissioner. Waldo was more amenable. He "possessed the charm of the social graces and did not try to ruffle or talk back to the Mayor". One of his early acts was to abolish the Italian Squad, as part of a general redistribution of the detective force to the precincts evidently directed by Mayor Gaynor. There were immediate protests from the Italian community. "Commissioner Waldo has injured the Italian colony," said the *Bollettino*, "by abolishing the detective squad which sent back such dangerous criminals as Enrico Alfano, chief of the Camorra in Italy." Petrosino had died in performing the great duty of listing dangerous Italian criminals here. Lieutenant Vaccarezza (Vachris) had worthily succeeded him. But there were now in New York six hundred thousand Italians, and there were only sixty men to police them. "Now Commissioner Waldo abolishes these. The Italian colony is sad. The Italian merchants once responded to the call for funds and will do so again; but a proper squad of Italian detectives is necessary, men who are familiar with the dialects, customs, habits, and methods of the criminals who prey on the Italian people by blackmailing, extortion, kidnapping, and other outrages. . . . Let us not waste time, but restore the detective squad."

Vachris, too, protested in vain the breakup of his squad, taking his case directly to Commissioner Waldo. As he testified later, men had been taken from his squad at the rate of four or five a week, and then they all had been transferred to the precincts. He had talked to Inspector Russell about it. Russell was sympathetic but said he could not help it. "You know this is a funny administration," Russell told him. "We have to do what we are told." Vachris said he was going to Waldo about it, and Russell went with him. As Vachris recalled it, Waldo did not even know what sort of work he was doing. Vachris explained and showed him documents that he had received from the Italian government on a criminal wanted for murder and extortion. Waldo took the papers and accompanying photograph and dismissed him. Vachris was then called to testify before a grand jury in Brooklyn, where Judge Dike had made some critical remarks from the bench about the action of the police commissioner in destroying the Italian Squad. Vachris was questioned on the subject. That same day he was transferred to the Bronx, then to remote City Island, from which it took him four hours to get to his home in Brooklyn. He soon retired from the force.[21]

A recent writer on the Mafia, who has the society flourishing in the United States all through the period, attributes the disbanding of the Italian Squad to its propaganda, "playing on the ethnic sensibilities of New York's large Italian voting population," the argument being that to maintain a special Italian Squad in the New York Police Department was vicious and unfair. Its existence was a libel on the fair name of all Italian-Americans. "New York politicians, never a notably courageous breed, ran scared at the possibility of losing all those Italian-American votes. The Italian Squad that had been Petrosino's pride was quietly disbanded." No doubt there was always some sniping at the Italian Squad, but the weight of evidence is that the Italian community as a whole consistently demanded more, rather than less, police protection. Gaynor's own prejudices were probably the controlling factor here. He did not believe in having special squads at headquarters. He abolished not only the Italian Squad but also a number of other special squads. "Following the persistent protests of Italians," according to Park and Miller, "the Italian detective squad was restored in July, 1913." This seems, however, to have been only a temporary arrangement. A few months later, when a Black Hand gang was cracked, Italian detectives had to be called in from various precincts to carry on interrogations.[22]

In August a letter from Coney Island, signed by "Several Italian American Citizens," was sent to Mayor Gaynor complaining of the deterioration of conditions of vice and crime in their neighborhood. It was detailed and specific, giving a large number of names and addresses of disorderly houses in the Italian section of the island. When Vachris and his Italian detectives had covered Coney Island, it said, "The Black Handers, Camorrists, and thieving prostitutes were afraid and most of them had been handled by the Italian Squad." Since the transfer of Vachris to Manhattan, restriction in the Brooklyn office, and the abolishing of the squad altogether, these people had become bolder, "and carry on their nefarious trade without hindrance, and the poor victims and neighbors are afraid to open their mouths because they do not have the protection of the Italian squad; but the evil doers have that of the police":

> These cases we give as a sample of what was done when the Italian squad was well directed and encouraged, there are many other instances we could cite to show the necessity of the Italian (good) detectives in certain Italian cases, where the American police officer can not expect to make any headway through his lack of knowledge of their language or dialects, habits, inclinations, temper, surroundings etc., our countrymen are generally good, they want to be let alone, they expect justice and real protection.

Gaynor referred the letter to Waldo, Waldo sent it to the district inspector, and the inspector dismissed it as untrue and doubtless based on mercenary motives. There had been no Italian crime in Coney Island lately, he said; "In fact the general condition of Coney Island has vastly improved over preceding years." Waldo returned the letter to the mayor without comment, obviously taking the inspector's word for the true situation without question.[23] This sort of trustfulness got him into trouble later.

At the end of the year the *Times* ran an illustrated Sunday feature article, "Black Hand Crimes Doubled in Year Just Ended." Decorated with photographs of noted Black Handers and of detectives who had fought them, it declared that "The year 1911 in this city was richer in Black Hand outrages than any other." In 1910 there were thirty-five Black Hand bomb explosions in New York City; in 1911 there were seventy, "a number which broke all records." Kidnapings, "the other leading branch of the Black Hand industry," remained about the same from year to year; it was the bombings that were alarming. What was still more sinister was the fact that a new development had appeared in their pattern. "Heretofore all the operations of the Black Hand were directed against Italians, but in 1911 there were revealed several attempts against people of other nationalities. It looks as if the Black Handers, finding themselves more at home and getting better acquainted with America, had begun to look about them and discover, with interest, that there are other people besides Italians who have money." A list of the bombings, by month, day, and address, was presented to readers. Most of the names of victims were Italian, but some were Jewish or German. As for kidnappings, the article noted, Flynn's work had probably thrown a scare into operators of this type for a time; but their work had begun again after he was taken out of the police department. "The Black Hand situation has gotten beyond the control of the police."

Commenting editorially on this article the next day, the *Times* pointed out that a number of people well informed as to the methods of Italian criminals insisted that there was "among them no such thing as an organization, at least in this country;" that "these criminals at most have only small groups, in nowise affiliated with each other." Their solidarity was only apparent, the result of a mere similarity of method. "This may be true," the editor observed. "The fact remains, however, that what has been happening in the various Italian colonies is about what would happen if there were a Black Hand exactly like the one of popular belief." It made little difference how much or how little of an organization existed. There was a situation before which the police, as then organized, seemed almost helpless. While they had captured not a few of the blackhanders, their efforts seemed ineffectual "either in discouraging the criminals or in encouraging their chosen victims to assist in bringing them to justice." There were more Black Hand murders, kidnapings, and explosions in 1911 than in the year before and no probability that they would be decreased in the coming year. The most promising remedy so far suggested was the establishment of a secret police; "but that would be one of those choices between two great evils which we particularly detest, and it is not likely soon to be made."[24]

In 1911 there had begun the trial for murder at Viterbo, Italy, of a large number of alleged members of the Neapolitan Camorra, including their leader Alfano, or Erricone. This trial was held far from Naples, as earlier trials of the Mafia chief Palizzolo and his associates had been held far from Palermo. Alfano, following his deportation from the United States, had been kept in prison for nearly four years before the Italian government was ready to bring him to trial. There was great interest in both countries in the case, which lasted for seventeen months before he and a number of his associates were convicted. Former Mayor McClellan, who spent much time in Italy, covered some of the early court sessions for *Cosmopolitan*. A number of the defendants recognized him, he noticed. The Italian police, he reported, believed that if they succeeded in convicting the thirty-seven Camorrists they would go far toward blotting the society out of existence. "The trial is therefore doubly vital to us here in America," McClellan said, "for the reason that the so-called Black Hand societies, which in most of our big cities have defied and made the police a laughing-stock, are nothing but the trans-Atlantic manifestation of the Neapolitan Camorra." McClellan, of course, made no reference to any part he might have played in bringing about this deplorable state of affairs. For a time the name *Camorra* became popular in accounts of Italian crime in New York and elsewhere.[25]

In May 1912, Arthur Train, former assistant district attorney of New York County who had also attended some of the court sessions at Viterbo, tried to set the record straight in an article in *McClure's*. There were far more Sicilians than Neapolitans in New York, he pointed out, and more criminals of Mafia background than of the Camorra. The two societies together, he said, were known as the "Mala Vita." There were geographical and other differences between them; "but they are all essentially of a piece, and the artificial distinction between them in Italy disappears entirely in America." It was impossible to estimate their numbers correctly, of course, but "Whatever their actual number, they are quite enough, at all events." In New York City, he said, Italians headed the list of those convicted in some classes of crime—murder, assault with intent to kill, blackmail, and extortion. In Naples and Palermo the societies were highly organized; but in New York their organization was loose, and such gangs had no such political power as at home, where their influence was everywhere. They enjoyed, however, a certain amount of political protection extending into the Board of Aldermen, in exchange for assistance at election time. They sometimes worked in harmony and were sometimes in open conflict with each other, but all were united as against the police "and exhibit much the same sort of *Omertà* in Chatham Square as in Palermo":

The overwhelming majority of Italian criminals in this country come from Sicily, Calabria, Naples, and its environs. They have lived, most of their lives, upon the ignorance, fear, and superstitions of their fellow countrymen. They know that so long as they confine their criminal operations to Italians of the lower class they need have little terror of the law, since, if need be, their victims will harbor them from the police and perjure themselves in their defense. For the ignorant Italian brings to this country with him the same attitude toward government and the same distrust of the law that characterized him and his fellow townsmen at home, the same Omertà that makes it so difficult to convict any Italian of a serious offense. The Italian crook is quick-witted and soon grasps the legal situation. He finds his fellow countrymen prospering, for they are generally a hard-working and thrifty lot, and he proceeds to levy tribute on them just as he did in Naples or Palermo. If they refuse his demands, stabbing or bomb-throwing shows that he has lost none of his ferocity. Where

they are of the most ignorant type he threatens them with the
"evil eye," the "curse of God," and even with sorceries.
The number of Italians who can be thus terrorized is astonishing . . . . medievalism would be comparatively unimportant
did it not supply the principal element favorable to the growth
of the Mala Vita, apprehended with so much dread by many
of the citizens of the United States.

A disturbing factor, Train noted, was that "a majority of
the followers of the Mala Vita—the Black Handers—are not
actually of Italian birth, but belong to the second generation." They were recruited by some experienced *capo maestro*, who gathered about him associates from his own part of
Italy and the sons of men he had known at home. "To them
he is a sort of demi-god, and they readily become his clients
in crime, taking their wages in experience or whatever part
of the proceeds he doles out to them." They were usually
told nothing of the inner workings of plots. Generally each
capo maestro worked for himself with his own handful of
followers, and each gang had its own territory. The leaders
knew each other but did not trespass on each other's pre-
serves. They rarely attempted to blackmail or terrorize anyone but Italians. Their followers merely carried out orders,
"to deliver a letter or to blow up a tenement," but in time
they became bad men on their own hook. Joseph Petrosino,
Train reminded his readers, "was while he lived, our
greatest guaranty of protection against the Italian criminal.
But Petrosino is gone. The fear of him no longer will deter
Italian ex-convicts from seeking asylum in the United
States."[26]

There is evidence that the Camorra had its agents and
sympathizers in Viterbo during the trial. When it was over,
"the judge, the jurymen, the prosecutor, and other court
officials were escorted to their homes by the police because
of the fear of attempts on their lives by friends of the prisoners." That the Camorrists knew Train and viewed him as
a threat seems apparent. While he was in Viterbo attending
the trial, his auto had been maliciously set on fire when he
and his wife were in it and it was being refueled. "It is believed," said the correspondent of the London *Daily Chronicle* who reported the incident, "that the outrage was provoked by the fact that Mr. Train was on a mission to study

the relations between the Italian secret societies and the Black Hand gangs operating in the United States."[27]

Gino Speranza had meanwhile been made chairman of a committee on aliens and crimes in the American Institute of Criminal Law and Criminology, reflecting the growing national concern over alien, and particularly Italian, crime. On the committee were some of the leading settlement workers, reform politicians, jurists, and scholars in the country. The group was so widely dispersed physically that Speranza was never able to call a meeting, but he kept in touch with individual members, personally labored hard to collect data, and occasionally submitted reports. Among others that he approached for information, shortly after Train's article appeared in *McClure's*, was Police Commissioner Waldo of New York City. Waldo did not even bother to answer his inquiry personally, much less to invite him in for an interview. "The Police Commissioner directs me to acknowledge your letter," Waldo's secretary wrote him, "requesting his views on bomb explosions and socalled blackhand outrages. He regrets that he cannot comply with your request, as he does not enter into discussions of this character."

Without whatever assistance Waldo might have been able to give, Speranza soon submitted a brief report giving his own definition of the Black Hand. The "spectacular cases of extortion commonly called 'blackhand outrages' are," he said, "in the opinion of police officers and others with whom I have discussed the subject, but a very small part of a system of extortion practised among groups of foreigners in our great cities and even in some labor camps." While it was true that petty sums only were extorted, they were paid "under the threat and compulsion of fear by honest men who appear to have no reliance on our system of defenses against crime." It should not be imagined that such blackmailers and extortioners were many or that they were organized. "There is no such thing as a Black Hand Society either here or abroad, but there does exist what I might term a Black Hand spirit of terrorism which until recently was practically unknown in this country." In its shadow practiced not only men with criminal records "but also some shrewd apprentices of criminal tendencies who make an easy living by spreading the belief of a mysterious organization to which tribute must be paid.'' This class of evildoers had discovered the limitations of our law of evidence in reaching them. They knew exactly what evidence would convict them and took care that no such evidence should be found. ''That is why they can be so brazen as to explode bombs near police stations as they have been known to do. They count both on the limitations of our laws and the traditional unwillingness or the present fear of their victims to complain.'' This made the problem ''un-American and sinister in the eyes of thoughtful men.'' It was this that would make the situation worse and worse unless it was met aggressively.

In a fuller report a little later, Speranza urged closer international cooperation ''in preventing the coming into this country of alien criminals, ex-convicts and fugitives from justice.'' In a previous report, he said, he had pointed out what Joseph Petrosino of the New York police had attempted to do. ''What he attempted to do at the cost of his brave life the High Contracting Powers of this Republic and the Kingdom of Italy could do successfully by a stroke of the pen.'' It was true that a very small element of our alien population was involved in the types of crime that perhaps our entire structure of criminal law was not adapted to fight. But ''it matters little whether there are ten percent of immigrant criminals or one millionth percent; the point I wish to urge is that if an infinitely small fraction of immigrants transplant into this country a form of criminal life which we cannot fight with existing weapons, we must meet this new case, however rare it may be, just as one would try to suppress a single case of bubonic plague from Asia.'' Speranza, who had done much for the Italian immigrant in America, defending him against both economic exploitation and nativist attack, was becoming alarmed. He was on his way to the strident nativism that characterized his final years.[28]

Rising xenophobia in the United States long had been reflected in state legislation. In New York State laws were passed in 1911, going into effect September 1, illustrating the growing fear of the immigrant, particularly of the Italian. The penal law on extortion was so amended as to make an oral threat, as well as a written communication, ''with intent to extort or gain any money or property,'' a misdemeanor.

The law was further amended to make extortion punishable by imprisonment up to fifteen years. The law regulating the carrying of concealed weapons was tightened up greatly. The carrying of concealed weapons was made a felony, instead of only a misdemeanor, and gun dealers were forbidden to sell pistols or revolvers to anyone not producing a permit. They also were required to maintain full records of all such sales, open to police inspection. One provision in the new weapons law was that "Any person not a citizen of the United States, who shall have or carry firearms, or any dangerous or deadly weapons in any public place, at any time, shall be guilty of a felony."

This last provision of what was called the Sullivan Law was tested almost immediately. Giuseppe Costabile, who had been under police surveillance ever since he had been arrested in 1908 in connection with the bombing of one of the Spinella houses on East 11th Street, was picked up on Prince Street at noon by Italian detectives. "Police had been trailing him recently," the *Herald* learned, "because a former partner of his had recently been shot to death. He has returned to Italy more than once and the police have watched him constantly since his last trip." He was found to be carrying a large bomb that "contained enough high explosives to kill two or three men and to wreck the interior of an ordinary tenement."

Costabile was held in the Tombs prison for further examination under the new law which, the police contended, "makes it a felony for a foreigner to have in his possession any high explosive." He was held in $10,000 bail, while the police predicted more arrests within a short time. A police inspector revealed that more than one hundred reports had been received from merchants and peddlers in the vicinity where Costabile was arrested, that a band of blackmailers had been collecting monthly payments ranging from $20 to $50 each. However, "none of those who have been so treated would make a complaint or identify the blackmailers because of their fear of the other members of the band."

Costabile's lawyer made the defense that the new Sullivan act violated an existing treaty with Italy. He contended that the treaty specifically prohibited discriminatory legislation

against its nationals. Nevertheless, Costabile was quickly indicted on the bomb-carrying charge, and the district attorney
asked the Court of General Sessions for an immediate trial.
Speranza had already called the attention of the Italian consul general in New York to this new law, noting that it
raised the question of whether its discriminatory provision
against aliens was a violation of the existing Italo-American
treaty of commerce. Speranza's own opinion was that the
law did constitute a violation of the treaty, but he advised
against raising the issue as a matter of policy. "Public opinion has been shocked by the number of shootings by Italians
in this City and State and by the number of deadly weapons
unlawfully carried by Italians," he informed the consul general. He believed that the courts would reflect such public
sentiment "in any judicial proceedings that might be brought
to nullify the law."

The consul general evidently followed Speranza's advice
and seems not to have made an issue of treaty violation, in
connection with the Costabile case or otherwise. Costabile's
lawyer also soon shifted his ground, basing the defense
largely on the denial that a bomb was a weapon under the
Sullivan law. This argument was overridden, and Costabile
was found guilty of carrying concealed weapons. He was
sentenced to a term of up to seven years in Sing Sing.[29]

John Foster Carr, preparing a guide for the Italian immigrant in the same year, gave the newcomer much sound advice. The pamphlet was printed in both Italian and English
and evidently was intended for distribution at Ellis Island.
Carr warned the immigrant against various types of
swindlers and presented many factual data in compact form
on the United States and its Italian colonies, the means of
travel to them, and the like. Publication was under the auspices of the Daughters of the American Revolution, however; and, as might have been expected, the booklet had
rather a condescending and admonitory tone. In particular,
the Italian immigrant was warned against violence. "Italians
are too ready to have recourse to violence in quarrels," he
was told. "If this habit could be given up, Italian immigrants
would at once find themselves more welcome in America;
for this is the one thing that makes them distrusted." The

immigrant was urged to throw away all weapons he had with him. He was advised to study the laws against carrying concealed weapons, and the new legislation in New York State was presented with the erroneous implication that it was typical of the states as a whole. Several paragraphs on the subject were printed in heavy type. The immigrant was also warned about "Blackmail and Threatening Letters," and the penalties concerning them were noted.[30]

Commissioner Waldo had dispersed the detective force pretty largely to the precincts, but he had created what was called the Special Squad. Under a favorite of his, Lieutenant Charles Becker, this squad ranged widely over Manhattan, checking on gambling, vice, and dangerous gangs. Early on the morning of July 16, 1912, a well-known gambler by the name of Herman Rosenthal was murdered as he left a Times Square hotel. A group of gunmen met him with a hail of bullets, then fled in a waiting car. This affair became one of the most celebrated and controversial in New York police annals. Becker had some time before raided Rosenthal's gambling house in midtown Manhattan and kept it closed. Rosenthal had charged that this had been done because he refused to pay off at an exorbitant rate; he claimed that Becker had been his partner in setting up the establishment. He had taken his story to the *World*, which had given it flaring headlines; and information had been given to the district attorney. An official investigation had been announced. The murder, therefore, laid great suspicion on Becker.

Four gunmen, a mixed group ethnically, were soon picked up and finally went to the electric chair in Sing Sing. They were followed eventually by Becker himself. Mayor Gaynor's administration, which had another year and a half to run when the murder took place, was shaken badly. Commissioner Waldo, who has been described as "a pleasant young socialite who had a naive faith in the incorruptibility of his police force," was put under especially heavy fire by the press. Gaynor fought back, defending his police commissioner vigorously.

"The Mayor," says his biographer, "seemed to think that Rosenthal was murdered just to annoy him and bring discredit upon his administration." His "keen judgment was warped," and he became obsessed with the idea that the district attorney was "persecuting the police in an effort to undermine his reforms." Waldo hesitated to bring any departmental charges against Becker, and Gaynor at first told him to do nothing further than to take the lieutenant off his command and put him on a minor assignment. The newspapers were corrupt, he said, mere press agents of the gamblers; but "they cannot hurt an honest man." Waldo had, Gaynor assured him, "the hardest police situation in the world to deal with. We have in this city the largest foreign population of any city, and a large number of them are degenerates and criminals. The gambling of the city is almost all in their hands, not to mention other vices and crimes. "He promised to stand by the commissioner and did so in an investigation of the police department that Henry H. Curran, the new Republican chairman of the finance committee of the Board of Aldermen, launched after Becker was arrested on a murder charge.[31]

In the uproar over the Rosenthal murder, the Black Hand type of crime failed to get its normal quota of headlines. It may even have decreased for a time. Lawbreakers of all types seem to have been rather cautious in the uncertainty of the months that followed that event, with the district attorney, Charles Whitman, on the warpath and even the Board of Aldermen investigating crime. In 1913, however, it rose to new heights. Early in the new year the *Times* described a bombing on East 11th Street, commenting that bomb explosions in the tenement districts had been infrequent enough recently "to justify the hope that at last our police had about solved this one of their many problems." As so often happened, the inhabitants of the bombed tenement who came in terror down their fire escapes denied any knowledge of why they were attacked. "In other words, the population of the so-called bomb zone have not yet been convinced that the police are more powerful than the blackmailers, or else they have not yet freed themselves from the conviction, brought over in the steerage with other baggage, that he who for any reason whatever helps the police incurs a deep and lasting disgrace." The *Times* called again for a secret police, "repugnant to American instincts" as it was, to cope with the Black Hand dynamiters. "To exterminate them it would be worth while to pay a considerable price, and perhaps even one as large as the opening of as wide a door to other evils as the establishment of a secret police would unquestionably be."

A rapid succession of bombings had ushered in the new year. Caesar Conti, an Italian banker and president of the Italo-American Stores at 37 Broadway, had—according to the *Times*—"led a movement among the Italians of New York two years ago to co-operate with the police in exterminating Black Hand criminals." Conti announced that "I'm in favor of lynching any man who sets off a bomb." These continued outrages were a disgrace to the Italian race, Conti declared, "and I'm ready to lead a lynching party to administer justice to the first man caught in such a dastardly act as setting off a bomb. But we are unable to catch the guilty men." Conti's dramatic remarks made good copy, though he had perhaps exaggerated to the reporter his previous activities against the Black Hand. At the same time several members of the Italian colony reminded the *Times* that the Italian Squad at police headquarters, which had made notable arrests while under the direction of William J. Flynn, had been discontinued "and its members distributed throughout the different precincts containing Italian colonies." One well-known Italian, who had been associated with Mr. Conti in his efforts to stop these outrages, "lamented that the Italian Squad had been disbanded." He said that persons threatened had gone to police headquarters to report, "but not finding detectives of their own nationality in whom to confide, had returned home without telling of the danger which menaced them."[32]

As the hearings before the Curran committee continued, a number of men were called on to testify on the Italian Squad and the effect of its abolition. Judge Norman S. Dike, of the criminal side of the Kings County Court, who had himself received threats of death in the past, spoke highly of its work, especially when Lieutenant Vachris had headed its Brooklyn branch. He did not know why it had been dispersed, nor why Vachris had been banished to remote precincts and had left the service. He remembered the work of

Petrosino; but since he had been assigned to Manhattan almost entirely, Petrosino rarely came to his court. Lieutenant Vachris, on the other hand, had been many times in his court. "I regarded him as one of the most splendid and efficient officers and detectives," Dike testified, "a splendid successor to that great detective, Petrosino."

A squad with a majority of Italian detectives was very useful in his experience. Italians were likely to seal their lips when they were in serious trouble. If there was a detective who knew how to handle them in a quiet way to gain their confidence, witnesses at first disinclined to talk would sometimes come upon the witness stand and give valuable information, feeling that they would be protected. "In one case," Dike related, "when a woman, the mother of a kidnapped child, in my presence, from the defendant received the death sign and collapsed, and had to be taken away for an hour, came back again and courageously gave her testimony, although at first she declined to talk to any detective, or to anybody." But he reminded the committee that criminality was by no means confined to the Italians. "Yes," he said, "there should be Italians there and other nationalities, as I say, as well, because there are witnesses of course, of various kinds to be met on occasions, and of course, other nationalities."

Dr. Pecorini, testifying a few days later, was questioned closely about the Italian-American Civic League, of which he had been managing director and the memorial that it had presented to Acting Mayor Mitchel in 1910. Did he still believe that there should be an Italian Squad? Pecorini did believe in this kind of specialization for every kind of work in the police department. "It just happens that Italians are committing certain crimes which are not usually committed by other nationalities." He thought that they had a better record than some other nationalities, because some kinds of crime were almost unheard of among Italians; but such things as "kidnapping and blackmailing and bomb throwing" were perhaps committed more by Italians than by other nationalities. The only way to deal with such a situation was by a specialized detective force.

Judge Dike, Pecorini was informed, had testified that the

Italian, when preyed upon, was more likely to seal his lips than men of other races. Did this accord with his own experience? It did, Pecorini said; the Italians "come from abroad with certain prejudices, and the greatest of all prejudices is the one that makes them feel that the police and every authority is opposed to their welfare." He was sorry to say that they had not received enough protection to take this prejudice from their minds. How could the police department gain the confidence of the honest Italian, he was asked. There should certainly be a well organized squad to deal with Italian crimes, he thought; but it should not be made up exclusively of Italians. There should also be Americans who had learned the language and customs. In an exclusively Italian squad there would be some men who would be subjected to influences that they could not be expected to withstand. "I do not believe that the leading forces in the Italian community in this city are such as would help in any way the total eradication of crime." Here Pecorini was no doubt referring to the Italian press as a whole, with which he had a standing feud.

Although the former Italian Squad had not been properly organized and had not been given a free hand, Pecorini felt that while Petrosino was alive and Vachris was active, Italian crime had been kept under a measure of control. Since the squad had been disbanded "nine out of ten of the people who receive blackmailing letters prefer to pay rather than enter a complaint, and they do pay actually." There were, he added, "many, many people who live exclusively on this business."

Like Speranza, Pecorini thought that close cooperation with the Italian government would be very helpful. Little use had been made of the seven hundred records that it had supplied to the New York police, and was prepared to continue to supply, of criminals who had crossed the border and escaped to America. Would the Italian government like to have them back? "Yes," said Pecorini, "and the Italian government is ready for them. Send them where they ought to be." The Italian government felt that it did not help either the commerce of Italy or the good name or the welfare of the Italian masses in this country "to have a number of criminals, which is very limited, but which is sufficient to disgrace the whole community.''

Ex-Lieutenant Vachris, called to the stand, was made to recount in detail his own experience on the Italian Squad, including his mission to Italy after Petrosino's murder and all that had happened to him afterward. Among many other things, he testified that he and Crowley had brought back four hundred criminal records and that three hundred more had later been sent on by the Italian authorities. A year afterward, when he had been brought back from Brooklyn to head the squad in Manhattan, he had checked up on these records. ''When I came back to New York,'' he said, ''I found them all upset in a bureau drawer in one of the desks. They had not been—I don't know that any action had been taken on them at all.'' They could, of course, be used for deportation only for three years from the time that the criminal came from Italy. While he was left in charge and until the Italian Squad was broken up, he had been able to get about 200 men on the list deported, although the certificates were rapidly losing their value. Vachris's account of his subsequent treatment at the hands of the police department, and his resulting resignation, was received with considerable apparent interest. He testified further on the need for central detective squads specializing in the various types of crime.

Arthur Woods, former deputy police commissioner under General Bingham, told the committee, ''I do not see how you could handle this blackmailing crime among the Italians without a special squad.'' Crime did not prevail among Italian residents of New York any more than it did among others. ''Of course the enormous majority of the Italian community is just as law-abiding as any other community, but there has been a peculiar form of blackmail which seems to be prevalent there.'' The police had found that most of these Black Handers were men who had criminal records in Italy. ''They worked only among their own countrymen, and the reason they had such a good time here was because our laws and judicial procedure seemed to them so made to order for their purpose.''

In Italy, Woods understood, the practice in criminal trials was that both the witness and the defendant were encouraged to talk all they could, sometimes both together, even to lose their tempers; the theory was that the truth would come out with all the other things. The Italian criminal used to this, coming to this country, found that for some strange reason the effort was to keep the truth from coming out. The witnesses were not allowed to tell the truth. "The thing seems to be made to order for him. It is the finest thing he ever struck." All he had to do, Woods said, was "to give the high sign to some witness and the witness is terrified and does not say much, and he gets off and begins all over again." Like Speranza, Woods had begun to doubt that the American system of law and court procedure, with its strict rules of evidence, was able to cope with Italian crime. He praised the memory of Petrosino and the work of Vachris and Crowley, deploring the fact that the criminal records brought back from Italy had not been properly used. As to why this was so, as to why the Italian criminals had not been shipped out wholesale at once, he said, "You will have to ask someone else."[33]

In March the *Times* announced that "50th Bomb Outrage Wrecks a Tenement." Fifty bombs had been exploded in Manhattan and the Bronx since the first of the year, it said. By the first week in April the bomb score was reported at fifty-six. One explosion on Grand Street a few days later was so violent that it threw a patrolman off his feet two blocks away and shook police headquarters. A. J. Oishei, an Italian lawyer on lower Broadway, had meanwhile sent a client to the mayor with a long letter of introduction asking that he be given a pistol permit. The man, Giovanni De Marco, was foreman of a construction company and a U. S. citizen. He had received Black Hand letters demanding $200 and, after consulting the police, had informed them who the sender was. The blackmailer, Luigi Pernicci, was arrested and was now being held for the grand jury, but the lawyer's client lived in terror of the Black Hand, the letter said. Italian strangers appeared near his home and kept him under observation. They obviously were watching for an opportunity to "do him up" so that he could not appear and testify against Pernicci in court. Oishei had a number of clients who had received Black Hand letters, "and something ought to be done to protect the good, honest law-abiding citizens.'' The Black Handers were fully aware that citizens were not allowed to carry revolvers and were helpless to defend themselves against ''any assaults which may be committed upon them.'' A police investigation confirmed the facts stated in the letter, adding that De Marco, who lived in Brooklyn, ''never comes home from his place of employment in Manhattan twice in succession by the same route.'' The police had instructed him in the proper procedure for getting a pistol permit and placed a guard on his home.[34]

The boldness of the Black Hand operators was sometimes astonishing. In May a group of five Italian gunmen took over the saloon of Frank Di Scipio at 2129 Lexington Avenue, beating him over the head with revolver butts and forcing him to sign a bill of sale, already made out in legal form. They gave him a dollar bill from his own till, to complete the legal formula of transfer of property, and kicked him into the street, beginning the serving of drinks themselves. They were still there the next day, including the new ''owner,'' when police came to pick them up on extortion charges. Di Scipio admitted that he had been paying money to Black Hand agents for months but had not been able to meet the last payment. The police had investigated after he had gone to Harlem Hospital for repairs and detectives had gotten his story out of him.

At about the same time, a number of residents of Chrystie Street near what the *Times* chose to call ''Black Hand Square,'' a neighborhood where Italian and Jewish communities abutted, combined in a protest to Police Commissioner Waldo against the police attitude on the Black Hand problem:

> In the complaint of the residents, which was forwarded through an Italian editor, it was set forth that the idea that the Black Hand was merely an Italian organization, attacking only Italians, had ceased to be true. Cases were cited in which the Black Hand operators in the district levied tribute against persons regardless of their nationality.
>
> In the letter to Commissioner Waldo the police methods were described as clumsy and ineffective and as indicating a spirit of indifference. It was held that even the babies and children in the district gossip of men who are ''to be blown

up in a little while," the explosion often bearing out the advance gossip of the streets, while children are able to point to men known as "big men" in the graft levying organization.

A settlement worker living near this centre of the bomb zone described conditions yesterday. She said her name was known to the police and that she had joined in the movement to present a statement of the police situation to Commissioner Waldo.

The social worker described conditions in the neighborhood at some length to a reporter. On one occasion, she heard "the familiar noise of a bomb" ahead and found a grocer picking up fragments of his stock in the street. The policeman on the corner merely watched, and told another who came running up: "You should worry. It's only one of them Wop affairs. I know all about it. Back to your post for yours and forget it." She knew a Hebrew grocer who paid tribute since his horses died of eating ground glass. "A young Italian girl pointed out to me the most prosperous and portly man in the district. She told me that all her people knew he was a big man of the Black Handers." Commissioner Bingham, she remarked, "really went after these people. He got results. Photographs of Italian criminals obtained from the Italian Government were an invaluable aid" to him. "People who knew their pictures were in that collection were afraid to operate." One of the things that the protestors demanded of Waldo was that "the Bingham method of dealing with the bomb situation be revived."[35]

After Cropsey resigned as police commissioner he returned to Brooklyn, where he became district attorney of Kings County. Speranza, still methodically collecting data on the Black Hand problem, now wrote to his office for information. Cropsey's chief clerk told him that he could not give him a separate report on Italians involved in blackmail crimes. Many indictments did not involve Italians, and there was no method of classifying Italian cases alone. He could report, however, that while there had been only one conviction for blackmail in 1912, and four convictions for extortion, the picture was changing. "The figures for 1913 will show considerably in excess of this, for we have twelve or fifteen indictments for blackmail and extortion, all involving Italians, which have been founded by this County's Grand Jury within the past three months."[36] Black Hand activity had evidently been increasing in Brooklyn as well as in Manhattan, but Cropsey was going after it much more vigorously than had been done before.

The Society for the Protection of Italian Immigrants, in which Speranza had been active from the beginning, had shortened its name to the Society for Italian Immigrants as more in line with its broad objectives. Its report for 1913 contributed its bit to the mounting evidence that the so-called Black Hand problem and that of crime in general was becoming more acute. "Since the distribution of the detectives by the Police Department among all city precincts instead of the local central bureaus," it said, "our immigrants as well as those of other nations have been preyed upon as never before." In one month, eight Italians had been robbed within two hundred feet of the society's office. "When the Italian Bureau was in existence, whether they knew the thieves or 'confidence men' better than others, or whether they were better men, we do not know." The fact was that "never as at the present time have the immigrants been given so little protection."[37]

Frank White, who had written a number of articles on the Black Hand, announced in the *Outlook* in August that the Black Hand was in control in Italian New York. He traced the problem from its beginning, declaring that it had grown steadily worse since Mayor McClellan had removed Commissioner Bingham from office and the Italian ex-convicts learned that Bingham's scheme for their wholesale deportation had been frustrated. White recalled the case of Mr. Spinella, whose houses on East 11th Street had been bombed beginning in 1908. Bombings continued, White charged, and Spinella was a ruined man. He slept little, fully dressed, and with pistols ready. His hair had turned white and he had aged twenty years in appearance. "The Spinella case is known in the Italian settlements throughout the United States, and his sorry plight is accepted as proof of the boast that the police cannot prevent the vengeance of the Black Hand upon those Italians who defy its mandates."

"During the first seven months of 1913," White stated, "Italian criminality broke all previous records." In 1909 he had presented in an article figures approved by the Italian Chamber of Commerce of New York, showing achievements on the part of Italians during the previous twenty-five years that could scarcely be equaled by any other nationality among us. It was a startling fact that, according to Secretary Schroeder of the same Italian Chamber of Commerce, the holdings of New York Italians in real estate and general commerce not only had failed to increase in the last few years but were probably considerably less than in 1909. Other factors might be involved, "but it is a fact that the falling off in these indicated totals of material prosperity among the Italians of New York is synchronous with the presentation of the freedom of the city to the Black Hand."

Such men as Alberto Pecorini, now editor of his own newspaper, *Il Cittadino*, "the aim of which is the uplift of the Italian masses in the United States;" Umberto Coletti, who had succeeded Speranza as secretary of the Society for Italian Immigrants; and Lieutenant Corrao, "who perhaps comes nearer to holding the position formerly occupied by Lieutenant Petrosino than any other member of the Detective Bureau," were in agreement, White stated. They "do not hesitate to say that the Black Hand has ruined and driven out of the United States thousands of honest and industrious Italians who might otherwise have made the best kind of citizens."[38]

The *Times*, which had changed its mind more than once about the existence of the Black Hand, reviewed White's article editorially, concluding, "The Black Hand is organized, triumphant, it is constantly recruited from the prisons of Italy. A vast population is at its mercy. Will Mayor Gaynor start anew the work that Mayor McClellan so mysteriously abandoned?" A letter to the editor from one Gualtiero Campino, a well-informed member of the local Italian community, followed immediately. Ex-Mayor McClellan could not afford to ignore the charges made in the *Outlook*, he said. The destruction of the criminal certificates should be brought before a grand jury. The immediate situation was disastrous:

> But this is not the only effect. The fact that few cases of attempted blackmail are now reported to the police, while in the last seven months there have been no fewer than seventy

Black Hand murders and over one hundred bomb explosions
in the Italian colony, and not a single indictment, offers conclusive proof of organization among the criminals and the
utter inadequacy of the police under Commissioner Waldo
and the present Mayor to cope with the situation. What must
be the moral influence of such a situation upon the thousands
of young and growing Italo-Americans who are destined to be
citizens of the United States?

The Curran committee had twice asked Commissioner
Waldo for the certificates, Campino said. "At first he inno-
cently replied that they did not exist, and never had existed.
When proof was laid before him that they had been in existence, had been classified and indexed, he replied that he
would look for them. He is still looking."

Pecorini, whose Italian-American Civic League's joint
committee with the City Club seems to have died aborning,
had meanwhile founded his own newspaper. He had long
been critical of the Italian press as a whole, going so far as
to charge it with actually fostering crime by its extreme
parochialism. He now wrote to the *Times*, commending its
editorial and endorsing the idea of a grand jury investigation
of the disappearance of the records brought back from Italy
by Vachris and Crowley. Commissioner Baker, he said, had
told him that the police department was in possession of 742
penal certificates of deportable Italian criminals. Commissioner Cropsey, who succeeded Baker, said he knew nothing
of such certificates. Commissioner Waldo, who succeeded
Cropsey, had never seen them. Now nobody knew anything
about them; the Curran committee could not get them, "and
in fact it is known that they have been destroyed at Police
Headquarters, probably under the pressure of politicians allied with the deportable criminals."

Pecorini was wrong about this. The records, under this
publicity, were soon reported as "found," long after they
had ceased being of any practical use. Detectives seem to
have been able to lay their hands on them meanwhile, when
they wanted to get more information on some Italian suspect
that they had picked up. But they had never been used for
the comprehensive cleanup campaign that Bingham and
Woods had visualized and that Petrosino had died for, except for a time when Vachris got control of them and they

were rapidly expiring as instruments that could be used for deportation. Commissioner Waldo, the *Times* pointed out, had not "sought to obtain fresh lists on the criminals from Italy who are constantly recruiting the secret regiment of Black Handers." The situation, in which the Black Hand, it seemed, was aided by "powerful political influences," was unprecedented. "It seems incredible that a great Italian population, equal to that of the City of Rome, should be overridden by desperadoes unchecked and unhindered by the American police."[39]

Mayor Gaynor, who had been at odds with Tammany Hall much of the time since it had put him in office, was planning to run for re-election in 1913 on an independent ticket. Boss Murphy had refused to endorse him as the Democratic candidate. He was going to "strip the Tammany gang bare" in the campaign. But Gaynor's health had never been good since he had been wounded, and on his way to Europe for a short vacation in September he died of a heart attack. John Purroy Mitchel already had been nominated and won the election on a new Fusion ticket, drawing most of Gaynor's former supporters to him and making "the need to eliminate police corruption" a principal campaign issue, along with economy and efficiency in government. Meanwhile Ardolph L. Kline, who had succeeded him as president of the Board of Aldermen, had been sworn in as mayor.[40]

Curran's investigating committee of the Board of Aldermen had conducted many months of hearings on the doings and misdoings of the police department. It had published the entire body of stenographers' notes of the hearings in six fat volumes, and its recommendations for action were submitted in a separate report. The report gave a devastating statement of Waldo's failings as police commissioner, but Mayor Gaynor refused to remove him. Among many other charges against him were that he had failed to prevent "a wide-spread system of blackmail and extortion by certain of his subordinates"; that he had failed to secure or make effort to secure from his subordinates accurate information on crime conditions in the city; that he had seriously impaired the efficiency of the Detective Bureau by his frequent changes of personnel and by using it for individual reward and preferment rather than for developing detective ability;

and that he had abolished the squads specializing in particular crimes such as pocket picking, "black hand outrages," etc. The report, which declared that "Public Interest requires the immediate removal of Commissioner Waldo," made numerous recommendations in the way of organization and procedure, including the re-establishment of the homicide squad, "the Italian and pickpocket squads," and the formation of other squads to specialize in the detection of various crimes.

An even more damning indictment of Waldo's regime was contained in a letter from a veteran police reporter to Mayor-Elect Mitchel after the election. He had heard rumors that Waldo was being considered for reappointment and was horrified. He had been the representative of a newspaper at police headquarters for twelve years, he wrote, and he gave Mitchel his estimate of every commissioner in office since 1902. McAdoo, Bingham, and Cropsey all received high marks. Of Baker, "the least said the better." Waldo had been appointed in May 1911. "With his man 'Friday' (Secretary Sheehan) he has succeeded in putting the New York Police Department in such a state of chaos that his successor will have a gigantic task to bring it back to anything like its former condition under Commissioner Cropsey." The Detective Bureau, which had been "at its highest state of efficiency," had suffered particularly, experienced men being sent out to the precincts to do patrol duty, their places being taken by "old ex-ward men of the Devery regime, and proteges of district leaders." Qualifications for detectives were pull or willingness to split salary increases with superiors. Inspectors were appointed, apparently, on no qualification but ability to "gather." The lineup was abolished. "So too was the Italian Squad, and the Missing Persons Squad." Pictures and records of known criminals were destroyed by thousands. "The city became a mecca for burglars, pickpockets, thieves and hold-up men. We had a carnival of crime." Waldo's personal secretary, he charged, was the intimate friend of notorious gamblers and gangsters. "The operations of the gang became so bold that conditions were apparent to every one, except Waldo." The trail led right into his office.[41]

Commissioner Waldo, whom Gaynor had kept in office throughout the Rosenthal murder scandal and whom Mayor Kline left there until the end of the year, had one major triumph to record in his last months of service. More or less by accident, his detective force picked up some members of a gang of blackmailers, counterfeiters, horse thieves, and holdup men who talked freely. They talked, it developed, because they felt they had been cheated by their bosses. They took the risks and others collected the fees. One was a German, another was a Pole, and another who talked was an Italian. The bosses and most of the members were Italians.

Following their statements there was a general roundup, and there were soon charges that third-degree methods were being used. Of course these were denied by the police. As there was no longer an Italian Squad at headquarters, Italian detectives had been called in from various precincts. They apparently brought in for questioning not only men mentioned by the captured gangsters but also some of their own favorite targets. A number of the Italian detectives had been reduced in grade for previous failures, or perhaps for other reasons, and no doubt made the most of this opportunity to rebuild their status. Additional confessions were sweated out after the roundup. Arson and murder were added charges. Some men had been picked up in company with Secret Service men on counterfeiting charges and were arraigned before the U.S. commissioner in New York.

The gang, it appeared, levied blackmail on anyone who seemed to have money and could be frightened, practiced horse stealing and armed robbery, and was also available to anyone able to pay its fees. A client for a bomb attack might be a businessman fearing competition, a striking labor union, or even a jealous swain. The gang was divided, according to intelligence and skill, into letter writers, "lighters" of bombs, "lighthouses" or watchmen, and other specialists. Counterfeit money was found on some members of the gang, and a Black Hand letter on one. He admitted writing it himself. He had also a pocketful of cards printed in Italian, announcing that Il Signor Antonio Levantino was to give a grand ball at 203 Chrystie Street, and tickets were one dollar apiece. "If a man received notice that $200 or $300 was needed to keep his premises clear of bombs, the proper course would be for him to purchase 200 or 300 tickets," the *Times* explained.

One member spoke of a rival gang, the "Lynch gang," which had gotten in the way of a planned robbery. On the whole, this "Black Hand" outfit resembled in many ways the well-known East Side gangs that had flourished for years, to which the label was not ordinarily applied. While it apparently had contacts in Troy, New York, and members sometimes ranged far afield (the case had actually broken in Hackensack, New Jersey), efforts were largely concentrated on the lower East Side. The German and the Pole, both graduates of state reformatories, had been admitted to the gang only after a period of apprenticeship and probation. They often were used to plant and light bombs at the points selected by others, because everybody assumed that the bombers were Italian and they could pass without notice.

Inspector Owen Egan, of the Bureau of Combustibles in the Fire Department, cooperated in the search for the gang's dynamite supply. It seems to have come largely from laborers in the excavations for the Lexington Avenue subway, who sold it to a broker for the gang's use. Sometimes expeditions were made to upstate counties, to New Jersey, and even to Philadelphia, in search of dynamite, which was not so tightly controlled outside New York City. Egan told reporters that there had been 112 bomb cases between the first of the year and the beginning of October, and he believed that the gang now rounded up was responsible for three-quarters of them. Deputy Police Commissioner George S. Dougherty, chief of detectives, said optimistically that "he believed that the era of bomb explosions was at its end in this city." The *Times* had its doubts. The capture of the gang was lauded editorially, "But fifteen Black Handers are not the whole 'trust,' if trust there be."[42]

Trials of members of the gang began the following January, though Giuseppe Ferrara, alias Joe Fay, alleged leader, and some others had disappeared at the first alarm and were believed to be in Italy. Alfred Lehman, the German, known as Smitty; Anthony Sadaitys, the Pole, known as Burke; and Rocco Pucielli, known as Zump, all had turned state's evidence and were given immunity. They entertained the district attorney's office and the court with a vast amount of detailed information and probably misinformation, including much bragging, about the gang's operations. As so often happens in criminal investigations, the trials and actual convictions did not come up to advance billing. Indictments were narrowed down to specific charges that could be proved against individuals actually in custody. Angelino Sylvestro, of 250 Elizabeth Street, was convicted, partly on the evidence of gang members but largely on that of his intended victims, of having planted a bomb at 170 East Houston Street. This particular bomb had failed to go off, as a young woman had thrown a bucket of water on it. The jury was out only five minutes. Sylvestro had made a bad impression, charging that he was the victim of a conspiracy on the part of the Joe Fay gang. He was sentenced by Judge Rosalsky of the Court of General Sessions, who had himself received bombs in the mail a year or two before, to a three- to six-year term in Sing Sing. Pietro Giambruno, now identified as the leader of a separate gang, surprisingly pleaded guilty to planting a bomb on East 167th Street and received a sentence of from three to nine years. Antonio Levantino, known as Scapone, who had a grocery store at 187 Chrystie Street, was convicted on Pucielli's evidence of having had a part in a bomb explosion on Prince Street. Scapone was the bomb-maker for Giambruno's outfit, Pucielli said, but he didn't pay off his assistants properly; Pucielli and Lehman had blown up his shop to get even with him. Scapone got five to ten years in Judge Malone's court.

The code of *omertà* seems to have broken down badly in this group. Even some of those convicted had talked at length with members of the district attorney's staff. There was talk among prosecutors of investigating stories of "men higher up, of whose existence the ordinary bomb throwers were not aware." These men were said to have dealt only with the leaders of the gangs, "whose movements they directed, and with whom they split up the profits."[43] No doubt this very active and diversified band of Black Handers did have outside connections, both criminal and political. The business of stealing horses, for instance, in which they engaged, was well organized for years in Manhattan, involving a stable in Harlem where they were disposed of. It was virtually impossible that the gang could have operated so long and so freely without political protection also. By the time the trials were held, the city was under a reform administration, and criminal gangs were being pursued relentlessly. Confessions from this gang of malefactors probably helped considerably in this campaign.

David Chandler, who finds the Mafia active in the United States from a comparatively early date, insists that "The Black Hand and the brotherhood were separate phenomena." In fact, real Mafiosi and Camorristi despised Black Handers as operating outside the rules of organized crime. "The very existence of the Black Hand," he says, "was damaging to the societies' reputations. Most contemptible of all, from the crime families' point of view, was the Black Handers' tendency to sign their extortion notes 'the Mafia.' No true Mafioso would ever sign such a note, for it would amount to signing his own death warrant." This rather dogmatic view is not sustained by the evidence. Lupo and Morello, for instance, maintained affiliations with Mafia chiefs on their home ground in Sicily; they were also certainly Black Handers, though it is doubtful that they used a Mafia signature. Other Italian criminals of the Black Hand type frequently made voyages back to Italy. It would be astonishing if they did not maintain some contact with the Mafia or the Camorra there. But there is some indication that in New York, at least, there developed an Italian crime syndicate that at one time did profess to view the Black Hand as outside the pale. This, however, was obviously part of their racket.

Some time before his lucky break with the East Side Black Hand gang in the fall of 1913, Deputy Commissioner Dougherty, in concert with the district attorney's office, had come to the conclusion that the policy game, or lottery, was the source of a large proportion of Italian crimes. The mayor's office had long been receiving letters from Italians, usually anonymous, complaining of both blackmailers and gambling joints. Sometimes these complaints were signed:

New York June 1st, 1912.

Onorabel Mayor Gaynor:
Dear Sir:
We desired to inform you of the location of notorious Blackmail and Gam-

bling place, at 119 Mulberry St. & 121 Mulberry St. first floor front. 2 bros. Joseph Tudishi & Luigi Tudishi. the are the wholesale Peoples in this Gamme of polasi This Gang ov Crooks ruined Meny Femelies. The Captain of 12th precinct he have a men by the name Nicola Roberti, that Getting from avery place in this precinct, $50.00 & $25.00 for avery Week for Police Protation. We to inform you of this Blackmail Gang the are very Dangerous Peoples. We desired to notify you as Mayor of this large City, you are in position to punish this Peoples, af you Wandted.

Please, Mr. Gaynor We cannot see why that such Gang should be in existence in this fine City.

   We sendet to you the paper with number on

Remain Yours Truly

Luisa Ferrandina & Maria Frank

Luigi Laborio and Alfonso Bracco.

Such complaints were investigated after a fashion, but reports almost invariably, as in this case, "failed to find any evidence of Gambling" or "anything that warranted police action." There was no mention in this case of the precinct captain and his alleged bagman.[44]

While he must have been aware that there were influences in his own department that might hamper his efforts, Dougherty, with evident encouragement from the district attorney's office, eventually decided to do something about the situation. After careful preparation, with the use of Italian and other detectives, thirty-five Italians were arrested on charges of operating policy shops. "Policy King of Little Italy in Bomb Dragnet" was the headline in the *Herald*. Dougherty and Assistant District Attorney Murphy had formed a "clean-up" squad of detectives armed with "John Doe" warrants, who made simultaneous arrests "in those parts of Manhattan between Mulberry Bend and Upper Harlem." Young Italian policemen, not long enough in service to be known to the criminals, had been selected by Dougherty personally, carefully coached by experienced detectives, and sent out weeks before to mingle with suspected persons all over the city.

One of the men arrested with his bodyguard was Gabriel Bova, of Paterson, New Jersey, whom detectives believed to be the ringleader of the policy shop operators. He was said to be worth two hundred thousand dollars and to enjoy the exclusive right to receive from Italy weekly the results of the national Italian lottery and to pass them on to operators in

the city. Also brought in were Giosue Gallucci, of 318 East
109th Street, his nephew and bodyguard John Russamano,
and Joseph Nazzaro, of 339 East 108th Street, all charged
with carrying concealed weapons. Tony Vivola, another of
Gallucci's bodyguards, it was said, had been killed not long
before. Detectives said that "Gallucci's consent was necessary before anything out of the way could be done in Harlem's Little Italy."

The *Herald* quoted a formal statement that Dougherty
gave reporters in explanation of the arrests:

> "For more than six weeks we have been working to com-
> plete this dragnet," said Mr. Dougherty last night, "and I be-
> lieve that with these arrests we will be able to solve some of
> the mysterious shootings and bomb outrages. There is no
> doubt in my mind that the policy ring is the cause of a great
> many of the Italian crimes. The agents to whom the players
> pay their money for a ticket in turn deliver the money to the
> runners or collectors and these men take it to their em-
> ployers, who communicate with the game in Italy, where it is
> tolerated, as the government receives revenue from it.
> "If a policy man has a good collector and by some chance
> another policy man engages him at a higher salary im-
> mediately we hear of a building wrecked by a bomb."

The Black Hand label was, of course, by this time almost
universally applied to Italian crimes of violence, and
Dougherty told the press that he hoped to get enough confessions "to tear apart the Black Hand gangs that have terrorized the city." As the investigation developed, it appeared that the policy operators were piously disclaiming
any Black Hand connection.

The prisoners were displayed in a line-up, the first that
had been held in several years, to all the Italian-speaking detectives on the force. They were described as the leaders in
a system of blackmail by which prosperous merchants who
declined to buy a specified quantity of tickets in the Italian
lotteries were bombed. "In the investigation of complaints
by both officials it was learned that the big blackmailers of
the Italian colonies do not use the crude methods of the
mere bandits in the same business. Those responsible for
Black Hand letters do a small change business in comparison
with the tremendous returns obtained through the lottery

game intimidation." The extortionists of the lottery type not only robbed the respectable members of their nationality who were worth robbing, but also resented and punished quickly "any interlopers of the Black Hand letter type who seek blackmail from the lottery ring's appointed victims." When an Italian merchant balked at buying lottery tickets in quantity on a weekly or monthly basis, his place would be blown up. The next day lottery men would come around "and tell him that if he had bought lottery tickets as requested the lottery ring would have protected him from the Black Hand." Runners of rival lottery gangs competing for business also fought among each other, adding to the shooting and bombing.

A number of the prisoners were taken to court on charges of violating the antipolicy law or of carrying concealed weapons, but there seems to have been no continuation of the raids, though Dougherty had talked of a campaign—of "spreading a net of constant surveillance over the lottery ring." He had put his finger on an interesting development in Italian crime but was evidently called off. Much painstaking detective work seems to have gone down the drain. In any case, Dougherty welcomed the capture of the East Side Black Hand gang a few months later and was happy to blame it for most of the bombing in the city. Gallucci and his associates, competitors, and successors in crime were to figure in the headlines again.[45]

CHAPTER V

The Passing of a Symbol

When Mitchel took office at the beginning of the new year, Arthur Woods became his private secretary. Woods had campaigned actively for him, and, as Woods had special knowledge of the police department and its problems, it had been rumored that he would be appointed commissioner. But Mitchel was after Colonel George W. Goethals, then at the height of his fame as the builder of the Panama Canal. In the meantime he left in office Commissioner Douglas I. McKay, who had for a time been Waldo's first deputy without becoming involved in the scandals of the office. He had been promoted to commissioner at the end ·of the year, when Waldo was finally dismissed, and was popular in the department.

A prominent citizen was accidentally killed in a gang battle on the East Side early in January, and McKay was ordered at once to use the agencies of the department vigorously "to rid the City of professional criminals and so-called gunmen." Mitchel authorized the use of nightsticks, which Gaynor had forbidden, in dealing with gangsters, assuring the patrolmen that they would not be brought up on charges if they found it necessary to use them. Robert Rubin, who had served in the district attorney's office, replaced Dougherty as second deputy in charge of detectives, and close relations with the district attorney were predicted.

After Goethals had declined the appointment, Woods replaced McKay as police commissioner in April, a move not unexpected; and Mitchel announced that "Police policies

will be settled by Commissioner Woods and myself in conference. The administration of the department will be left entirely in his hands." He promised that there would be con-
structive changes. He expected the commissioner and the
force "to preserve diligently the peace, order and decency of
the community." But the police department was also to become active in crime prevention, as the fire department was
in fire prevention, and no longer be "merely the instrument for the
detection and punishment of crime." The *Times* welcomed
Woods's appointment and the news that he was to have a free
hand, but warned Mitchel of powerful pressures that would be
brought to bear on him personally if Woods should, as expected,
be found unapproachable.[1]

Woods and Rubin worked together in a general reorganization of the Detective Bureau. This work was based largely
on a plan that McKay had drawn up in conformity with the
recommendations of Curran's aldermanic committee of investigation, and it was carried out in part before he left
office. The system of branch bureaus was revived, and a
good many older men of experience, who had been reduced
to patrol duty under Commissioner Waldo, gradually were
brought back into detective work. The city was divided into
nine detective divisions—four in Manhattan, two in Brooklyn, and one each in the Bronx, Queens, and Richmond—
and special squads of detectives were created for the various
major types of crime. The line-up, in which half the detectives daily scanned the faces of prisoners brought in the day
before, had been abolished under Gaynor and Waldo. It was
now revived in modified form. "In this connection," the
Times said, "Woods laments the fact that the identification
bureau of the department has been sadly handicapped by the
wholesale destruction of photographs of criminals ordered in
the Gaynor administration." Under Gaynor, a man could
have his picture removed from the rogues' gallery simply by
writing a letter to the mayor, unless he had a serious conviction on his record. Woods also sought to improve morale by
better housing in the precinct stations, increased annual
leave, and extra duty in place of fines for infraction of rules,
and promised promotion on merit rather than precise civil
service rating. He announced that he would always be avail-

able to any police officer with a sincere grievance. Crime statistics were to be kept by districts, so that the comparative effectiveness of inspectors could be checked.

Woods prepared a report to the mayor describing all these changes covering the first half of 1914. It was made public in August, and the *Times* commended it highly. It did not at first include a statement of convictions and criminal cases pending in the city, as compared with the same period in 1913. After his attention had been called to this deficiency, Woods obligingly prepared a supplement giving the data. It showed a considerable improvement. Not only had the number of complaints of crime diminished and the number of arrests increased, but there were both absolute and relative gains in convictions. Complaints of homicides, in particular, had decreased, while convictions and pending cases had increased very markedly. "That indicates," said the *Times* approvingly, "that the gangs of Blackhanders and professional gunmen that distracted Mayor Gaynor's Administration are being rounded up." As Asbury, in his study of the gangs of New York, puts it, "the Tammany Hall district organizations had been temporarily demoralized and discredited by the result of the election which had put Mitchel and a reform administration in City Hall, and the Wigwam politicians were unable to protect their hereditary allies . . . . the gangsters against whom conclusive evidence could not be obtained were fiercely clubbed by the uniformed patrolmen and closely watched by the detectives."[2]

The roundup of the lower East Side blackmailing gang the autumn before probably had helped to improve these statistics. Some of the gang's leading members had escaped, to Italy or elsewhere, but a number had been convicted on extortion and other charges and sent up river for considerable stretches. More important was the tough new policy on gangsters in general. Nevertheless, the new year was by no means free from the Black Hand type of crime. In May, in rapid succession, a bomb exploded on the second floor of a tenement house at 222 First Avenue; the house of Dr. Benjamin Maggio at 691 Bushwick Avenue, Brooklyn, was damaged by a bomb; and the kidnaping of an Italian boy, another member of the Longo family, was reported in Greenwich Village. Another kidnaping had taken place shortly before. The kidnaping cases, at least, were solved after painstaking effort by the detective force, and ten members of the gang responsible for both were captured. There were seven convictions. "These seven convictions," the annual report of the district attorney's office announced with satisfaction, "have dispersed the gang that operated so extensively in this city and caused so much terror, especially to the Italian-American families who live here." Kidnaping became a rare thing in the Italian community for a long time. Sporadic bombings were reported throughout the year; but such activity, at least as a form of blackmail, seems to have tapered off rapidly. Some of the bombs now being used, moreover, were filled with black powder, indicating that tight regulations on the sale of and accountability for dynamite were having an effect.[3]

Police Commissioner Woods, in an interview at the end of the year, talked frankly about the problem of the gunmen in New York City, after the *World* had published what he said were inflated figures on recent crime and asked what the police were doing about this type of criminal. He laid no particular stress on the Italians and did not even mention the Black Hand. Gunmen were discussed as a class without ethnic designation. He thought they were coming under control. "During the year 1914 up to date," he said, "we have behind the bars over two hundred professional gunmen." A roster was kept of all gangs in the city, and a special squad of detectives was designated to cover each one. Gunmen had been given three alternatives: "to mend their ways, get out of town, or go behind bars." Unfortunately, he added, "there is a demand for the dirty work that is the chief stock in trade of these gentlemen that we call gunmen, gangsters, or gorillas." In the forefront of those who made this kind of work a marketable commodity, he put "certain politicians of the district leader class." It was only through their brazenly frank influence or backing that the gunmen had developed "the reckless defiance that has characterized their activities in recent years."

Most gangs, Woods thought, should be called by the names of district leaders rather than by the names of the thugs in immediate command. Their work, especially on election day, now had been considerably curtailed. About five hundred of the gangsters, he said, worked for gambling houses. Many were employed by businessmen as strike breakers; some now worked for the unions. Business rivals could be beaten up or even killed. They also used and sold cocaine and other drugs. When they were hard up, they made their women work as prostitutes. They did a great deal of holdup work and had had the East Side terrorized, "but we have changed that." "No," said Woods, "the east side will no more stand for the gangster, gunman, and gorilla than an honest Italian will stand for the Mafia. The east side is as sound as any part of the city. Its sentiment is for right thinking and doing. It has simply been preyed upon." A few weeks before Woods gave his interview, the inspector in charge of the Detective Division had sent him a memorandum on progress in the war on the gangs. It showed 175 leading members of 30 different gangs as having been arrested and convicted on charges up to and including murder, or with cases pending. Judging by the names, the gangs were chiefly Irish, Italian, Jewish, and some German, with a number of gangs ethnically mixed.[4]

While bombings that could be identified clearly as blackmailing attempts declined in number, there developed a rash of bombings with political implications. A period of depression had set in late in 1913, and anarchist propagandists, led by the veterans Alexander Berkman and Emma Goldman, took full advantage of it. The more violent members of the movement took to bombing. A new terror to established society was the syndicalist Industrial Workers of the World, better known as the IWW, which had conducted some successful and near-successful strikes and upset the authorities no end. The police tended to lump the anarchists and the IWW together, and there seems actually to have been some cross-fertilization. When a terrific explosion in a tenement on upper Lexington Avenue killed four people and injured many others, the dead were identified as members of both groups. They seem to have been manufacturing bombs, presumably for use at John D. Rockefeller's residence in Tarrytown, when their dynamite supply exploded prematurely.

A bomb was found in the building that housed the Italian consulate. Consul General G. Fara Forni could not explain its presence but admitted that there had been IWW threats against the office. He pointed out, also, that his office had been instrumental in a good many deportations. Bombings of the new Bronx County courthouse and of the Tombs court left the authorities puzzled. There was in this period a continuing crusade against the so-called White Slave trade, or organized prostitution. County Judge Louis D. Gibbs of the Bronx recently had sentenced a gang of Italian white slavers to long prison terms, and he had been getting threatening letters. It was not believed that white slavery was part of the anarchist program, but some of these letters contained anarchist literature and threatened Gibbs with the death "which King Humbert received." Magistrate John A. L. Campbell of the Tombs court was about to ascend the bench one morning when a policeman discovered a lighted bomb under a seat in the courtroom. Judge Campbell had some months before sentenced a large number of the "Army of the Unemployed" and imposed prison terms on Berkman and other known anarchists. Commissioner Woods had been informed of an anarchist plot against Mayor Mitchel and other officials, and a special squad of detectives had been keeping an eye on known anarchist gathering places.

A few months later there was a bomb lighted in St. Patrick's Cathedral during a mass, but it was at once extinguished and the bomber captured. A plot had been discovered, it was said, involving not only St. Patrick's but also attacks on Andrew Carnegie and the Rockefellers. The foiling of this plot was pronounced as "the culmination of one of the most intricate pieces of detective work ever achieved by the New York police." Commissioner Woods and Mayor Mitchel were elated, and the mayor said that it showed "what the police can do when they have support in working out the plans of the department without being subjected to clamor and criticism." One of the two men picked up, both Italians, was identified as a member of the Gaetano Bresci Circle, an Italian anarchist group named for the man who had once lived in Paterson, New Jersey, and had gone back to Italy to assassinate King Humbert. Known anarchists denied his membership and called the whole affair a "police frame-up."

Carlo Tresca, who had been forced to flee Italy because of

his Socialist political activities, had come to America to help the immigrant workers improve their economic position. He founded and edited in New York the anarchist newspaper *Il Martello* but always insisted that he sought "only freedom, not anarchy." In this period he usually was found wherever there was a strike, taking the side of the strikers, working with the IWW. Tresca now called the St. Patrick's Cathedral bombing case "the police farce." However this may have been, and provocateurs seem to have been used, the New York authorities were taking the anarchist threat seriously, while the Black Hand was no longer even mentioned very often. The supposed anarchists both received stiff sentences. Woods, in reorganizing the detective force, had not revived the Italian Squad under that name; instead, there was now a Bomb and Anarchist Squad.[5]

There were other activities of the sort practiced by the more violent wing of the anarchist movement in 1915, still further complicated by the fact that there was general war in Europe and that American bank loans and munitions were beginning to flow to the powers allied against Germany. A bomb exploded in the United States Capitol, and there was an attempt, almost successful, on the life of J. P. Morgan, the financier, at his summer home on Long Island. While Commissioner Woods and police officials were investigating the attack on Morgan, a bomb exploded in the basement of police headquarters. Frank Holt, a former German instructor at Cornell, was captured and confessed to both the Capitol bombing and the wounding of Morgan, declaring that he wanted the export of munitions to the Allies stopped. He committed suicide in jail a few days later. As for the bombing of police headquarters, it was recognized as a protest of some sort, and "confederates of Holt, Black Hand sympathizers, and anarchists were all mentioned." The new Bomb and Anarchist Squad, headed by Captain Thomas J. Tunney, handled this sort of problem. It had also taken over the functions of the old Italian Squad and had handled the kidnaping case the year before.[6]

The year 1915 was not without events of the clearly defined Black Hand type as well. Early in January, Dr. Balderesco Baldereschi, president of the Italian Hospital, turned over to the police letters demanding $1,000 and threatening that the Mano Mera would make sausage meat of him if he failed to comply. He was told that he was dealing with "people who are able to do anything in the world." Andrew Postiglione, a prosperous tailor of 471 West 153rd Street, had been receiving Black Hand letters and had informed the police. He also bought a revolver and a police whistle. One night he was waylaid and traded shots with his assailants, blowing his police whistle at the same time. Police, though sympathetic, locked him up for carrying a revolver without a permit.

One night a bomb exploded on the roof of a tenement at 323 East 48th Street. Inspector Egan of the fire department, who lived in the neighborhood and heard the explosion, found it an interesting case; a bomb on a roof was unusual. It was soon learned that Charles Baldercano had a boarding house on the top floor and had been receiving threatening letters. Michael Delia, a manufacturing tailor of 203 Union Avenue in Brooklyn, turned over blackmail letters to the police, a trap was laid, and the extortionist was picked up when he accepted some marked bills. Frank Razzo, a barber of 430 Second Avenue, found a bomb at the door of his shop one morning. He had his assistants put it in a pail of water. It stayed in the shop all day, and he took it to the police in the evening. It was found that the fuse had burned out just short of the cap. Razzo insisted that he had received no threatening letters. Detective Michael Fiaschetti, of the erstwhile Italian Squad, caught three Black Handers who had threatened a fish peddler on Amsterdam Avenue, after he had disguised himself for days as a fish salesman there.[7]

Woods's annual report for 1915 showed an encouraging reduction in most types of crime and a record rate of convictions. There was a falling off in the homicide rate, in assault with firearms, in burglaries, and in grand larceny. As for the Black Hand, an article in the *Outlook* said that Commissioner Woods, in addition to "the really marvelous results he has already accomplished in the Department," had been quietly giving particular attention to it. It was Woods, the author noted, who, under Police Commissioner Bingham, had conducted the negotiations with the State Department at

Washington in 1908, through which the Italian government made arrangements to turn over the penal certificates of malefactors of that nationality to agents of the New York Police Department. If political pressure on Mayor McClellan had not brought about the dismissal of General Bingham and the resignation of Mr. Woods in 1909, with the subsequent suppression of the penal certificates, "it is probable that the Black Hand would have been extirpated before the end of 1910. As it was, the evil order grew and thrived."

Woods had put the campaign against the Black Hand under the general direction of Deputy Commissioner Guy Scull. "So successful had been the policy of close surveillance and quick arrest of these malefactors on the commission of any crime, no matter how trivial, with the detention of witnesses and the skilled 'working up' of evidence," the *Outlook* declared, "that in two years the *omertà*, or conspiracy of silence, once the most effective factor in preventing the convictions in Italian cases, has practically disappeared from the courts." Respectable Italians now carried complaints of the Black Hand to the police of their own accord, "and there is comparative peace in the Italian settlements of New York." Arrests for bombing had been 151 in 1913, 65 in 1914, 45 in 1915, and only three in the first quarter of 1916. As Dwight Smith remarks, "*omertà* turned out to be not so much a conspiratorial code as the pragmatic response of the beleaguered immigrant who had calculated the odds of law enforcement all too well."[8]

Judges seem to have been cooperating by handing out stiffer sentences to Black Handers and gangsters in general. Judge Nieman in Brooklyn had in August imposed a sentence of ten to twenty years in Sing Sing on Francesco Giarraputo, "reputed Black Hand leader," convicted of having placed a lighted bomb in the drug store of Joseph Ingoglia at 1081 Flushing Avenue. Judge Dike had imposed a similar sentence the week before on Anirea Guatfeo, an accomplice in the same crime. The police department's annual report made no mention of the Black Hand, as Woods obviously did not believe in giving it free advertising, but did stress success in coping with gangsters. It called attention to "The general absence of complaints and the peace and quiet existing in heretofore turbulent districts." It noted with interest and evident approval "that the sentences imposed by the courts in 1915 were much heavier than those of the year before."[9]

By the end of 1917, in spite of sporadic outbreaks of the types of crime that for years had been labeled Black Hand, Frank White, who four years before had declared the Black Hand in control in New York, thought that under Woods they had been brought practically to an end. The capture of the kidnaping gang in 1914 had "ended kidnapping in the Italian settlements of New York." It was "the beginning of the end of Black Hand crime." But the most frequent crime committed by the Black Hand was that of bomb throwing, "thus wrecking houses and killing and maiming the inhabitants, as a delicate protest when the householder failed to respond to a demand for money." The police measure of Italian crime was the number of arrests for bomb throwing, since other crimes were found to be on the same scale. Tighter regulations on the use of dynamite had helped, and the capture of one Leonardo di Vizio, who operated a dynamite and bomb factory on his premises, had virtually stopped bomb throwing:

> Close surveillance, quick arrest, and, by arrangement with the district attorney, immediate trial in the event of crime committed, was Commissioner Woods's policy in dealing with the Black Hand. No matter how trivial a case of extortion or blackmail it might be, it was followed up with all the energy and resources of the police department. The incorrigible criminals among the Italians began to discover that what they considered to be their constitutional rights were not being respected by the police. Their homes were searched for stolen property, whether there was likely to be any stolen property there or not, at all hours of the day or night, and protest often resulted in rough handling. It became so that Black-Handers, who for years had been swaggering among their honest compatriots in the Italian settlements, could not come into the streets without being hustled by policemen in uniform or "plain-clothesmen," who bade them to pursue themselves elsewhere in a hurry on pain of arrest for disorderly conduct, with the penitentiary in view. The result of these indignities constantly practised upon them was that hundreds of the Black-Handers shook the dust of New York from their feet

within a year after Woods became police commissioner. Today the people in the Italian settlements sleep as tranquilly as other residents of the city.

The great rush of Italian immigration began with the century, White pointed out, and "The jailbirds of the race were among the earliest arrivals." They were being driven from home by the punitive supervision of the Italian police, "and conditions here could not have been better for them." Congress practically invited them in by refusing to ask for passports. Under the symbol of the Black Hand they had "piled up a record of crime here unparalleled in a civilized country in time of peace. The bringing of these desperadoes under police control in New York has crippled their activities throughout the United States, and there is every reason to believe that the words black and hand in conjunction will soon cease to have a sinister connotation in this country." Schiavo, in his study of the Mafia, gives Woods equal credit. Speaking of the Black Hand, he says that Woods, as police commissioner, "stamped it out by instructing his policemen to club the Black Handers mercilessly. Soon most of them were in jail; the others saw the handwriting on the wall and simply quit."[10]

Allowing for some exaggeration, this was no mean achievement. The Black Handers and other gangsters had been riding high under Gaynor and Waldo. They were sharply checked, if not destroyed, under Mitchel and Woods. This was done at some cost to civil liberties, without doubt. It illustrated the problem of controlling violent crime in a great, modern, American city, inundated by successive waves of largely poverty-stricken immigrants of varied cultural background, without some sacrifice along this line. Mayor Gaynor had had no fondness for criminals and had hated bitterly the corrupt politicians that he blamed for protecting them. But his libertarian instincts were so strong that he held the police department under a tight rein in all the minutiae of the Bill of Rights. At the same time his ego was such that he could not endure as a subordinate in the office of police commissioner a man strong enough to cope with the problem of crime or to keep really massive corruption out of the police department itself. Gangsters, including

Black Handers, had flourished. Woods, with the approval of Mayor Mitchel and the close cooperation of the district attorney's office, used authoritarian methods. They seem to have worked, at least for a time.

There was protest, of course. A. J. Oishei, the same Italian lawyer who had complained of the Black Hand in 1913 and asked for a pistol permit for one of his clients so that he could protect himself against it, three years later filed a complaint of the violation of the rights of another. He wrote Mayor Mitchel "asking for the names of the two detectives who entered and ransacked the house of Ferdinando Castaldo, 735 East 205th Street." Woods obviously ignored the request, which had been forwarded to him. Three months later Oishei wrote again to the mayor, and again his letter was called to Woods's attention. "Mr. Oishei complains," said Mitchel's secretary, "that although he has called at the Police Department on several occasions, he has been unable to secure any satisfaction. Won't you send for him and give him a few moments of your time?"

Whether Oishei ever got any satisfaction is not shown in the records, but Woods was obviously in no mood to interfere with the work of his detectives, no matter how high-handed their methods might be. On the other hand, Mitchel and his administration had strong support in the Italian community. *La Follia di New York* praised him highly, noting in particular the fact that he had appointed six Italians to important office. "This is 'Some Record,' " the Italian paper proclaimed, "which, heretofore, has never been equalled by any of his predecessors." On the whole, the Italians of New York seem to have responded with relief and cooperation to the campaign against the Black Hand.[11]

Though Black Hand activities undoubtedly had been cut down sharply, they had by no means been eliminated. On May 21, 1915, Guy Scull, then Commissioner Woods's secretary, had forwarded to the mayor's office a summary of murders reported to the police department since the beginning of the month. There were eleven such cases, six of them of persons with Italian names. These included Giosue Gallucci of 318 East 109th Street and his son Lucca. Gallucci was referred to as "the famous blackhand king in Little Italy," by which Scull obviously meant the Italian quarter in

Harlem. Lucca had died of his wounds; the father was still alive. Scull said that the shooting was undoubtedly the result of a feud among criminals. Gallucci had refused to assist the police in any way, saying that he would settle the matter himself in his own way when he got out of the hospital. The department was trying in every way to find the perpetrators.

Gallucci subsequently died and the case had not been solved when, in the following year, the *Herald* announced, "Nineteenth Man Falls in Italian Feud in Harlem." Gaetano Del Gaudio had been shot in his restaurant at 2031 First Avenue. If he died, as expected, "his will be the nineteenth assassination in the 'Murder Stable Feud,' regarded as the most active vendetta ever waged in an American city." George Esposito, Del Gaudio's bodyguard, had been killed opposite the "Murder Stable" on East 108th Street a few weeks before. Esposito once had been Gallucci's bodyguard but had deserted him. Gallucci and his son both had been killed in May 1915. "That was a heavy blow," said the *Herald*, "as Gallucci was the wealthiest man in 'Little Italy' and a political power among the Calabrians there." The Little Italy around Mulberry Bend and Mott Street, it explained, was composed of Sicilians; the Little Italy adjacent to Greenwich Village was populated by North Italians; and Harlem's Little Italy was composed of natives of Calabria and the "heel" of Italy. This was an oversimplification, of course; there were settlements of people from different parts of Italy in all the larger Little Italies. There were a great many Sicilians in Harlem, for instance, though Gallucci may have been a Calabrian.

The *Herald* described a number of murders in sequence, all of which, it affirmed, "radiate from the 'Murder Stable,' a shack in East 108th Street, and the sawed off shotgun has been the favorite weapon for both sides in the feud." The vendetta had started among men who stole horses in the city streets and stabled them there for sale. Six successive owners of the establishment had been murdered. The feud had branched out in various channels, "involving political leadership and control of 'Black Hand' revenue."[12]

None of these murders had been solved when Ralph Daniello, known as Ralph the Barber, began to talk a year later. Daniello had been extradited from Reno, Nevada, on a murder charge in Brooklyn. He had written his pals, "members of the gang known as the Neapolitans," for money and had been ignored. The police had learned of the letter and through it of his whereabouts. "Realization of his own serious situation and a savage desire to be avenged on the men whom he thinks have 'double-crossed' him caused him to tell the story the details of which have shocked the police and the District Attorney," said the *Herald*, obviously making the most of the gory details.

Daniello had been jailed in Brooklyn, but "He made such startling disclosures," the *Times* learned, "that the Manhattan District Attorney was notified and Daniello was brought across the bridge. There he made a full confession." In District Attorney Edward Swann's office he had been secretly pumped for ten days while detectives rounded up material witnesses whom he named. These included Ciro and Vincent Morello, brothers, and Nicholas Arra, all of Harlem's Little Italy. Arra was identified as a nephew of Lupo the Wolf, who was serving time in Atlanta for counterfeiting. Daniello then appeared before the grand jury.

The district attorney, the *Herald* understood, "expects to tear the veil from the operations of three bands of criminals who for nearly ten years have levied tribute and exacted vengeance in the Italian sections of the city." Henry S. Renaud, of the homicide bureau in Swann's office, told reporters that Daniello had made revelations extending over a period of eight or ten years and that, where they could be checked, he seemed to be telling the truth. They involved a small group of Sicilians and Neapolitans who had set out to gain a monopoly on Italian gambling. They were organized in three bands, in downtown Manhattan, in Harlem, and in Brooklyn. Although they were supposed to be a close combination, they sometimes fought each other. The leaders, who were known by name to the police, gave the orders and reaped the profits. Daniello and other subordinates simply carried out orders. These orders often involved the killing of an enemy or of someone who opened a gambling house and refused to pay tribute. The murder of Gallucci and his son two years before as well as a good number of others were the work of the combine. The leaders, Renaud said, "had been long under suspicion but until now it was not known what their crooked work was." They had been frisked time and again, but no case could be built up against them. Daniello told of twenty-three murders, in many of which he had taken part.[13] This was obviously the same organization that Deputy Police Commissioner Dougherty had uncovered in 1913.

The *Herald* followed Daniello's revelations with evident relish, boasting that it had a private index of the murders circling about the murder stable, "the old headquarters for horse thieves at No. 334 West [East] 108th Street," which was "much more complete than that of the Police Department." The police had come to it for information. District Attorney Swann and the police hoped to obtain the testimony necessary to send to prison or the electric chair "the men who have ruled the Italian colonies of the city by murder and robbery of every form."

The gang collected graft only from Italians. Certain members were allowed specific monopolies. One controlled the sale of olive oil. The three Morello brothers, one of whom had been murdered and the other two of whom were now under arrest, had the exclusive right to sell artichokes in the Italian colonies. Gallucci, until he was murdered, had operated a lottery under the name of the Royal Italian Lottery. He had agents in many cities. The lottery was operated in his home, only a few doors from the murder stable. There was one prize of $1,000 monthly, and the man who drew it was always robbed just as he left. "Many crap games and other forms of gambling developed, however, and operators were murdered if they did not obtain 'licenses.'" Daniello and others were graft collectors, sold lottery tickets, and were expected to murder when instructed to do so. Gallucci had run things in Harlem with a high hand until the Brooklyn gang became jealous and tried to encroach. A feud began, and Gallucci and his son were the first victims. The Morellos had succeeded him in Harlem. There had been a dozen murders since. "In 'Little Italy' they usually knew who would be the next to be slain. They always had their 'marked men,'" said the *Herald*.

In the wake of Daniello's confessions, the grand jury in Manhattan handed up seventeen indictments for murder in the first degree. Most of the men were charged with more than one murder. District Attorney Swann declined to discuss the matter. "The greatest danger," he said, "is that some of the indicted men may be able to escape to Italy. . . . We have a large number of detectives out looking for them and hope to get them all very soon." Arrests were expected as far away as Chicago. Criminals had begun to leave town the minute it was whispered that Daniello was talking. Renaud told reporters that the investigation was still in progress. Only the first phase had been completed. "Yes," Swann interrupted, "we want to keep at this investigation until we break up the blackmail bands which have been levying tribute in the Italian sections of the city. We want to show these fellows that they can't get away with organized murder in this town indefinitely."[14]

In the following February trials began. The focus of attention had shifted to Brooklyn. Daniello had been turned over to District Attorney Harry E. Lewis of Kings County and made further revelations. On the stand he testified against one Alessandro Vollero, indicted with others for the murder of two men, Nicholas Morello and Charles Umbriacco, near his coffee house on Navy Street in Brooklyn in 1916. The Brooklyn gang was composed of Neapolitans, Daniello said, whereas the victims were Sicilians. They had been lured to Brooklyn to meet a supposed Camorra chief and arrange a truce. Vollero was said to have a personal grudge against the Morellos, though a dispute over the sharing of the graft was basic. He was himself a Sicilian but had allied himself with the Brooklyn Neapolitans. After the murder the Neapolitans had prospered, controlling most of the rackets in the whole Italian community and even taking over, for the time, the artichoke monopoly in the city. A Harlem gambler testified that he had had to come to Brooklyn every week to have his books examined by Vollero.

The illness of the judge, real or feigned because Daniello had begun to talk about police protection, brought about a mistrial in Vollero's case. He was tried again before another judge, however, a few weeks later and convicted of first degree murder, chiefly on the evidence of Daniello and other former associates. In April further murder trials began in Manhattan. One Antonio Notaro, who had turned state's evidence, gave the court lurid details of murders in various parts of the city. He had come to the United States eight years before and had since taken part in at least thirteen murders. Daniello corroborated much of his testimony. "Most of the murdered men," the *Times* noticed, "were gamblers who refused to share their money with the gang leaders." Details of the trials faded from the press just when they were getting well under way. World War I was approaching its climax, and the United States was becoming heavily engaged. The mighty German offensive of the spring of 1918 was on, and New York journals were choked with war news. Even the *Herald*, normally avid for news of Italian crime, ignored the trials.

Space was found, on the other hand, for occasional news reflecting favorably on the Italians. The *Sun* noticed the formation of the "Roman Legion of America" among prominent Americans of Italian descent to counter German propaganda in the Italian community. A good number of convictions did result from the trials, however. Most of them were of members of the Brooklyn Neapolitans. Perhaps a dozen gangsters were sent to Sing Sing for long terms, and at least one went to the electric chair.[15]

When Daniello had first begun to talk, the *Brooklyn Eagle* had spoken of his revelations as describing "a murder pool," headed by "padrones." They were worse than the Old World criminal societies, it proclaimed:

> The Camorra of Naples and the Mafia of Sicily never held life so lightly as did these "padrones." Murder as an adjunct of a petty larceny game is not part of the Camorra or the Mafia scheme. Each of these organizations has killed for money, but only when the stakes were large. And the peculiar but real code of bandit ethics governing the Neapolitan and the Sicilian defiers of law had no counterpart in this murder pool.

During the trials the Italian gangsters involved were sometimes referred to in the press as Black Handers, sometimes as Sicilians and Neapolitans, and often simply as "the murder gang." The bosses were sometimes identified as "padrones." The Brooklyn gang came often to be identified as Camorra, and some witnesses spoke of having been initiated into the society. Their enemies were usually referred to as the "Harlem Sicilians" or the "Harlem Morellos." The term *Mafia* was seldom used, apparently having gone almost completely out of fashion. Modern writers, however, since the term has become popular again, tend to call the whole affair Mafia, or a Mafia-Camorra feud. Chandler regards it as the culmination of guerrilla warfare between the Sicilian Mafia and the Neapolitan Camorra, that had gone on ever since Inspector Byrnes of the New York police had washed his hands of Italian intramural crime. The Camorra had never been strong outside Brooklyn and suffered complete disruption from the sentences imposed on its leaders. "After the trial," says Chandler, "the Camorra-Mafia war ended. Following the events of 1918, the Camorra vanished and was heard from no more, although individual Neapolitan criminals did appear afterward."

Dwight Smith, who finds no Mafia or Camorra established in the United States, does not discuss the affair. He notes, however, in another context, that "willingness to accept hypothetical relationships as real is a continuing gift of writers about organized crime." Whatever these gentry called themselves, the confessions of Daniello and Notaro revealed the widespread, long-time, and diversified activities of as vicious a group of associated criminals as had often had their affairs aired in American courts. Very few of them, apparently, were the product of American slums but brought their criminal habits, or at least proclivities, with them from elsewhere.[16]

The Lupo-Morello gang, though its leaders were out of circulation at the time, had intimate connections with some of the sinister characters exposed in 1917 and 1918, notably the Harlem Sicilians. In 1903, at the time of the barrel murder investigation, letters had been found in Giuseppe Morello's rooms addressed to him by the name of Giuseppe Terranova. When he was asked about this, he finally had admitted that he was sometimes known as Giuseppe Terranova; his stepfather's name was Terranova and his own Giuseppe. The Morello boys who operated later in Harlem also used the name Terranova. This might be regarded as mere coincidence, but one of the material witnesses picked up in 1917, along with two of the Morello boys, was identified as a nephew of Lupo the Wolf. Lupo and Giuseppe Morello, leaders in Italian crime in New York and farther afield until 1910, had not only come from the same town in Sicily but were also brothers-in-law. There seems good evidence here of what Ianni calls the "web of kinship" in Italian crime, which he holds to be the real cement of Italian-American criminal syndicates, now disintegrating, and which he has explored in detail for a later period. Chandler ties the group together as "one extended family from the town of Corleone."[17]

While the trials of the Brooklyn, Harlem, and downtown gangsters were still going on in the county courts, the Secret Service scored another victory in the federal courts in New York. Antonio Puglisi and others were convicted on counterfeiting charges. Puglisi, considered the chief conspirator in a scheme to make and sell spurious Federal Reserve banknotes, received a fifteen-year sentence. Several others were sentenced to lesser terms. Giovanni Infantino, a member of the band, gave evidence and was let off with three years. "Puglisi, a swarthy Sicilian of massive frame," said the *Herald*, had "boasted of his Mafia and Camorra connections." While he was being led in handcuffs to the Tombs prison, he turned and shouted at Infantino in Italian, "Your wife, your three girls and baby will have their throats cut by the Mano Nera." Here was a use of terminology that might confuse anyone trying to establish organizational labels in Italian crime. It might be dismissed as the mere mouthings of a desperate man, but Infantino took the threat seriously and begged the marshals to protect his family while he was in prison.[18]

Mayor Mitchel had failed of re-election in 1917. The United States had entered the war, and he had pitched his campaign on a high patriotic level, going so far as to question the patriotism of his Democratic opponent. German and Irish voters had been alienated, along with others who thought that a mayoralty campaign should be fought on local issues. The Socialists for the first time ran strongly, their candidate capturing much of the Jewish vote. Mitchel had made no effort to build up a personal machine. The Republicans had run their own candidate, greatly weakening the Fusion movement. Hearst had made a temporary alliance with the Democrats. Boss Murphy's Tammany organization, long starved for patronage, returned to power with its Democratic allies in Brooklyn, electing by a tremendous plurality John F. Hylan, a former Brooklyn judge. "Joy filled the Tammany wigwam," said the *Herald*. "The leaders there, who for so many years have been close to political starvation, were in ecstasy. . . . The Tiger has bagged his first square meal of years."[19]

Tammany's rule this time was destined to be long. While good men, such as Al Smith and Robert Wagner, Sr., rose through its ranks to national prominence, the culmination was the scandals of the Jimmy Walker administration. For some time the police department seems to have kept up a relatively high state of morale and efficiency under Commissioner Richard E. Enright, a veteran professional policeman popular with all ranks. Frederick H. Bugher, who had served as a deputy commissioner under both McClellan and Gaynor, was first appointed, but his resignation was forced a few weeks later after he had expressed a lack of harmony with Mayor Hylan. Enright made many administrative changes in the department, but there was at first no perceptible letup in the war on the gangs, including Black Handers. The homicide rate for 1918 was practically the same as that for 1917, although some types of crime actually declined.[20]

The New York Police Department was even able to aid other cities materially in coping with the Black Hand type of crime, or at least with Italian crime. In May a detective from Akron, Ohio, came to New York looking for one Pasquale Manfredi, for complicity in the killing of several policemen. Acting Detective Sergeant Michael Fiaschetti promptly picked up the fugitive and an associate in Brooklyn. He took them to Akron, on the way extracting confessions from both men. One Rosario Borgia of Akron had paid them $150 for each murder. Borgia had done time for maintaining a disorderly house and carrying concealed weapons. On his release the police had searched him for weapons whenever he passed them. Borgia had evidently had contacts in New

York and hired gunmen there to rid him of this annoyance. Fiaschetti, in cooperation with local authorities, made further investigations in Ohio and picked up another suspect in Sandusky. Four men, including Borgia, were convicted of murder in the first degree and went to the electric chair in Columbus. Two others received life sentences from an Akron judge.[21]

According to John Landesco, who made an exhaustive study of organized crime in Chicago in the late 1920s, it was also in 1918 that John Torrio went there from New York to help his uncle, "Big Jim" Colosimo, run his vice and gambling syndicate. Some time later Torrio brought Alfonse Capone, a protege of his in the Five Points or a successor New York gang, to assist him. Colosimo, it seems, had been threatened by Black Handers. Capone appears to have been at first a bodyguard to Colosimo and a pimp for one of his brothels. Big Jim died violently in 1920, at the instigation of his nephew, it is believed. The ambitious Torrio saw the possibilities opened up by Prohibition, but Colosimo hesitated to move into the new field of bootlegging. Torrio, with Al Capone as his lieutenant, took over his uncle's interests and became a contender for the overlordship of Chicago's underworld. Landesco does not suggest that Chicago was a better field for gangsters of all types than New York when Torrio went there, but this is a reasonable inference.

The Black Hand type of criminality had flourished in Chicago since the White Hand Society had given up its efforts in the face of obvious local protection to criminals. The only serious attempt to curb the Black Handers appears to have been made in the federal courts, where Judge Kennesaw Mountain Landis in 1911 began sentencing them for mail fraud. Two years later the judge said that he had received twenty letters threatening to blow up his home but that he always gave the maximum sentences in such cases. These sentences were usually served in full, as local politicians were unable to give help to the convicted extortionists. In 1915, after Woods's campaign against gangsters in New York had gathered momentum, it was reported that Chicago had appealed for additional help from federal authorities to stamp out the Black Handers, "who have terrorized 'Little

Italy' in defiance of the local authorities.'' Much was expected from increased federal activity, but Black Handers continued active in the city for some time.[22]

Grace Abbott, able lieutenant of Jane Addams, founder of the pioneer settlement Hull House, and director of the Immigrants' Protective League of Chicago, found crime of the Black Hand type flourishing there in 1917, just when New York was reporting its practical disappearance. One newspaper had reported forty-five murders in seven months that the police charged to the Black Hand. Prominent Italians and the leading Italian newspapers believed that there probably was a Black Hand organization, she said, but that "very little of the murder, bomb-throwing, blackmailing, and kidnapping charged to such a society are really committed by its members." Their view was that the police were protecting some other band of criminals and covering up their failure to arrest the offenders to the satisfaction of the American public by attributing such crimes "to Italian Black-Hand organizations."

This seemed a reasonable theory to Miss Abbott, in view of the inability of the police to find Italian perpetrators. She was, of course, conditioned by long experience in an immigrant community to accept its views against those of the police. "The result of all this," she said, "is that the Italian suffers at every turn. He is not protected against the criminal inside or outside of his own ranks; and the general public grows increasingly indignant, not at the police but at all the Italians."[23] There may have been something in the congenial theory advanced by the Italian community, but a criminal exodus from New York during the preceding two or three years probably had much to do with the deplorable situation in Chicago.

Some optimists at the time of Commissioner Woods's vigorous campaign against the Black Hand expressed the belief that it had cut down this type of crime all over the country, since it was to some extent controlled from New York. The exact reverse seems to have been what happened. Black Handers undoubtedly left the city in numbers. Black Hand operations, involving threatening letters and bomb explosions, were for the first time reported in Orange, New Jersey, in 1915. They may have been the work of refugees from New York. Some presumably sought the more hospitable climate of Chicago; others ventured farther afield and resumed their customary activities. In 1919 there were alarming reports from Kansas City to the effect that Black Hand-type operations had been going on there for some time in the city's Little Italy and were increasing. Blackmail and murder were frequent. Killers now operated in pairs with sawed-off shotguns. They usually came from other cities, it was believed. Some local officials denied the existence of a Black Hand organization, but it was noted that the methods used were exactly the same as those of the Mafia of Sicily. The Kansas City *Star* attributed the growing crime in large part to successful repressive activities in New York, "the former center of the Black Hand."[24]

In 1920 there began the great experiment of national Prohibition, and the whole crime problem took on new and vastly enlarged dimensions. New York was affected disastrously, as were Chicago and all other cities and even the small towns and villages of the United States. When Detective Sergeant Fiaschetti of the New York police, with the temporary grade of captain, was sent to Italy late in 1920, the term *Black Hand* was still very much in vogue. He was to track down, with the aid of Italian authorities, a number of criminals who had fled from the United States and were badly wanted here. Black Hand was still being used, as had long been the practice, to cover almost any violent crime committed by or against Italians. "Seek Black Hand Assassins in Italy" was the headline in the *Times*. Fiaschetti had been promoted primarily in reward for his work against the Black Handers and was now seeking to have arrested and extradited a considerable number of men who had gone home to escape the electric chair. He had other missions, as well; he had federal sponsorship and was looking for some escaped counterfeiters, and he was hoping, even at this late date, to track down the men who had killed Petrosino.

Fiaschetti talked freely to reporters when first in Italy (later he went underground) and consistently used the term *Black Hand* in discussing his mission. "The mission with which the Washington and New York departments intrusted me," he said to a *Times* correspondent, "is a very vast and

complex one. I have come to Italy to secure justice for thirty
or more Italian and American subjects who, after perpetrat-
ing homicidal crimes in America, have sought refuge in
Southern Italy." These men all subsisted habitally on robbery and blackmail. Fiaschetti did not mention Mafia or
Camorra but talked of "the new campaign for the extermina-
tion of that tremendous network of dangerous criminals who
constitute the Black Hand gang and who come to us princi-
pally from the Sicilian provinces of Trapani, Girgenti and
Palermo." It was a sad fact that some of them were recruited from the professional classes. He had tracked down
such men in a raid in a New York suburb. Three of them
were "Italian medical men, men who were specialists in the
department of the Black Hand concerned with the fabrica-
tion of false dollars." In a follow-up case he had captured
four men who confessed to a double murder. "They confessed that the murders were wrought with their own hands
in the execution of a mandate from the Black Hand, or La
Mano Nera, as they call it," because the victims were supposed to have betrayed to him "the subterranean meeting
place of several chiefs of the organization."

Fiaschetti's mission was a limited success, at best. Some
of the men had already been arrested and others were picked
up by the Italian police after he had located them. But
difficulties arose over their extradition. The Italian government pointed out the long delay in extraditing one Porter
Charlton, who had murdered his wife in Italy and fled back
to the United States. The Italian judicial authorities further
held that the extradition treaty should not apply in the case
of Italian fugitives who had been condemned in the United
States to death in the electric chair. Italy had "long
abolished capital punishment," they said, "as a relic of bar-
barism." Some of the men were eventually tried and convicted in Italian courts, after the Italian authorities had registered some points in one-upmanship. Fiaschetti, though he
tried hard and took long chances in the slums of Naples, had
no luck in finding Petrosino's killers. A tip he considered
valuable had sent him to Naples instead of Palermo. He was
finally recalled, because Commissioner Enright believed that
his life was in danger.[25]

Fiaschetti had not been in Italy long when the effects of

Prohibition became noticeable, not only in crime but also in the terminology applied to it. The killing of an Italian who had a long and varied police record and the wounding of his female companion were headlined in the *Times* as "Hundreds See Two Shot in Rum Feud." The shooting took place at noon in Mulberry Street, almost in the shadow of police headquarters, where a whiskey "curb market" for the convenience of bootleggers was flourishing. The victim, Alberto Altieri, had engaged in various nefarious activities over a period of ten years under a respectable front as an importer but had recently concentrated on bootlegging and had contacts extending into New England. He had made much money in the new enterprise and was about to return to Italy with a friend to spend some of it. A former associate from Providence, Rhode Island, evidently representing a disgruntled gang there, caught up with him. On the same day there was reported the holdup of an illicit whiskey truck in New Jersey with the killing of two men, one Italian and the other apparently a native American. The bootleg wars of the 1920s had begun.[26]

The term *Black Hand* did not disappear at once. In the summer of 1920 the town of West Frankfort, Illinois, in a coal mining section, was taken over by a mob seeking vengeance for the kidnaping and murder of two boys. The region had a violent history, there was a strike going on, and the miners were idle. There had been a series of robberies, the boys were said to have knowledge of them, and it was believed that they had been killed to silence them. When their mutilated bodies were found, the town exploded in riot. The robberies, the kidnaping, and the murders were charged to an alleged Black Hand Society that had its headquarters in the town. A pool hall operated by an Italian and patronized by Italians was supposed to be the headquarters. It was wrecked and burned, along with a neighboring Italian clubhouse. Settine de Sesnis, a Sicilian, arrested for the kidnaping and murder, was rushed to the jail in a neighboring county, but the mob followed him there. He and other suspects were spirited away to a distant town for safekeeping.

For nearly three days the mob surged through West Frankfort, beating and clubbing all foreigners, invading the Italian section and burning houses. Hundreds of foreigners, mostly Italians, fled in terror. Even after a large detachment of National Guard troops arrived to restore order, the rioting broke out again as soon as their patrols left the streets. One Italian was killed in the house where he had taken refuge with his children. Eventually the troops regained control, and the outburst of xenophobia subsided. As Higham says, it was "only the gaudiest of the portents signaling another great nativist wave." When the Ku Klux Klan became powerful in the same region a few years later, the Italians suffered again, but this time the Black Hand cry seems not to have been raised. It was going out of style. This time the charge against the Italians was bootlegging.[27]

In 1921 a story from Scranton, Pennsylvania, "Informer is Killed for Black Hand Raid," told of a spectacular raid by the state constabulary on the headquarters of a "black hand society" in Carbondale. Fourteen members of the band were arrested on the charge of a murder plot against an Italian detective. They had hardly withdrawn with their prisoners and lodged them in jail when another member of the gang, apparently suspected of having turned informer, was shot to death. Neither the local police nor the state troopers, naturally, admitted that he had been an informer. More arrests were expected, and local authorities considered the band "one of the most desperate gangs of criminals in the country."[28]

Not long after his return to New York, Fiaschetti's services were demanded in a kidnaping case on the lower East Side. It was still referred to as Black Hand work. Young Giuseppe Verotta, five years old, of 354 East 13th Street, had been abducted in the belief that his father had recovered $50,000 in a lawsuit. He was told to put $2,500 in a shoe box for someone who would call for it, or "you will never see your boy again, dead or alive, for he will be drowned and the rest of you all will be killed and the house burned." Verotta did not have the money, and he was too frightened to tell the police; but neighbors gave them the story. An older brother of Giuseppe had been badly injured at the Army camp in Yaphank during the war, and some wealthy volunteer women workers there had helped the father to institute proceedings.

According to the *Times*, the neighborhood had been for

twenty years "the rendezvous of Black Hand bands," and the police had never been able to cope with the extortionists because their victims would not testify against them.

Detectives under Fiaschetti's direction combed the vicinity and trailed a number of suspects. An Italian woman detective was placed in residence in the Verotta home, and a trap was finally sprung when a neighbor came to collect a scaled-down ransom. Five men were soon arrested, and three of them confessed to the kidnaping, persuaded by a ball bat in Fiaschetti's hands; but the boy was not returned. His body was found a few days later in the Hudson River. Fiaschetti told reporters that this was not a professional job but "a clumsy neighborhood conspiracy." There was a large funeral for the boy, who had been strangled before being thrown in the river, and one group of neighbors presented the Verottas with a gold plate inscribed in Italian: "Victim of the Black Hand. We demand justice. Let justice be vindicated." Justice was vindicated. Two men were sent to the electric chair and others were given life sentences, with the help of testimony from the Verottas. But the police, who had kept their home under guard for two years, eventually had to smuggle the whole family out of the city, with private assistance, and give them a new identity elsewhere. There had been constant threats and several attempts to kill them.[29] Here was a case, no doubt often repeated over the years, of an entire Italian-American neighborhood tragically caught between two conflicting social traditions.

In 1922 a letter from "Big Tom" Foley, powerful Tammany sachem on the lower East Side, told of his tour of the Mediterranean with Mrs. Foley. In Italy he had met Anthony Ferrara, a baker of Grand Street and one of his district captains, who told him that bomb and death threats had forced him to leave America. Foley wrote that "the police should tell the Black Hand that he had ordered Ferrara to return and that he, Foley, would not be intimidated by attacks on his aide." Foley probably wasn't afraid of the Black Hand—upper echelon Tammany men had little reason to be—but it would seem that Italian underlings of the organization were not always immune. Two years later Salvatore Bichiano, an ice cream manufacturer of Port Richmond,

Staten Island, received a Black Hand letter demanding $1,000. He refused to comply with the demand and turned the letter over to the police. Ten days later, as he was returning home, he was stopped by two men who robbed, shot, and stabbed him. A large group of young men saw the attack and gave chase, capturing one of the assailants. He was charged with felonious assault after Bichiano, who obviously had no use for *omertà*, had identified him in the hospital.[30]

Sometimes the term *Camorra* popped up again in accounts of Italian crime. Along with the Verotta case, Fiaschetti had charge of an investigation revolving around the confessions of Bartolomeo Fontano, picked up for the murder of Camilio Calazzo, whose body had been found in a sack in New Jersey. Fontano had been chosen to do the killing by his gang, he said, which had been hired for the job. He evidently believed that he was soon to be killed to destroy evidence, so he talked freely. He had also had hallucinations of Calazzo's ghost. They had been fellow townsmen in Castellamare, Sicily, and they had roomed together in New York. He implicated a number of men in a series of killings over a period of years. Some of these men were rounded up, and three of them admitted to having been involved in the Calazzo murder. There were also revealed lurid details of killings in several cities.

Fiaschetti, who recently had spent some time in Naples looking for Petrosino's supposed assassin, talked of "Camorra gangsters in Cleveland, Buffalo and Denver," who would be run to earth by Fontano's evidence. He used the term *Camorra* generally when discussing the case, even though the men involved seem to have been Sicilians. He had found the Camorra very much alive on its home ground and was convinced that it had its American affiliations. Mafia was also mentioned briefly, but the gang, who seem to have specialized in murder for hire, apparently called themselves "the Good Killers." The term *Black Hand* did not come up. It was beginning to go out of style, and Mafia had not yet had its resurrection. Even the *Times*, in introducing the story, had referred to the gang only as an "Italian Band."[31]

Black Hand and Camorra were referred to as synonymous in a case in West Virginia two years later. A story from Clarksburg told of eight men held in jail there on murder charges in connection with a "black hand reign of terror" that reached into four states. Records and books of the "Camorra Society" were found in a trunk seized when the arrests were made. On being grilled, the gang members admitted that these were part of their "black hand" literature. The books had been printed in Barcelona, Spain, and were being translated.[32] Just what sort of an organization the men really belonged to, if any, it would be hard to say. The anarchist tradition was strong in Barcelona. The local police in Clarksburg seemed rather foggy on the point.

As late as 1926 there were panics at schools in Italian neighborhoods in Brooklyn, Manhattan, and the Bronx when the cry of "Black Hand" was raised. In one case the alarm seems to have been raised by boys who didn't want to go to school that day. It spread all through the neighborhood, and police reserves were called out before order was restored. In other schools a lollypop vendor who sold lollypops in the form of a black hand was blamed as indirectly responsible for the scare. The lollypop was used to frighten some of the smaller children and kept the minds of all on the Black Hand idea. Older boys trying to break up the school routine would raise the cry, "Look out, Black Hand," or "Black Hand. Kill them." At one school boys covered their hands with lamp black and ran about leaving their prints on other children's blouses and on walls. The police were instructed to take "proper action" whenever they caught anyone selling black hand lollypops. Some boys found with blackened hands were picked up, hauled into Children's Court, and placed on probation.[33]

A Black Hand outcry could still alarm Italian children and even a whole Italian neighborhood in New York, but as a criminal technique the Black Hand had long passed its peak. Fiaschetti, born in Rome and recruited by Petrosino, retired from the New York police force in 1924. Some years later he recounted his experiences to a ghost writer. He had some blood-curdling tales to tell. While he had done sleuthing of all kinds and among all kinds of people, he "especially blew kisses at the Black Hand." This was a dark and savage corner of the underworld with a charm all its own, he said. "We broke the Black Hand, kept after the gangs, sent leaders and members to prison and the electric chair, until the reign of blackmail and terror in the Italian quarters was toned down and became a shadow of what it had formerly been. Today the Black Hand is almost gone. Prohibition helped a lot. It took a bad thing and turned it into something much worse."

What had happened, as Fiaschetti saw it, was that the Black Hand had become a millionaire. "Put it this way: Prohibition has thrown millions into the lap of the Black Hand gangs. Often the racketeers, especially the dominant leaders, are former members of the old-time blackmailing, kidnapping, and shakedown mobs, or they are of the tradition." The Black Handers operated in obscurity and for comparatively little money among the Italians. "Prohibition created a situation for which they were ideally constituted. The Eighteenth Amendment endowed the Black Hand with fabulous funds and took it from the isolated Italian quarters and bestowed it on the cities at large," with all the gaudy and bloody trappings of big-time gangsterdom that followed.[34]

This was, of course, a highly simplified version of what took place in the world of crime from 1920 to 1933, when a great part of the American public, otherwise more or less law-abiding, defied the drastic antiliquor laws and when bootleggers became more heroes than criminals in their eyes. Nevertheless, the coming of Prohibition did form a disastrous watershed in the annals of American crime. Captain Cornelius Willemse, another tough cop who entered the New York police force in 1900 when Tammany was in complete control, wrote his autobiography toward the end of the period. Corruption was almost universal when he was a rookie. "But after that, under commissioners like General Greene, General Bingham, Colonel Woods and others, the Department improved and conditions were better all around until the Eighteenth Amendment came into vogue. That threw a monkey wrench into the machinery of police departments and sheriffs' offices all over the country." Graft was now worse than ever before. "The bootlegger has waxed rich over night and money spells power. The crooks welcomed the Eighteenth Amendment as their great opportunity and went straight into the bootlegging and racketeering games."[35]

If men with Italian names, in Chicago and New York and elsewhere, often fought their way to the top in the bloody rivalry for control of the illicit alcohol supply, it was over the bodies of a swarm of competitors—Irish, Italian, Jewish, German, Scandinavian, Polish, Greek, and native American. Speaking of Chicago, Humbert Nelli says that "Black Hand activities . . . virtually disappeared in the 1920's." He traces this decline to three factors: the dwindling of the supply of simple, pliable victims after World War I and the succeeding quota immigration laws had cut it to a trickle; federal prosecutions for use of the mails to defraud; and, by far the most important, the "new Federal laws prohibiting the manufacture and sale of alcoholic beverages." Many American criminals left their former fields of labor for the more lucrative work offered through Prohibition, and Black Handers "forsook the less-profitable extortion rackets of the Italian quarter in order to join the liquor-traffic scramble."

Immigration restriction and Prohibition "marked the end of the Black Hand era," according to Nelli. Prohibition formed a Golden Age for American gangsters and especially for ambitious youngsters among second-generation South Italians, to whom many avenues of advancement were closed. A criminal syndicate under Italian leadership was already in existence. With Prohibition it moved out into the larger world of American crime, competing for control. "During Prohibition professional criminals—pickpockets, extortionists, safe crackers and others—abandoned their former practices in the Italian community and joined the growing ranks of bootleggers. The last vestiges of the Black Hand disappeared as members . . . entered the 'syndicate.' "[36]

Kobler, in his biography of Al Capone, lays a good bit of stress on federal prosecutions for mail fraud in the decline of the Black Hand in Chicago. Not that extortion ceased, but that "The dread letter signed *La Mano Nera* was replaced by a voice on the telephone or a personal visit." He notes also that the supply of malleable victims had dwindled with the sharp restriction of immigration. Like Nelli, however, he points to the richer opportunities beckoning to the professional extortionists in "the city which Lincoln Steffens described as 'first in violence, deepest in dirt, loud, lawless, unlovely, ill-smelling, irreverent, new, an overgrown gawk of a village, the tough among cities, a spectacle for the nation.' " The skill developed in long years of bomb throwing and practice with the revolver and the shotgun was not wasted. "Many an ex-Black Hander became a prized technician in the swelling ranks of gangdom" in the 1920s.[37]

The term *Black Hand* and the basic technique with which it was associated did not disappear all at once in Chicago any more than they did in New York or elsewhere. Early in 1923 Tito Schipa, tenor of the Chicago Civic Opera Company, turned over to postal inspectors a "black hand" letter demanding $50,000 under penalty of death. There were rumors that other singers had received similar letters. Schipa's letter, written in Italian, as translated read in part:

> We need desperately $50,000 to help our friends. We pray you and your comrades to furnish it to us. Not more than three days are given you for this; that is to raise this amount of money. If you think this communication is a joke you are mistaken. Give us all your consideration. If you refuse this request calamity will befall you. You must realize that we have an organization that at any place we can kill you.

It is interesting, as reflecting on local conditions, that Schipa did not look to the Chicago police, but rather to federal authorities, for help.[38]

In the same year a "black hand clique," possibly the same gang, was rounded up by the chief of postal inspectors. Capture was effected through a letter received by Giorgio Arquilla, 8348 Cottage Grove Avenue, which demanded $10,000. Landesco, whose work for the Illinois Crime Survey published in 1929 constitutes almost an encyclopedia of organized crime in Chicago for the first quarter of the twentieth century, treats this as practically the end of the Black Hand. While Judge Landis had begun imposing maximum sentences on Black Handers for mail fraud as early as 1911,

Landesco lists a great many Black Hand cases during the intervening years. He calls attention to the fact that others than Italians were using the technique. This, of course, had been noticed in New York. Summing up the Black Hand phenomenon over the years, he makes the point that the Italians in Chicago found conditions under Irish politicians not much different from those in Sicily under the Mafia. "In Chicago there developed a pattern like the Mafia among groups, such as 'Racketeer' organizations and trade associations, which did not import the pattern as an old-world trait. Not only has the extortionist thrived among the Italians in Chicago, but other national groups to whom violence was very foreign have developed methods of extortion."

Gino Speranza had made much the same point about New York in 1903, when there was a great hue and cry about the Mafia. The Mafia, he insisted, had never existed outside Sicily, and even there it was only "a sort of Tammany Hall in its worst form." Lindsay Denison confirmed this in 1908. "The secret society of Sicily is the Mafia," he noted. "It is a criminal machine like our own Tammany Hall. Nobles and men of high standing belong to it, as well as leaders of gangs of bad men." Vance Thompson, an American writer covering the Camorra trial in Viterbo in 1911, compared the Camorra to Tammany Hall. "Since 1890," he said, "the Camorra has been the most powerful political organization—with the exception of Tammany Hall under Tweed—that modern civilization has known." Its evolution, however, had been the reverse of that of Tammany Hall. It started in the jails of Naples and moved into politics afterward. Tammany began as a political society, and its alliance with crime came later. Thompson did not think the Viterbo trial would end the Camorra. Alfano was gone, but he had a successor. By the same token, "Tammany did not perish with Tweed nor end with Croker." Crime conditions in New York had improved considerably, if erratically, over the years, until the coming of Prohibition. In Chicago, according to Landesco's findings, they had not, except for limited federal intervention.[39]

That the Black Hand sprang from Mafia and Camorra roots cannot be doubted. Most transplanted Italian criminals, like those of other nationalities, worked in small groups or even alone. After 1903 they operated most often under the terror-inspiring symbol of the Black Hand. Here and there Italian practitioners of the criminal arts, including blackmail, kidnaping, and counterfeiting, attempted with more or less success to reproduce the Old World societies on a local scale, or even to create cells over extensive areas. Compared to the criminal organizations of Palermo and Naples, long entrenched in congenial environments, they were embryonic. Often they were broken up, occasionally by local law agencies but more often by federal action. Sometimes they persisted in one form or another and helped to lay the foundations of later and more elaborate structures of crime. That the Black Hand was only the trans-Atlantic manifestation of the Sicilian Mafia, as Flynn of the Secret Service came to believe and as some recent writers would have it, is, however, a good bit of an oversimplification.

Michael Fiaschetti of the New York police spent most of his professional life fighting the Black Hand. "The Italians came to America to work," he says. "Crooks followed to prey on them, most of whom had been members of the criminal societies." Victims would not talk. What could Irish cops do?

> And the Black Hand rode the crest, with blackmail, kidnapping, and murder. It never was a single, unified organization, but a number of criminal terrorizing gangs which might disband and come together as leaders arose or disappeared. It had its connections with the Camorra and Mafia in Europe, mobs keeping in touch with the underworld in the Old Country. It was flexible and many-headed.

As Italians began to enter police forces, Fiaschetti notes, a good number of them became detectives to cope with the problem. Naturally they were more effective than the others.

Landesco strangely ignored one of the effects of Prohibition on crime in Chicago, even though he was writing in the midst of it. He saw the Black Hand disappearing, and noted the success of federal agencies in combating it. He put the two together to the exclusion of another and probably more important factor. Later writers have convincingly demonstrated its significance. The disappearance of the Black Hand, in Chicago and New York and elsewhere, with some help from federal prosecutions for mail fraud, seems to have been one of the curious side effects of Prohibition. Basically, though the term came to be loosely applied to almost any violent crime among Italians, the Black Hand was only a technique that anyone so minded could practice. Many—Sicilians, Italians, and others—followed this route to easy money or revenge. With changing conditions, the professionals turned to richer pastures on the whole, and the amateurs gradually abandoned the no longer fashionable field.

The gangs that fought for mastery in the streets of American cities during the period of Prohibition and for years thereafter were usually labeled just that. Whatever their ethnic origin, their members were known as "gangsters," "racketeers," "hoodlums," often as "mobsters." Ethnic labels disappeared. "Many of the most successful operators were Italians," Dwight Smith notes, "but the names of a previous generation were not transferred to them . . . . The southern Italian criminals and 'death-bound assassins' thus were not resurrected, even though the gang fights of New York and Chicago provided almost daily opportunities for that to happen."

As Prohibition faded into the dark backward and abysm of time, entrepreneurs of the criminal world, many of them Italians, developed more fully other profitable specialties to replace bootlegging—prostitution, gambling, labor racketeering, loan sharking, and the drug traffic. As certain of these activities burgeoned across the land in the lush years following World War II, the term "organized crime" came into vogue to describe them. In the hearings led by Senator Estes Kefauver on organized crime beginning in 1950, the term "Mafia" was revived after having been very little used for many years. It has had great currency since then, except for a brief period after Joe Valachi, the informer, told of what he called "Cosa Nostra." Black Hand was not revived, except for occasional brief mention when it was simply equated with Mafia. But the memory and the terror of the Black Hand were a long time in fading from Italian communities, if, indeed, they have faded completely today.[40]

The terrorist symbol of the black hand, if not the name Mano Nera, continued in use in some Italian communities for a long time. As recently as 1971, Mayor Frank L. Rizzo of Philadelphia, in an interview on the Mafia, took the occasion to refer to its use as within his own experience. The mayor didn't like the term *Mafia*, "because other ethnic groups are involved in organized crime," he said, though he did concede that there were Italians at the top. Rizzo preferred to call it "the mob." Recalling his boyhood in South Philadelphia's Little Italy, he had a vivid recollection of the black hand as still in use as an instrument of terror. "I lived in an area where several gang killings took place," he told reporters. "If the mob even thought you were thinking of talking to the police, they'd put a black hand on your window at night. You'd wake up, and it would be there, in coal dust."[41]

Just where and when the print of a black hand was first used as a terrorist symbol has been much disputed. The point will probably never be determined. It is always a little unsafe to declare anything the first of its kind. Certainly it was known and probably used, along with other threatening symbols, in Sicily among the Mafia and elsewhere in South Italy, before it came into vogue in the United States, whether the device was imported from Spain, as seems probable, or not. Most writers have discounted a real organization called the Black Hand anywhere in Italy.

Norman Douglas, the novelist, who spent most of his life in Southern Italy, does speak in *South Wind* of the Black Hand as the real power in the local metropolis, presumably Naples. A literary device, perhaps, but the Black Hand was certainly spoken of from time to time as another name for the Camorra. There are suggestions that it was a bloody hand in Neapolitan understanding; dried blood, of course, does turn black. It is known that Serbian expansionists picked up and used the term *Black Hand* as the unofficial label for the *Narodna Odbrana*, the patriotic society that planned and carried out the assassination of Archduke Francis Ferdinand of Austria, thereby lighting the fuse that touched off the tremendous explosion of World War I. Whether they picked it up from Spain, or Italy, or from the United States, is unknown. Certainly Black Hand, as a term with a very sinister implication, had a wide vogue in the first decades of this century. It was known all over Europe by 1902.[42]

In this country, although it had been used before, the black hand got its start as a well-known symbol in 1903, when a newspaper reporter spotted its use and popularized it. Its vogue for a long time completely overshadowed Mafia and Camorra, the traditional labels for Sicilian and Neapolitan crime. Oddly enough, there is evidence that the first gang to use the term *Mano Nera*, or Black Hand, with the implication that it was the name of a society, was neither Sicilian nor Neapolitan but Calabrian. Italian-American newspapers, like the American press as a whole, quickly accepted and used it, as preferable to the Old World labels with which the Italian community had been belabored. They soon had reason to regret it. The American newspapers and periodical press found Black Hand as handy a designation as Mafia or Camorra to apply to the Italian community's criminal problem and sometimes to Italians in general. The label came, unfairly and tragically, to dominate news of Italian America, as Mafia had done before and was to do again.

The problem was appallingly real, without any doubt. Italian ex-convicts and fugitives from justice did come in considerable numbers, in defiance of Italian and American law, especially from the turn of the century onward. They found the United States, flush with a revived prosperity, its immigration laws easily evaded, its cities corruptly governed, with no national police force, and with vast numbers of impressionable fellow countrymen to prey upon, a happy hunting ground. When the Black Hand label was publicized, they picked it up and used it with great effect. That they were and remained largely unorganized seems clear. That there was a tendency toward coalition and considerable continuing contact with Old World criminal societies, which they sought to emulate, is equally clear. That the period up to the time of Prohibition was too short for such a coalition to develop beyond a relatively rudimentary stage appears a sound conclusion.

In summary, the term *Black Hand* was generally applied to Italian crime, and sometimes to the Italian community as a whole, for more than fifteen years. The basic technique and the label were imitated among other new immigrant groups and even among native Americans. With the coming of Prohibition, and the opening of a vast and highly profitable new field of endeavor for criminals in general, the Black Hand began to go out of fashion, but it had a lingering death.

FOOTNOTES

CHAPTER I

A New Name for an Old Crime

1. *New York Herald*, September 13, 14, 18, 19, October 3, 1903; *Brooklyn Daily Eagle*, September 13, 14, 17, 18, 21, October 1, 2, 21, 1903.
2. Lindsay Denison, "The Black Hand," *Everybody's Magazine*, XIX (September 1908), 293-295; *Herald*, September 13, 1903; New York *World*, September 14, 1903; New York *Sun*, April 19, 1903.
3. *Eagle*, November 29, 1903; *New York Tribune*, December 1, 4, 1903; *New York Times*, March 8, October 8, 1904; Denis Tilden Lynch, *Criminals and Politicians* (New York, 1932), 11; Humbert S. Nelli, *Italians in Chicago, 1880-1930: A Study in Ethnic Mobility* (New York, 1970), 132; *Annual Report of the Commissioner-General of Immigration*, 1904, 45. One Italian-American scholar suggests that the term *Black Hand* was coined by the editor of *Il Progresso Italo-Americano* in order to avoid using the word *Mafia*. Giovanni E. Schiavo, *The Italians in Chicago: A Study in Americanization* (Chicago, 1928), 125.
4. Luigi Monti, "The Mafiusi of Sicily," *Atlantic Monthly*, XXXVII (January 1876), 58-75. A very similar account, "The Mafiosi," appeared in *Chambers's Journal of Popular Literature, Science, and Arts*, Fifth Series, IX (June 18, 1892), 385-387. The author was convinced that the power of the society was growing.
5. *Times*, November 25, 1877; February 23, 1878.
6. "The Camorra," *Saturday Review of Politics, Literature, Science, and Arts*, LIX (January 17, 24, February 7, 1885), 76-77, 108-109, 171-172; "The Two Sicilies and the Camorra," *American Catholic Quarterly Review*, XVI (1891), 724-725; Jessie White Mario, "Italy and the United States," *Nineteenth Century*, XXIX (May 1891), 711-712.
7. John E. Coxe, "The New Orleans Mafia Incident," *Louisiana Historical Quarterly*, XX (October 1937), 1067-1110; Joseph E. Persico, "Vendetta in New Orleans," *American Heritage*, XXIV (June 1973), 65-72; David L. Chandler, *Brothers in*

Blood: The Rise of the Criminal Brotherhoods (New York, 1975), 41-51, 73-98.

8. "The Mafia," *The Nation*, LII (April 9, 1891), 296; Henry Cabot Lodge, "Lynch Law and Unrestricted Immigration," *North American Review*, CLII (May 1891), 602-612; "Immigration," *Public Opinion*, XI (May 16, 1891), 126; *Eagle*, March 15, 1891; *Herald*, March 15, 1891; *Sun*, March 16, 1891; *Times*, March 16, 1891; *Tribune*, March 15, 1891; *World*, March 16, 1891.

9. Chandler, *Brothers in Blood*, 109-110; *Times*, October 16, 17, 22, 1888; March 27, 30, April 2, 3, 1889; The People vs. Vincenzo Quarteraro, impleaded with Carlo Quarteraro, Minutes of the Sessions, 1889-1890, Court of General Sessions, New York County.

10. *Tribune*, March 15, 1891; *Times*, April 27, 1891; *Sun*, June 28, 1891; John Higham, *Strangers in the Land: Patterns of American Nativism 1860-1925* (New York, 1965), 90.

11. *Times*, May 16, 22, 1893.

12. Jacob A. Riis, *How the Other Half Lives: Studies Among the Tenements of New York* (New York, 1890), 49.

13. *The Illustrated American*, XIV (September 30, November 18, 1893), 387, 629.

14. *Harper's Weekly*, XLII (October 22, 1898), 1045-1046; Harold C. Syrett, ed., *The Gentleman and the Tiger: The Autobiography of George B. McClellan, Jr.* (Philadelphia, 1956), 158; Morris R. Werner, *Tammany Hall* (Garden City, N.Y., 1928), 451-458, 464-466; *Times*, January 1, May 22, 1898, February 2, June 17, 1899.

15. Frank M. White, "The Black Hand in Control in Italian New York," *The Outlook*, CIV (August 16, 1913), 860.

16. Rudolph J. Vecoli, "Contadini in Chicago: A Critique of *The Uprooted*," *The Journal of American History*, LI (December 1964), 407-409.

17. *Historical Statistics of the United States, 1789-1945* (Washington, D.C., 1949), 33; S. L. Martin, Executive Secretary to Commissioner Woods, April 3, 1917, Mayors' Papers, Box 186, Municipal Archives and Records Center, New York, N.Y.; *Times*, February 27, 1898, November 19, 1899, October 12, 1913; *Tribune*, May 26, October 17, 1901.

18. Vecoli, "Contadini in Chicago,'" 409; *Times*, April 15, 16, 18, 1907.

19. *Times*, April 18, 20, 23, 1907; October 11, 1913.

20. Kate H. Claghorn, "The Foreign Immigrant in New York City," U.S. Industrial Commission, *Reports* (19 vols., Washington, D.C., 1900-1902), XV, *Immigration*, 472-478; Theodore A. Bingham, "How to Give New York the Best Police Force in the World," *North American Review*, CLXXXVII (May 1908), 702-703; Herbert Asbury, *The Gangs of New York: An Informal History of the Underworld* (New York, 1928), 252-254, 268-269, 275-278; Alfred Henry Lewis,

The Apaches of New York (Chicago and New York, 1912), 52, 73-74; Werner, *Tammany Hall*, 434, 438-440; Lewis J. Valentine, *Night Stick* (New York, 1947), 125-126. Mariano, in his study of second-generation Italians in New York, says that the Five Points gang was composed entirely of Italians and that the Monk Eastman gang was 50 percent Italian, but he gives no evidence for his statement. John Horace Mariano, *The Second Generation of Italians in New York* (Boston, 1921), 309-310.

21. *Times*, March 16, 1909; Prison Association of New York, *Annual Report*, 1908, 34-35.

22. John Kobler, *Capone: The Life and World of Al Capone* (Greenwich, Conn., 1972), 21-22, 26, 28-29; Arthur A. Goren, *New York Jews and the Quest for Community: The Kehillah Experiment, 1908-1922* (New York, 1970), 148-150; Martin A. Gosch and Richard Hammer, *The Last Testament of Lucky Luciano* (New York, 1976), 17-20, 26-27, 30-32; Hank Messick, *Lansky* (New York, 1973), 19-23; Thomas Coyle to Mayor Gaynor, May 22, 1910, Mayors' Papers, Box 72.

23. Jeremy P. Felt, "Vice Reform as a Political Technique: The Committee of Fifteen in New York, 1900-1901," *New York History*, LIV (January 1973), 24-51; Syrett, *The Gentleman and the Tiger*, 167-168; Werner, *Tammany Hall*, 470-474, 476; Steven C. Swett, "The Test of a Reformer: A Study of Seth Low, New York City Mayor, 1902-1903", *The New-York Historical Society Quarterly*, XLIV (January 1960), 20, 28-29; *Tribune*, January 2, December 13, 24, 1902, January 2, August 23, 1903; New York *Evening Post*, December 12, 1902; *World*, February 18, May 2, 1903.

24. William J. Flynn, *The Barrel Mystery* (New York, 1919), 8-12; *Eagle*, July 24, 25, 26, 30, October 5, 1902, April 14, 16, 17, 20, 1903; *Times*, April 15, 17, 1903; *Tribune*, April 16, 21, 1903; *World*, April 16, 18, 21, 1903.

25. *Eagle*, March 11, 1903; *Herald*, April 17, 26, 1903; *Sun*, April 19, 1903; *Times*, January 18, 1896, April 17, 1903; Robert E. Park and Herbert A. Miller, *Old World Traits Transplanted* (New York, 1921), 250.

26. *Times*, April 17, 1903; *Eagle*, April 17, 1903.

27. *Times*, April 18, 1903; *Tribune*, April 26, 1903; *World*, April 19, 1903.

28. Gino C. Speranza to Comm. G. Branchi, St. Louis, Missouri, April 12, 26, 1904, and Paul U. Kellogg to Speranza, April ? 1904, Gino C. Speranza Papers, New York Public Library; Gino C. Speranza, "How It Feels to Be a Problem" *Charities*, XII (May 7, 1904), 459-460; *Times*, April 26, 1903.

29. *World*, May 17, 18, 1903; *Eagle*, May 18, June 14, 1903.

30. Charles W. Heckethorn, *The Secret Societies of all Ages and Countries* (2 vols., London, 1875) *passim*; S. Merlino, "Camorra, Maffia and Brigandage," *Political Science Quarterly*, IX (September 1894), 481; Major Arthur Griffiths, *Mys-*

teries of Police and Crime (2 vols., London and New York, 1899), II, 421; John H. Thacher, "Black Hand in Puerto Rico," *Harper's Weekly*, XLII (November 12, 1898), 1100-1112; Marcel Colliere, "La Mano Negra," *La Revue Blanche* XXX (1903), 161-173; Gerald Brenan, *The Spanish Labyrinth* (Cambridge, England, 1960), 160; Chandler, *Brothers in Blood*, 67-72; Dwight C. Smith, Jr., *The Mafia Mystique* (New York, 1975), 47; *Herald*, August 18, 1882; *Sun*, August 18, 1882; *Times*, August 18, 20, 1882.

CHAPTER II

A Growing Police Problem

1. Arrigo Petacco, *Joe Petrosino* (New York, 1974), 11-14; Flynn, *The Barrel Mystery*, 14-17; *Eagle*, April 29, June 25, 1903; *Herald*, April 26, 30, May 1, 2, 1903; *Tribune*, May 2, 1903; *Times*, February 20, December 11, 1910, May 1, 1911, September 10, 1915; *World*, April 26, May 1, 9, 1903. Mario Puzo, in his bestseller, *The Godfather*, has his hero come from Corleone as a boy in fear of Mafia vengeance and adopt the name of the town as his own. Mario Puzo, *The Godfather* (New York, 1969), 194.
2. *Tribune*, April 27, 1903; *World*, April 28, 1903.
3. Nancy Joan Weiss, *Charles Francis Murphy, 1858-1924: Respectability and Responsibility in Tammany Politics* (Northampton, 1968), 97; Lincoln Steffens, *The Autobiography of Lincoln Steffens* (New York, 1931), 430-434; Syrett, *The Gentleman and the Tiger*, 169; Werner, *Tammany Hall*, 482-483, 491-492, 497; *Eagle*, November 4, 1903; *Times*, November 4, 1903.
4. *Times*, December 25, 1903; Syrett, *op. cit.*, 184-185; Mayor McClellan to Robert William Welch, London, February 6, 1904, George B. McClellan, Jr., Papers, New-York Historical Society.
5. Syrett, *op. cit.*, 202-206; *Times*, February 7, March 8, May 30, 31, July 28, 29, 1904.
6. *Times*, August 12, 13, 1904.
7. *Ibid*, August 13, 17, 21, 1904; *Tribune*, August 18, 19, September 24, 1904.
8. *Tribune*, August 21, 1904; *Times*, August 25, 1904.
9. *Times*, September 14, 1904; Petacco, *Joe Petrosino*, 31-33.
10. Eliot Lord, John J. D. Trevor, and Samuel J. Barrows, *The Italian in America* (New York, 1905), 219-220; William McAdoo, *Guarding a Great City* (New York, 1906), 150-155.
11. *Times*, January 8, 1905.
12. Luciano J. Iorizzo and Salvatore Mondello, *The Italian-Americans* (New York, 1971), 95; *Times*, January 5, February 12, May 3, September 2, 11, 21, 22, October 25, 1905; *Tribune*, August 21, 31, October 28, 1905. At a much later date Petrosino

told an assistant district attorney "that there were five thousand Italian ex-convicts in New York City alone, of whom he knew a large proportion by sight and name." Arthur Train, *Courts, Criminals and the Camorra* (New York, 1912), 226-227.

13. *Tribune*, October 18, 21, 1905; *Times*, December 19, 1905.

14. *Times*, October 13, December 29, 1905.

15. Mayor McClellan to Commissioner of Police McAdoo, October 3, 1905, McClellan Papers; Syrett, *The Gentleman and the Tiger*, 24-26, 199-201, 221-222, 234-235; Werner, *Tammany Hall*, 510-511; Weiss, *Charles Francis Murphy*, 39-42; *Times*, December 30, 31, 1905.

16. Police Commissioner Theo. A. Bingham to Mayor McClellan, April 5, 30, 1906, Mayors' Papers, Box 25; White, "The Black Hand in Control in Italian New York," 859; *Times*, January 2, 7, May 31, December 20, 21, 1906; *Herald*, December 20, 1906. Petrosino's biographer has Bingham concentrating on the Black Hand problem from the beginning of his term. Petacco, *Joe Petrosino*, 67-69.

17. John Foster Carr, "The Coming of the Italian," *Outlook*, LXXXII (February 24, 1906), 419-431.

18. *Times*, November 14, 1906; *Tribune*, November 14, 1906.

19. Broughton Brandenburg, "Our Imported Criminals," III, "The Truth about the Mafia," *Collier's*, XXIV (December 10, 1904), 15, 18, 27-30; *Ibid.*, "Blows Out of the Dark," *New York Tribune Sunday Magazine*, May 27, 1906, 7-8.

20. U.S. Industrial Commission, *Reports*, XV, *Immigration*, 158; *Herald*, April 6, 22, 1903; *Tribune*, April 6, 1903; *World*, April 7, 1903.

21. *Times*, September 20, December 12, 1904; *Tribune*, July 9, 1905.

22. *Times*, May 7, 1905, July 20, August 12, 22, September 30, October 2, 1906; *Tribune*, August 19, 1906.

23. *Times*, October 25, 27, 1906; *Tribune*, February 29, 1908.

24. *Eagle*, September 12, 1903; *Tribune*, August 18, 1904; *Times*, May 23, 1905.

25. *Times*, January 26, February 25, September 3, 1906.

26. *Ibid.*, July 27, 1907.

27. *Ibid.*, July 30, 1907.

28. *Ibid.*, March 3, August 15, 27, November 18, December 1, 1906.

29. *Ibid.*, December 7, 1903; *Tribune*, June 24, 1907.

30. John Landesco, *Organized Crime in Chicago* (Chicago, 1929 and reprint 1968), 109-110, 116-117; The Italian "White Hand" Society in Chicago, Illinois, *Studies, Action and Results* (Chicago, 1908), 1-2, 3-5, 21-27; Vecoli, "Contadini in Chicago," 414-415; Nelli, *Italians in Chicago*, 134-136; Herbert Asbury, *Gem of the Prairie: An Informal History of the Chicago Underworld* (New York, 1940), 235-236.

31. "The Black Hand," *Watson's Magazine*, III (August 1909), 613; *Herald*, January 30, 1910; *Times*, June 9, 10, 11, 13, 16, 18, 20, August 7, 1909; *Tribune*, December 12, 1909.

32. *Annual Report of the Chief Clerk of the District Attorney's Office, County of New York*, 1907, 59; *Times*, April 18, 20, 23, 30, 1907.
33. U.S. Immigration Commission, *Reports* (41 vols., Washington, D.C., 1911), XXXVI, *Immigration and Crime*, 277-278; Frank M. White, "Fostering Foreign Criminals," *Harper's Weekly*, LIII (May 8, 1909), 7-8; *Herald*, July 24, 1907; *World*, July 24, 1907. Petrosino's biographer identifies Alfano as the first victim of the new law. Petacco, *Joe Petrosino*, 71-73. Actually, Alfano was deported under existing legislation some time before the new law went into effect.
34. *Times*, January 25, February 21, 22, 24, 1908; White, "Fostering Foreign Criminals," 8. Kidnaping, blackmail, and extortion now were called Black Hand crimes in the district attorney's office. There were only five convictions for blackmail out of seventeen cases in New York County in 1907, eight convictions for extortion out of twenty-nine cases, and two convictions for kidnaping out of eight cases. *Annual Report of the Chief Clerk of the District Attorney's Office, County of New York*, 1907, 7, 10-13, 59.
35. Commissioner of Immigration Watchorn to Secretary of Commerce and Labor Straus (Confidential), February 29, 1908, Oscar S. Straus Papers, Library of Congress; Straus to Watchorn, March 2, Watchorn to Straus, March 7, and Straus to Watchorn, March 19, 1908, *ibid.*; McAdoo, *Guarding a Great City*, 154-155; *Herald*, February 22, 25, April 13, 1908; *Times*, February 24, March 4, 1908; *Tribune*, March 3, 4, 5, 6, 1908; *World*, March 4, 1908. The use of Secret Service personnel for general criminal investigation was stopped shortly afterward by congressional action, over the vehement opposition of President Roosevelt. Arthur C. Millspaugh, *Crime Control by the National Government* (Washington, D.C., 1937), 72-76.
36. Gaetano D'Amato, "The 'Black Hand' Myth," *North American Review*, CLXXXVII (April 1908), 543-549; Mayor McClellan to Ettore E. Nicoletti, January 15, 1908, McClellan Papers.
37. William B. Howland to the President, September 9, 1908, Straus Papers; Robert Watchorn, "The Black Hand and the Immigrant," *Outlook*, XCII (July 31, 1909), 796; *Times*, April 5, 14, 1908; *Herald*, April 15, 1908.
38. *Annual Report of the Police Commissioner, City of New York*, 1907, 24; *Proceedings of the Board of Aldermen of the City of New York*, 1908, II, 4, 139-141; Theodore A. Bingham, "Patrolling 3095 Miles of Streets," *Harper's Weekly*, LI (November 9, 1907), 1648; *World*, July 21, 1907; *Times*, July 23, 24, 25, 1907, January 6, 25, February 26, 27, April 14, 22, 27, 1908.
39. Park and Miller, *Old World Traits Transplanted*, 250-251; Mariano, *The Second Generation of Italians*, 128-129; *Tribune*, August 18, 21, 1904, April 19, 1907. At a later date the immigration authorities at Ellis Island did ask Italian men for penal cer-

tificates, though there was no provision in law requiring their presentation. Acting Commissioner, Ellis Island, to Commissioner-General of Immigration, December 27, 1910, William Williams Papers, New York Public Library; Arthur Train, "Shall He Go Back?" *Saturday Evening Post*, CLXXXII (March 5, 1910), 17, 47.

40. Park and Miller, *op. cit.*, 248-249, 252; *Times*, January 6, 24, 26, February 8, March 8, 1908; *Tribune*, March 8, 1908; Train, *Courts, Criminals and the Camorra*, 243-244.
41. *Tribune*, April 30, 1908; *Times*, May 2, 10, 1908; Watchorn to Straus, May 8, 1908, Straus Papers.
42. House Committee on Immigration and Naturalization, *Hearings*, 60th Cong., 1st Sess., February 18, 1908.
43. National Liberal Immigration League, *The Press on the League* (New York, 1907), 3; William S. Bennet, "Immigrants and Crime," American Academy of Political and Social Science, *Annals*, XXXIV (July 1909), 120.
44. *The Press on the League*, 1-2; *Congressional Record*, 60th Cong., 1st Sess., 2752-2758; *Ibid.*, 60th Cong., 2nd Sess., 1707; *Annual Report of the Commissioner-General of Immigration*, 1912, 25.
45. *Ibid.*, 1908, 122-123.
46. *Times*, July 7, 25, 1908.
47. *Ibid.*, July 25, 27, 1908.
48. Denison, "The Black Hand," 291-301.
49. Theodore A. Bingham, "Foreign Criminals in New York," *North American Review*, CLXXXVIII (September 1908), 385-393; *Tribune*, May 25, 1908.
50. Moses Rischin, *The Promised City: New York's Jews 1870-1914* (New York, 1964), 243; Goren, *New York Jews and the Quest for Community*, 25-42, 49-56; Syrett, *The Gentleman and the Tiger*, 295-297; Francis J. Oppenheimer, "Jewish Criminality," *Independent*, LXV (September 17, 1908), 640-642; *The American Hebrew*, September 11, 18, 1908, March 5, 1909; *Times*, September 2, 17, 1908; *Herald*, September 4, 1908; New York *Globe and Commercial Advertiser*, September 3, 1908.
51. *Report of the Police Department of the City of New York*, 1891-1899, 1901-1905; *Annual Report of the Board of City Magistrates of the City of New York (First Division)*, 1900, 1904-1906.
52. *Ibid.*, 1905, 16-17.

CHAPTER III

The Petrosino Mission and Its Aftermath

1. *World*, February 26, 1892; U.S. Industrial Commission, *Reports*, XV, 158, 185; Gino C. Speranza to the American Institute of Criminal Law and Criminology, August ?, 1912, Speranza Papers.

2. *Times*, Spetember 30, 1901; Eliot Norton to Luigi Badio, Director-General of Emigration, Rome, June 17, 1901, and Gino C. Speranza to Comm. G. Branchi, St. Louis, Missouri, April 12, 1904, Speranza Papers; T. Dorr, "Protecting Poor Italian Immigrants," *Leslie's Weekly*, XCVIII (January 7, 1904), 14; Gino C. Speranza, "The Italian Emigration Department in 1904," *Charities*, XV (October 21, 1905), 114-116; "Our Italian Immigration," *Nation*, LXXX (April 20, 1905), 304; Robert Watchorn, "The Black Hand and the Immigrant," *Outlook*, LXCII (July 31, 1909), 794-797.

3. *World*, July 25, 1907; Bennet, "Immigrants and Crime," 121-122; White, "The Black Hand in Control," 860-861.

4. Speranza, "The Italian Emigration Department," 115; U.S. Immigration Commission, *Reports*, XXXVI, 277-278.

5. *Annual Report of the Police Commissioner, City of New York*, 1908, 22-24; Petacco, *Joe Petrosino*, 110-117; *Herald*, March 13, 1909; *Times*, March 16, 1909.

6. Park and Miller, *Old World Traits Transplanted*, 252-253; *Times*, January 30, February 20, 1909; *Herald*, February 20, 1909.

7. White, "The Black Hand in Control," 861-862; Petacco, *Joe Petrosino*, 118-135.

8. *Ibid.*, 135-149; George E. Pozzetta, "Another Look at the Petrosino Affair," *Italian Americana*, I (Autumn 1974), 85-86.

9. *Herald*, March 13, 1909; *Sun*, March 14, 1909; *Times*, March 14, 1909; *Tribune*, March 14, 1909; Pozzetta, "Another Look at the Petrosino Affair," 87.

10. *Sun*, March 15, 1909; *Times*, March 14, 1909; Train, *Courts, Criminals and the Camorra*, 227.

11. Park and Miller, *Old World Traits Transplanted*, 253; *Times*, March 14, 1909.

12. *Il Progresso Italo-Americano*, 20 March 1909.

13. Iorizzo and Mondello, *The Italian-Americans*, 165-166; *Outlook*, XCI (March 27, 1909), 656-657; *Independent*, LXVI (April 1, 1909), 712-713; *American Review of Reviews*, XXXIX (May 1909), 628; *Survey*, XXII (April 3, 1909), 11-14.

14. Edward A. Ross, "Italians in America," *Century Magazine*, LXXXVIII (July 1914), 440; Pozzetta, "Another Look at the Petrosino Affair," 89.

15. Manuscript Autobiography of George B. McClellan, VII, 543, McClellan Papers; *Sun*, April 13, 1909; *Times*, April 13, May 3, 13, 1909; *Eagle*, May 18, 1909; *Harper's Weekly*, LIII (April 24, 1909), 27.

16. McClellan Autobiography, VII, 538-541; Petacco, *Joe Petrosino*, 87-89, 104-106; *Current Literature*, XLVI (May 1909), 478-480; *Herald*, June 11, 12, 1908; *Times*, June 14, July 7, 1908, March 14, 17, 28, 1909; *Eagle*, March 15, 1909.

17. Petacco, *Joe Petrosino*, 124-125, 144-145, 150-153, 164-181; Pozzetta, "Another Look at the Petrosino Affair," 86. Mack Smith

calls the period 1901-1914, when Giolitti was in power most of the time, "the age of Giolitti." He implies, but does not state, that ·Giolitti used the Mafia as a political asset. Denis Mack Smith, *Italy: A Modern History* (Ann Arbor, Michigan, 1959), 166-167, 214.

18. Luigi Barzini, *The Italians* (New York, 1964), 273, 275-276; Petacco, *Joe Petrosino*, 188-189; Michele Pantaleone, *The Mafia and Politics* (New York, 1966), 40-41; Norman Lewis, *The Honored Society: A Searching Look at the Mafia* (New York, 1964), 77-79; Albini considers Petrosino's death as still unexplained. Joseph Albini, *The American Mafia: Genesis of a Legend* (New York, 1971), 195-196. Schiavo is rather equivocal on the point. Giovanni E. Schiavo, *The Truth About the Mafia and Organized Crime in America* (New York, 1962), 138-139. Dwight Smith is not convinced of Cascio Ferro's guilt. Smith, *The Mafia Mystique*, 54.

19. Arthur Woods, "The Problem of the Black Hand," *McClure's Magazine*, XXXIII (May 1909), 40-47.

20. *Times*, March 14, 17, 1909; *Eagle*, March 15, 1909; White, "The Black Hand in Control," 862.

21. Arthur H. Warner, "Amputating the Black Hand," *Survey*, XXII (May 1, 1909), 166-167.

22. "The Black Hand Scourge," *Cosmopolitan Magazine*, XLVII (June 1909), 31-41.

23. Watchorn, "The Black Hand and the Immigrant," 794-795.

24. Frank M. White, "How the United States Fosters the Black Hand," *Outlook*, LXCIII (October 30, 1909), 495-500.

25. *Herald*, August 20, 1909; *Times*, August 20, 1909; *World*, August 20, 1909; White, "The Black Hand in Control," 862.

26. McClellan Autobiography, VII, 542-543; New York City, Board of Aldermen, *Records and Reports of Testimony before the Committee Appointed on Aug. 5, 1912 to Investigate the Police Department* (6 vols., New York, 1913), V, 3814-3815.

27. Testimony of Fourth Deputy Commissioner Arthur Woods in the matter of George B. Duffy, June 9, 1909, Mayors' Papers, Box 39; Mayor Geo. B. McClellan to Police Commissioner, June 30, 1909, *ibid.*, Box 55; McClellan to First Deputy Commissioner William F. Baker, June 30, 1909, *ibid.*; Police Commissioner Theo. A. Bingham to the Mayor, July 1, 1909, *ibid.*; McClellan to Baker, July 1, 1909, *ibid.*; Theodore A. Bingham, "The Organized Criminals of New York," *McClure's Magazine*, XXXIV (November 1909), 62-67; White, "The Black Hand in Control," 862; Syrett, *The Gentleman and the Tiger*, 295-297; *Times*, June 2, 3, July 1, 2, 1909; *Eagle*, June 2, 3, 1909.

28. Board of Aldermen, *Records and Reports of Testimony*, V, 3815; Syrett, *op. cit.*, 297-299; White, *op. cit.*, 862-863; Sydney Reid, "The Death Sign," *Independent*, LXX (April 6, 1911),

714; *Times*, August 20, 1909, August 17, 19, 21, 1913; *World*, August 20, 1909.

29. Louis H. Pink, *Gaynor: The Tammany Mayor Who Swallowed the Tiger* (New York, 1931), 134-135, 143-144; Edwin R. Lewinson, *John Purroy Mitchel, the Boy Mayor of New York* (New York, 1965), 57; Werner, *Tammany Hall*, 518; *Current Literature*, XLVII (December 1909), 594-598; Mayor McClellan to William J. Gaynor, October 19, 1909, McClellan Papers; Mayors' Papers, Boxes 72, 73, 80, 81, 103, 141 *passim*; *Times*, November 3, 1909; *World*, January 3, 1910.

30. Reid, "The Death Sign," 714.

31. Flynn, *The Barrel Mystery*, 23-43, 44-171; Daniel Bell, *The End of Ideology* (New York, 1965), 128-129, 138; *Herald*, January 27, 28, 29, February 19, 20, 1910; *Times*, February 20, December 2, 3, 11, 1910; *Tribune*, February 20, 1910; *World*, January 28, February 20, 1910.

32. *Annual Report of the Secretary of the Treasury*, 1910, 70-71; 1911, 69-70.

33. Flynn, *The Barrel Mystery*, 206-214, 243-261.

34. Petacco, *Joe Petrosino*, 6-8, 11-13, 56-58, 75-76, 90-95, 185; Michele Pantaleone, *The Mafia and Politics*, 34-35, 38-39.

35. Francis A. J. Ianni, "Mafia and the Web of Kinship," *An Inquiry Into Organized Crime* (Staten Island, N.Y., 1970), 11-13. Ianni does consider the gang war that broke out in New York in 1930 and that reverberated clear across the country as involving a real attempt to set up an American Mafia, after ten years of bootlegging prosperity and reinforcements of Mafiosi fleeing from Mussolini's campaign against them. What followed, however, was not a Mafia but a loosely integrated group of Italian criminal syndicates based largely on kinship. *Ibid.*, 15-19. He develops these themes further in a later study. Francis A. J. Ianni with Elizabeth Reuss-Ianni, *A Family Business: Kinship and Social Control in Organized Crime* (New York, 1972), 15-61.

36. Asbury, *Gangs of New York*, 267-268; Kobler, *Capone*, 29-30. Albini discounts the more sensational charges against Saietta. All that seems to be established about him, Albini says, "is that he was a Sicilian fugitive from justice who engaged in extortion, killing, and other crimes in New York during the early 1900s." Albini, *The American Mafia*, 157-159.

37. Arthur A. Carey, "Business Men at Arms," *Collier's*, LXXXV (February 15, 1930), 66.

38. *Times*, September 1, 1904, June 24, 1905, November 21, 1906, July 3, 1907, April 12, 1909, March 25, August 24ff., 1913, January 17, 1914; *Tribune*, October 2, November 3, 4, 1905; *World*, February 5, 1910; Denison, "The Black Hand," 296; Goren, *New York Jews*, 170; R. A. Schermerhorn, *These Our People: Minorities in American Culture* (Boston, 1949), 249-250.

CHAPTER IV

The Black Hand in Control

1. Reid, "The Death Sign," 712; Pierce Van Rensselaer Key, *Enrico Caruso: A Biography* (Boston, 1922), 267-269; Dorothy Caruso, *Enrico Caruso, His Life and Death* (New York, 1945), 193-194; Michael Fiaschetti, *You Gotta Be Rough: The Adventures of Detective Fiaschetti of the Italian Squad* (New York, 1930), 131-133; *Eagle*, March 5, 7, 8, 16, 22, 1910.

2. Arthur B. Reeve, "The Black Hand," *Cosmopolitan Magazine*, LI (September 1911), 479-496.

3. Notable Arrests by the Detective Bureau, 1911, Mayors' Papers, Box 103; *Times*, June 22, 23, 24, August 1, 1910, February 14, 1914; *Eagle*, September 10, 1910. The district attorney's office gave the name of the convicted kidnaper as Vito Micelli. Presumably he had an alias. *Annual Report of the Chief Clerk of the District Attorney's Office, County of New York*, 1911, 54-55.

4. Frank M. White, "Against the Black Hand," *Collier's*, XLV (September 3, 1910), 19; *Times*, September 4, 1910.

5. "Prevention of Alien Crime," *Survey*, XXV (December 24, 1910), 488-489; *Times*, December 15, 1910.

6. Vecoli, "Contadini in Chicago," 414-415; White, "The Black Hand in Control," 864-865; *Times*, December 15, 1910.

7. Alberto Pecorini, "The Italian in the United States," *Forum*, XLV (January 1911), 15-29.

8. Pink, *Gaynor*, 174; John Purroy Mitchel, Acting Mayor, to Commissioner of Police, September 16, 1910, and Robert Adamson, Secretary, to Commissioner of Police, September 21, 1910, Mayors' Papers, Box 141; F. H. Bugher, First Deputy Police Commissioner, to His Honor the Mayor, October 19, 1910, *ibid.*, Box 103; *Eagle*, April 18, September 20, October 21, 1910; *Times*, October 4, 21, 1910.

9. W. J. Gaynor, Mayor, to Winifred T. Denison, Assistant Attorney-General, October 25, 1910, Mayors' Papers, Box 103; *Times*, October 30, 1910.

10. James C. Cropsey, Police Commissioner, to His Honor the Mayor, with enclosures, November 7, 1910, Mayors' Papers, Box 73.

11. *Times*, November 18, 1910.

12. *Jewish Daily News*, May 14, 1911, translation in William Williams Papers; Goren, *New York Jews*, 150-151, 159-170; *Annual Report of the Chief Clerk of the District Attorney's Office, County of New York*, 1913, 43; *Times*, December 12, 1911, March 6, 25, August 24ff, 1913.

13. Reid, "The Death Sign," 711; *Times*, November 24, 25, 27, December 9, 10, 11, 14, 21, 23, 1910; *Eagle*, December 3, 9, 10, 22, 27, 1910.

14. *Eagle*, December 3, 1910; *Sun*, December 26, 1910.
15. Reid, "The Death Sign," 711.
16. Adolfo Valeri, *La "Mano Nera"* (New York, 1905), preface and *passim*. Chandler traces the Camorra back to Spain and argues that the Sicilian Mafia was a comparatively late offshoot of it. Chandler, *Brothers in Blood*, 14-31.
17. Iorizzo and Mondello, *The Italian-Americans*, 36-37; Puzo, *The Godfather*, 208-212; *Times*, March 25, 1906; *World*, March 31, 1907; James C. Cropsey, Police Commissioner, to His Honor the Mayor, March 9 and April 10, 1911, with enclosures, Mayors' Papers, Box 80.
18. *Times*, December 20, 1910, January 8, 1911; *Sun*, December 27, 1910; White, "The Black Hand in Control," 863-864.
19. Reid, "The Death Sign," 714-715; *Times*, April 1, 2, 20, 27, 1911; *World*, April 1, 2, 20, 27, 28, 1911.
20. *Times*, July 12, 1911.
21. R. Waldo, Police Commissioner, to Mayor William J. Gaynor, January 11, 1912, Mayors' Papers, Box 88; Board of Aldermen, *Records and Reports of Testimony*, V, 3817-3820; Park and Miller, *Old World Traits Transplanted*, 254-255; Pink, *Gaynor*, 174-176; *Times*, May 24, 1911; *World*, May 18, 24, 1911.
22. Fred J. Cook, *Mafia!* (Greenwich, Conn., 1973), 44-45; Park and Miller, *op. cit.*, 256-257; R. Waldo, Police Commissioner, to Mayor Ardolph L. Kline, November 1, 1913, Mayors' Papers, Box 98.
23. R. Waldo, Police Commissioner, to Mayor William J. Gaynor, with enclosures, September 18, 1911, Mayors' Papers, Box 81.
24. *Times*, December 31, 1911, January 1, 1912.
25. "The Trial of the Camorrists," *Independent*, LXX (March 16, 1911), 543-544; George B. McClellan, "The Terror of the Camorra," *Cosmopolitan Magazine*, LI (August 1911), 293-303; "Camorrists in Cages," *Outlook*, XCVII (March 25, 1911), 614-615; "The Camorra Trial," *ibid.*, XCIX (December 30, 1911), 1038; "The Camorra," *ibid.*, CI (July 20, 1912), 603-604; *Times*, July 9, 1912.
26. Arthur Train, "Imported Crime: The Story of the Camorra in America," *McClure's Magazine*, XXXIX (May 1912), 90-94. Train shortly afterward expanded this article into a book, *Courts, Criminals and the Camorra*.
27. *Outlook*, CI (July 20, 1912), 603-604; *World*, May 10, 1911.
28. Nathan W. MacChesney, President, American Institute of Criminal Law and Criminology, to Gino C. Speranza, December 1, 1910, Speranza Papers; Grace Abbott, Immigrants' Protective League, to Speranza, March 6, 1911, *ibid.*; Speranza to the American Institute of Criminal Law and Criminology, September 2, 1911, *ibid.*; W. R. Sheehan, Secretary to Police Commissioner, to Speranza, June 10, 1912, *ibid.*; Speranza to the American Institute of Criminal Law and Criminology, c.

June and August ?, 1912, *ibid*. For Speranza's views during the immigration debates of the 1920s, see Gino C. Speranza, *Race or Nation* (Indianapolis, 1925) *passim*.

29. Higham, *Strangers in the Land*, 72-73, 161-162; *Laws of the State of New York*, 1911, Chapters 121, 195, 602; Gino C. Speranza to Royal Consul General of Italy, New York, August 29, 1911, Speranza Papers; Police Department of the City of New York, *Annual Report*, 1911, 14; *Herald*, September 6, 7, 9, 1911; *Times*, August 29, September 9, 10, 12, 14, 16, 20, October 10, 11, 12, 18, 1911.

30. John Foster Carr, *Guide for the Immigrant Italian in the United States of America* (Garden City, N.Y., 1911), 34-35, 70-71.

31. R. Waldo, Police Commissioner, to William J. Gaynor, Mayor, July 25, 1912, Mayors' Papers, Box 103; Gaynor to Waldo, July 26, 1912, *ibid*.; Gaynor to Waldo, July 26, 1912, *ibid*., Box 144; *Proceedings of the Board of Aldermen*, 1912, III, 181-183; Pink, *Gaynor*, 191-194; Alfred Connable and Edward Silberfarb, *Tigers of Tammany: Nine Men Who Ran New York* (New York, 1967), 250-251; Henry H. Curran, *Pillar to Post* (New York, 1941), 145-147, 151-152; Goren, *New York Jews*, 149-151; *Times*, July 16, 1912; *World*, July 13-30 *passim*, October 27, 1912.

32. *Times*, January 16, 17, 1913.

33. Board of Aldermen, *Records and Reports of Testimony*, V, 3622-3624, 3805-3812, 3812-3824, 3942-3944.

34. *Times*, March 24, April 6, 11, 1913; R. Waldo, Police Commissioner, to Mayor William J. Gaynor, with enclosure, April 4, 1913, Mayors' Papers, Box 96.

35. *Times*, May 22, 23, 1913.

36. Chief Clerk, District Attorney's Office, County of Kings, to Gino C. Speranza, May 26, 1913, Speranza Papers.

37. The Society for Italian Immigrants, *Eleventh Annual Report*, 1913, 9.

38. White, "The Black Hand in Control," 857-859, 864; *Literary Digest*, XLVII (August 30, 1913), 308-310.

39. *Times*, August 17, 19, 21, September 9, 12, 13, 1913.

40. Lewinson, *John Purroy Mitchel*, 86-87, 95; Werner, *Tammany Hall*, 556-557; *Times*, September 12, November 5, 1913.

41. *Report of the Special Committee of the Board of Aldermen of the City of New York, appointed August 5, 1912, to Investigate the Police Department* (New York, June 10, 1913), 3-5, 18-19; Curran, *Pillar to Post*, 152-174; John J. Gordon to John Purroy Mitchel, December 22, 1913, Mayors' Papers, Box 210.

42. R. Waldo, Police Commissioner, to Mayor Ardolph L. Kline, with enclosures, November 1, 1913, Mayors' Papers, Box 98; Kline to Waldo, December 30, 1913, *ibid*., Box 146; *Times*, October 11, 12, 13, 1913.

43. *Ibid*., January 27-31, February 1, March 4, 5, 26-28, 1914.

44. Chandler, *Brothers in Blood*, 67-68, 72; R. Waldo, Police

Commissioner, to Mayor William J. Gaynor, July 25, 1912, with enclosures, Mayors' Papers, Box 89.

45. *Herald*, July 27, 28, 1913; *Times*, July 27, 1913; *World*, July 27, 1913.

CHAPTER V

The Passing of a Symbol

1. Mayor Mitchel to Charles S. Whitman, February 2, 1914, Mayors' Papers, Box 161; George W. Goethals, Culebra, Canal Zone, to Mayor John Purroy Mitchel, January 14, 1914, Scrapbooks of Mayor John Purroy Mitchel, 1914-1917, Municipal Archives and Records Center, New York, N.Y.; Mayor Mitchel, Statements to the Press, January 10, April 7, 1914, *ibid.*; Lewinson, *John Purroy Mitchel*, 117-120; *Times*, January 1, 8, 10, February 3, April 8, 12, 1914.

2. W. J. Gaynor, Mayor, to James C. Cropsey, Police Commissioner, February 28, 1911, Mayors' Papers, Box 143; D. McKay, Police Commissioner, to John Purroy Mitchel, Mayor, February 4, 1914, *ibid.*, Box 209; Lewinson, *op. cit.*, 120-121; Asbury, *The Gangs of New York*, 367-369; *Times*, June 28, August 23, 25, 27, 1914.

3. *Annual Report of the Chief Clerk of the District Attorney's Office, County of New York*, 1914, 57-58; Frank M. White, "The Passing of the Black Hand," *Century Magazine*, XCV (January 1918), 331-336; *Times*, May 11, 12, 16, 18, June 28, November 26, December 7, 9, 11, 15, 21, 28, 1914.

4. A. W., Police Commissioner, Memorandum for Mr. Rousseau, December 22, 1914, Mayors' Papers, Box 211; Joseph A. Faurot, Memorandum for the Police Commissioner, November 28, 1914, *ibid.*; *World*, December 3, 1914; *Times*, December 27, 1914.

5. A. Woods, Police Commissioner, to Mayor John Purroy Mitchel, January 14, 1915, and to Mr. Rousseau, March 1, 1915, Mayors' Papers, Box 220; Iorizzo and Mondello, *The Italian-Americans*, 200-202; William Preston, Jr., *Aliens and Dissenters: Federal Suppression of Radicals, 1903-1933* (Cambridge, Mass., 1963), 44-46; *Times*, June 16, July 5, November 12, 13, 15, 1914, March 3, April 20, 1915.

6. *Ibid.*, July 4, 6, 7, 1915.

7. *Ibid.*, January 6, 26, February 17, 20, March 8, July 20, 1915.

8. Police Department, City of New York, *Annual Report*, 1915, vii-viii; "The Police and the Black Hand," *Outlook*, CXIII (June 14, 1916), 347-348; Dwight Smith, *The Mafia Mystique*, 52; *Times*, February 9, 1916. Scull had been Woods's personal secretary but had been promoted. Even while secretary he had been looking into Black Hand activities. G. H. Scull, Secre-

tary, Memorandum for Mr. Cruger, May 21, 1915, Mayors' Papers, Box 220, and G. H. Scull, Fifth Deputy Commissioner, to B. de N. Cruger, Executive Secretary, Office of the Mayor, October 4, 1915, *ibid.*, Box 221.

9. *Times*, August 3, 1915; Police Department, *Annual Report*, 1915, vii-viii.

10. White, "The Passing of the Black Hand," 336-337; Schiavo, *The Truth About the Mafia*, 137.

11. S. L. Martin, Executive Secretary, to Arthur Woods, Police Commissioner, February 5, May 17, 1916, Mayors' Papers, Box 168; Arthur Woods, Police Commissioner, Memorandum for Mr. Rousseau, April 21, 1917, *ibid.*, Box 239.

12. G. H. Scull, Secretary, Memorandum for Mr. Cruger, May 21, 1915, Mayors' Papers, Box 220; *Herald*, December 1, 1916.

13. *Herald*, November 28, 1917; *Times*, November 28, 1917.

14. *Herald*, November 30, December 1, 1917.

15. *Ibid.*, January 27, February 15, 16, April 27, 1918; *Eagle*, March 5, 7, 8, 9, 11, 12, 14, May 6, June 7, 1918; *Sun*, June 15, 1918; *Times*, February 15, 16, 19, April 27, June 18, 1918; *World*, April 27, 1918; Lynch, *Criminals and Politicians*, 95-97.

16. *Eagle*, November 28, 1917; Lynch, *op. cit.*, 95-97; Nicholas Gage, *Mafia, U.S.A.* (Chicago, 1972), 15; Ed Reid, *The Grim Reapers* (New York, 1970), 25-27; Chandler, *Brothers in Blood*, 110-111, 124-126; Smith, *The Mafia Mystique*, 56.

17. *Herald*, May 8, 1903, November 28, December 1, 1917, January 27, 1918; *Eagle*, November 27, 1917; White, "Fostering Foreign Criminals," 7; Ianni, "Mafia and the Web of Kinship," 18-21; Chandler, *Brothers in Blood*, 112-113.

18. *Herald*, March 2, 1918.

19. Lewinson, *John Purroy Mitchel* 206, 227-245; Werner, *Tammany Hall*, 563; *Herald*, November 7, 1917; *Times*, January 2, 1918.

20. F. H. Bugher, Police Commissioner, to His Honor the Mayor, January 22, 1918, Mayors' Papers, Box 275; Edward Swann, District Attorney, to John F. Hylan, Mayor, January 24, 1918, *ibid.*, Box 267; R. E. Enright, Police Commissioner, to Hylan, February 13, July 26, December 31, 1918, and John R. Leach, Acting Police Commissioner, to Hylan, December 5, 1918, *ibid.*, Box 275; Police Department, City of New York, *Annual Report*, 1918, 40-41; *Herald*, January 28, 1918; *Times*, January 2, 26, 1918.

21. *Times*, May 11, 1918; Undated Memorandum for the Files, Police, Mayors' Papers, Box 275; Fiaschetti, *You Gotta Be Rough*, 131, 135-146.

22. Landesco, *Organized Crime in Chicago*, 25-26, 36-37, 112-113, 116-117, 118-119; Asbury, *Gem of the Prairie*, 233-234, 236; *Times*, April 8, 1911, December 24, 1913; *Literary Digest*, L (June 19, 1915), 1454. Asbury, like Landesco, has Torrio remov-

ing to the West in or about 1918. Asbury, *Gangs of New York*, 355-356. Nelli has him making the move as early as 1909. Nelli, *Italians in Chicago*, 149-150. Messick gives the date as 1910. Messick, *Lansky*, 58.

23. Grace Abbott, *The Immigrant and the Community* (New York, 1917), 118-119.

24. *Times*, February 16, July 13, 1915; *Literary Digest*, LXI (April 5, 1919), 51-54.

25. *Times*, December 16, 21, 1920, August 21, 1921; Tommaso Sassone, "Italy's Criminals in the United States," *Current History*, XV (October 1921), 23-24, 30-31; Fiaschetti, *You Gotta Be Rough*, 250-289; Albini, *The American Mafia*, 196.

26. *Times*, February 11, 13, 1921; Sassone, "Italy's Criminals in the United States," 31.

27. Higham, *Strangers in the Land*, 264-265; Paul M. Angle, *Bloody Williamson: A Chapter in American Lawlessness* (New York, 1952), 136, 138, 144-145; *Times*, August 6, 7, 8, 10, 15, September 9, 1920.

28. *Ibid.*, May 4, 1921.

29. *Ibid.*, May 29, 31, June 3, 12, 13, 14, 15, 1921, February 10, 1922, May 11, 12, 1923; Fiaschetti, *You Gotta Be Rough*, 233-242.

30. *Times*, March 14, 1922, August 19, 1924.

31. Dwight C. Smith, Jr., "The Mafia Mystique," *An Inquiry into Organized Crime*, 75-76; Albini, *The American Mafia*, 195-196; *Times*, August 17, 18, 21, September 11, 1921. In his memoirs Fiaschetti called the group "a savage Camorrist gang." Fiaschetti, *You Gotta Be Rough*, 70-77.

32. *Times*, February 13, 1923.

33. *Ibid.*, June 12, 18, 25, 1926.

34. Fiaschetti, *You Gotta Be Rough*, 13-15.

35. Captain Cornelius W. Willemse, *A Cop Remembers* (New York, 1933), 162-163.

36. Nelli, *Italians in Chicago*, 125-126, 139-140, 154-155, 219-220; Gage, *Mafia, U.S.A.*, 11; Lloyd Lewis and Henry Justin Smith, *Chicago: The History of its Reputation* (New York, 1929), 432-434, 436.

37. Kobler, *Capone*, 45. Ianni offers another explanation for the disappearance of the Black Hand. It was "the immigrants themselves who finally did away with the Black Hand," through a system of informal "courts" in the Italian communities, he says, but gives no specifics. Ianni, "Mafia and the Web of Kinship," 13.

38. *Times*, January 6, 1923.

39. Landesco, *Organized Crime in Chicago*, 112-113, 118-120; Denison, "The Black Hand," 296; Vance Thompson, "The Caged Men of Viterbo," *Collier's*, XLVII (August 19, 1911), 13; *Ibid.*, "The Cockpit of Viterbo," (August 26, 1911), 19, 26; *Times*, April 26, 1903.

40. Fiaschetti, *You Gotta Be Rough*, 82-83; Schiavo, *The Truth*

About the Mafia, 87-88; Gage, *Mafia, U.S.A.*, 78-79, 82-83; Lynch, *Criminals and Politicians*, 10-11; Reid, *The Grim Reapers*, 165-166; Dwight Smith, *The Mafia Mystique*, 63-64, 121-124, 148, 169; *Third Interim Report of the Special Senate Committee to Investigate Organized Crime in Interstate Commerce*, Senate Report No. 307, 82d Cong., 1st Sess., May 1, 1951, 2.

41. *Times*, November 12, 1971.
42. Norman Douglas, *South Wind* (New York, n.d.), 375-377; Henri Pozzi, *Black Hand Over Europe* (London, 1935), 78-81.

Elizabeth Street, lower East Side of New York City, a haunt of Black Hand criminals. *Everybody's Magazine* (September 1908).

Lieutenant Giuseppe Petrosino.

HERO AND MARTYR

Lieutenant Petrosino, of the New York police force, shot down in Palermo because of his activity against Black Hand criminals, was buried with high honors a few days ago. The king of Italy sent a wreath, and the flags on all municipal buildings in New York were put at half-mast.

Current Literature (May 1909).

Detective Charles Corrao of the Italian Squad,
New York City Police. Courtesy, Alfred J.
Young Collection, New York City.

LIEUTENANT VACHRIS, OF THE NEW YORK DETECTIVE
BUREAU (IN THE CENTER)

Vachris, who was Petrosino's chief assistant in Brooklyn,
now knows more than anyone else of the methods
of the Italian criminals in America

Cosmopolitan Magazine (June 1909).

*Cosmopolitan
Magazine*
(August 1911).

"Besides its activity in crimes of violence the Camorra [with its offshoot, the Black Hand] derives a very
great revenue from blackmail.   It not only levies on gambling hells, the social evil, and the
white-slave traffic, but forces a vast number of law-abiding people to pay
a species of insurance against molestation by its members"

Italians on
trial for
sending
Black Hand
letters.
*Everybody's
Magazine*
(September
1909)

This lurid cartoon in *Life* (April 8, 1909) illustrates the violent reaction to Petrosino's assassination.

McClure's Magazine (May 1912).

MICELLI PALLIOZZI, THE KIDNAPPER OF LITTLE MICHELE SCIMECA. FROM A ROGUES' GALLERY PHOTOGRAPH LENT TO McCLURE'S MAGAZINE BY THE NEW YORK CITY POLICE DEPARTMENT. TWO SIXTEEN-YEAR-OLD SCHOOL-GIRLS SAW THE KIDNAPPER WITH THE CHILD IN HIS ARMS, AND GAVE THE POLICE THE CLUE THAT LED TO HIS CAPTURE

THE RUINS OF A FRUIT STORE DESTROYED BY BLACK HAND DYNAMITERS.

Everybody's Magazine (September 1908)

Dynamite bomb planted by a Black Hander in the hallway of No. 356 East Thirteenth Street, New York City. *McClure's Magazine* (May 1912).

McClure's Magazine
(May 1912)

BLACK HAND DIRKS
THESE KNIVES WERE TAKEN FROM HAND PRISONERS BY THE NEW POLICE. ALL HAD RAZOR EDGES BORE EVIDENCE OF HAVING B⁵ REPEATEDLY GROUND AND SHARPENED

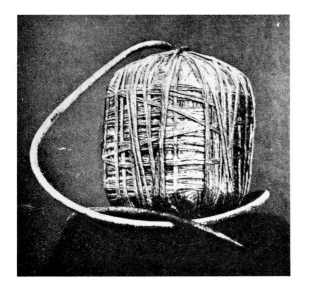

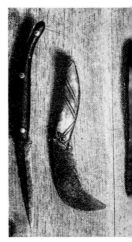

Caro Amico

Mercoledì prossimo

Black Hand letter turned in to the Italian Squad of the New York City police in 1906.
Courtesy, Alfred J. Young Collection, New York City

Police Van, 23rd Precinct (138 West 30th St., New York City)

BIBLIOGRAPHICAL NOTE

The Black Hand phenomenon developed in New York City and proliferated there as nowhere else, but official manuscript material concerning it is limited. The precinct records, or "blotters," of the New York Police Department have for years been systematically destroyed as they become fifty years old. The present policy, however, is to have them reviewed for historical value before destruction. This review, unfortunately, did not go into effect in time to preserve records of the Black Hand period. Departmental personnel records are destroyed ten years after the retirement or death of an officer. These are now microfilmed, but few if any such microfilms go back to the period. Only brief individual records ("yellow sheets") of individual criminals are maintained in the department, and these are destroyed on confirmation of death. A few such sheets are preserved in the Police Academy Museum. These are chiefly of more recent times. Also retained there is the Italian Branch Detective Bureau blotter for 1908-1909, covering the last service and death of Lieutenant Joseph Petrosino.

The records of the New York County Court of General Sessions, in which most of the more important Black Hand cases were tried, were hurriedly ordered into storage some years ago. They still exist, but are in such confusion as to be for all practical purposes inaccessible. Fortunately, the papers of the mayors of Greater New York, beginning in 1898, have been largely preserved and are accessible at the Municipal Archives and Records Center. A great many communications to and from the police department, including fairly numerous references to Italian crime and the Black Hand, are among them. These papers are also invaluable in helping to clarify the shifting political and administrative background of law enforcement in the city.

Most notable among the few available private manuscripts relating to the Black Hand is the voluminous collection of Gino C. Speranza Papers in the New York Public Library. Speranza, a prominent, second-generation, Italian-American lawyer, was engaged in a number of activities looking to the well-being of the Italian immigrant. He became greatly concerned at the rise of the Black Hand. His reports to the American Institute of Criminal Law and Criminology, as chairman of its committee on aliens and crime, are particularly illuminating. The George B. McClellan, Jr., Papers at the New-York Historical Society have some material on Lieutenant Petrosino, the Italian detective who was until his death the most effective enemy of the Black Hand. McClellan was mayor of New York from 1904 to 1909. There are a number of letters on the Black Hand problem, as it affected the immigration authorities at Ellis Island, in the Oscar S. Straus Papers at the Library of Congress. The William Williams Papers at the New York Public Library also contain occasional references to the problem of criminal immigrants including the Italian.

The picture is brighter in the category of published documents. The New York Police Department published an annual report under one title or another during the whole period. There are interesting statistics on ethnic crime in these reports to 1906, and some of them later deal with the Black Hand problem specifically, notably the *Annual Report of the Police Commissioner, City of New York*, 1907 and 1908. The *Annual Report of the Board of City Magistrates of the City of New York (First Division)*, 1905, has some interesting comment on the growth of alien crime in general. The *Annual Report of the Chief Clerk of the District Attorney's Office, County of New York*, maintained statistics on what it sometimes called "Black Hand" crimes—blackmail, extortion, and kidnaping—and summarized some of the more notable Black Hand cases, as in 1907, 1911, 1913, and 1914. The most illuminating single body of material among published official documents in New York City is the testimony presented to the committee of the Board of Aldermen investigating the police department in 1912-1913, in *Records and Reports of Testimony before the Committee Appointed on Aug. 5, 1912 to Investigate the Police Department* (6 vols., 1913). A number of law enforcement officers, judges, and Italian community leaders testified at length on the effectiveness of the Italian Squad of the detective force and the consequences of its disbandment.

A number of unofficial documents are helpful. The Prison Association of New York, in its *Annual Report*, 1908, spoke briefly of Black Handers paroled to it from the Elmira Reformatory, who ignored jobs provided for them and headed straight back to their old haunts in the Bowery. The Society for Italian Immigrants was concerned about the criminal element among Italians, as in its *Annual Report*, 1909, 1911, and 1913. The National Liberal Immigration League, *The Press on the League* (1907), noted widespread support for its proposed legislation "to secure the deportation of members of the Black Hand and of criminals of all races." For the Black Hand in Chicago, and even nationally, the report of The Italian "White Hand" Society in Chicago, Illinois, *Studies, Action and Results*, 1908, is outstanding if somewhat defensive in tone. John Landesco, *Organized Crime in Chicago*, Part III of *The Illinois Crime Survey 1929*, is an almost encyclopedic review of crime in the city for the first quarter of the twentieth century and pays due attention to the Black Hand. Landesco finds it to have been not an organization but a method of operation. This study was reprinted in 1968.

Among federal government publications, the U.S. Industrial Commission, collecting its data at the turn of the century, in *Reports*, XV, *Immigration* (1902), has some comment on the Italian and Jewish immigrants on the lower East Side of Manhattan, generally favorable but noting the corrupting influence of the "remnants" of the Irish in the area. The U.S. Immigration Commission, collecting its data on crime largely in 1907-1908, devoted Volume XXXVI of its massive *Report* (1911) to *Immigration and Crime*, in which the Italians figured prominently. The *Annual Report of the Secretary of the Treasury*, 1910 and 1911, commented with satisfaction on the breakup of the Lupo-Morello gang of

counterfeiters and Black Handers by the Secret Service. The
Black Hand problem was discussed in Congress from time to
time, in connection with the perennial debate over immigration legislation. Of particular interest are a committee hearing, House Committee on Immigration and Naturalization,
Hearings, 60th Cong., 1st Sess., February 18, 1908, and an
attempt to introduce stronger legislation against alien criminals a little later, in *Congressional Record*, 60th Cong., 1st
Sess., 2752-2758. The *Annual Report of the Commissioner-
General of Immigration* first took cognizance of the Black
Hand in 1904 and noted the problem of criminal immigration
almost yearly thereafter. The crimes of members of "the
'Black Hand' and other like societies" were discussed at
some length in 1907.

In this study, a principal reliance has necessarily been
placed on New York City newspapers. There are extensive
microfilm runs of a number of these journals in the New
York Public Library and the New-York Historical Society.
The *New York Times* began mentioning the Mafia on its
home ground in Sicily as early as 1877. In 1882, along with
other newspapers, it noticed extortionists as at work among
the Italians in the city but gave them no name. In 1888-1889
it carried the story of a supposed Mafia local murder case.
Along with other journals, it gave extended space to the
murder of the New Orleans chief of police in 1890, the Mafia
trial that followed, and the lynching that followed the trial.
From that time on, it seems to have accepted the existence
of Italian criminal societies in the city. The newspapers in
general consistently reported Italian crime as such, though
as *Il Progresso Italo-Americano* complained, Irish crime,
common enough, was no longer labeled *Irish*. The next great
Mafia alarm did not come until the spring of 1903, when the
Times, along with the *Herald*, the *Sun*, the *Tribune*, the
World, and the *Brooklyn Daily Eagle* played up the so-called
barrel murder as undoubtedly the work of the Mafia.

A few months later the *Herald* called attention to the
Mano Nera (Black Hand), a gang of Italian extortionists, as
at work in Brooklyn. One after another, the other journals
followed its lead. Within a few months the Black Hand had
practically taken the place of the Mafia (or occasionally the

Camorra) as the supposed prime source of crime in the Italian community. Even the Italian newspapers took it up, as preferable to Mafia. The Black Hand was good for headline stories in almost all the city's newspapers for the next fifteen years or more. For most of the period, the *Times* is easiest to follow simply because it has an index, though the *Herald* seemed to be most avidly interested in Italian crime. The *Times* could never make up its mind whether the Black Hand actually existed as an organization, but the *Herald* had no doubts. Other journals, including the *Sun*, the rather flamboyant *World*, and even the relatively unsensational *Tribune* were never far behind in playing up Italian crime, usually with a Black Hand label. The *Tribune*, for instance, carried a highly alarmist Sunday feature article on the Black Hand in 1906. Petrosino's assassination in 1909, generally attributed to the Black Hand, caused a sensation in all the New York City journals; the "Black Hand is Everywhere," the *Eagle* proclaimed. For a time, in 1911 and 1912, when the great Camorra trial was being held at Viterbo, Camorra tended to crowd out Black Hand, but by 1913 the Black Hand had returned to preeminence. With the 1920s, and the coming of Prohibition, it began to fade out as worthy headline material.

The periodical press followed much the same pattern. The *Atlantic Monthly* treated at some length the Mafia in Sicily as early as 1876. The Neapolitan Camorra was described as very powerful in the English *Saturday Review* in 1885. Alarm at alien crime, not exclusively Italian, was expressed in various American periodicals in the later 1880s. A spate of stories on Italian crime, with emphasis on the Mafia, accompanied and followed the New Orleans episode. There were also articles in the same period on the Camorra, sometimes asserting its infiltration into the United States. While a criminal label had been fixed on the Italians in the minds of many Americans, the Mafia, for the next ten years or so, was treated chiefly as it existed on its home ground. *Chamber's Journal for Popular Literature, Science and Arts* in 1892 described the society as becoming more powerful in Sicily. The *Political Science Quarterly*, on the other hand, in 1894 insisted that both the Mafia and the Camorra, as well as brigandage in general, were nearing extinction. The trial for murder of Raffaele Palizzolo, the reputed Mafia chief, and his lieutenant at Bologna early in the new century received a good bit of attention in American periodicals, but there was no great alarm expressed at the possible spread of the society in the United States.

Though *Harper's Weekly* noticed the discovery of a criminal society using the symbol of a black hand as at work in Puerto Rico in 1898, the term *Black Hand* was not recognized in the United States until several years later. Following the sensational newspaper accounts of the New York barrel murder case in 1903, the Mafia and Italian crime in general received renewed attention. The Italians were both attacked and defended in the *Outlook*, and Speranza in *Charities* was highly critical of the American press for headlining the Mafia. In *Collier's* appeared a series of articles expressing alarm at imported crime in general and at the Mafia in particular. The Black Hand, as operating in New York, was first noticed in the French *Revue Blanche* in 1903 but did not become a popular subject in the American periodical press for some time. Beginning in 1908, however, it received a great deal of attention. Gaetano D'Amato, a prominent New York Italian-American, presented a carefully written article on the subject in the *North American Review*. While acknowledging the widespread criminal activities of the so-called Black Hand, he held it to be mythical as an organization. The muckraking periodicals shortly took it up. Lindsay Denison, in *Everybody's Magazine*, took much the same view as D'Amato had done, finding the Black Hand an alarming development but discounting it as an organized society. Both writers stressed the Mafia and Camorra origins of the Black Hand. In the same year New York Police Commissioner Theodore A. Bingham, in the *North American Review*, charged the Jews with committing half the crime in the city but stressed Italian criminals, masquerading under the Black Hand, as more dangerous to law and order.

In the following year, after the assassination of Petrosino, there was a great burst of articles in *Harper's Weekly*, the *Independent*, the *Survey*, the *Outlook*, the *American Review of Reviews*, *Cosmopolitan Magazine*, and *McClure's Maga-

zine, stressing Black Hand crime, often linking it to the Mafia, and demanding more effective action against it. Perhaps the most thoughtful of these articles was by Arthur Woods, a New York deputy police commissioner, later to be commissioner himself. Woods, in *McClure's*, like D'Amato and Denison, traced the Black Hand back to the Mafia and the Camorra. He did not believe that the Black Hand was a great unified organization but thought it might become such. His remedy was tighter immigration and especially deportation laws, along with constant vigilance on the part of the police. Interest in the subject continued at a relatively high level thereafter. In 1911, when the Camorra trial got under way at Viterbo, there was a tendency to stress the Camorra as the origin of the Black Hand, notably in an article by former New York Mayor George B. McClellan, Jr., in *Cosmopolitan*. The *Independent*, the *Outlook*, and *Collier's* all gave much space to the trial, which lasted for seventeen months. Arthur Train, former assistant district attorney of New York County, in *McClure's* (1912), thought the Mafia was a more important source of Italian crime, commonly labeled Black Hand work, than the Camorra, at least in New York City. He linked them together as the "Mala Vita" and warned that a formidable group of second-generation criminals was developing under its tutelage. In 1913 Frank M. White, who had devoted a great deal of attention to the Black Hand in different periodicals, in the *Outlook* declared that the Black Hand was in control of Italian New York. In the following year, however, the reform administration of Mayor John Purroy Mitchel, with Arthur Woods as his police commissioner, took over in the city. Woods, with the active cooperation of the district attorney's office, made relentless war on Black Handers and other gangsters. White credited him with having brought the Black Hand under control locally, in the *Outlook* (1917) and *Century Magazine* (1918).

In 1919 the *Literary Digest* called attention to the proliferation of Black Hand operations in Kansas City, quoting local sources as attributing it to repressive action in New York City, the former center of the Black Hand. Tommaso Sassone, in *Current History*, as late as 1921 talked of the Black

Hand, an offshoot of the Mafia and the Camorra, as being very active in the United States but noted that many Italian criminals were now going into bootlegging. His article was almost the last of its type. After 1920, when the great experiment of national Prohibition began, little was heard of the Black Hand in the periodical press.

Recent articles, since the revival of the Mafia legend, occasionally add information or comment on the subject. Rudolph J. Vecoli, in *The Journal of American History* (1964), notes the rise of the Black Hand in Chicago and the unsuccessful effort of the White Hand Society to eradicate it. Humbert S. Nelli covers the same ground in the *American Journal of Sociology* (1969). Joseph E. Persico, in *American Heritage* (1973), reviews the Mafia affair in New Orleans objectively. He notes that blackmailing and extortion were common in the Italian community, but without mentioning a Black Hand. George E. Pozzetta, in *Italian Americana* (1974), throws new light on the Petrosino assassination from fresh material. Luciano Iorizzo and Salvatore Mondello, in the same periodical (1975), take a critical look at the traditional American emphasis on Italian crime, including the Black Hand. A group of Italian-American and non-Italian scholars contribute individual articles to *An Inquiry Into Organized Crime*, sponsored by the American-Italian Historical Association in 1970. An article by Francis A. J. Ianni seems authoritative on the Mafia in Sicily and discounts its penetration of the United States until late in the 1920s. There was then, Ianni says, a real but unsuccessful attempt to organize an American Mafia. Black Hand activities, he states, though a cultural offshoot of the Mafia, were unorganized. Dwight C. Smith, Jr., follows a roughly parallel course, devoting most of his attention to the period after the Black Hand had gone out of fashion and discounting any American Mafia. Pellegrino Nazzaro traces the evolution of the Mafia and the Camorra on their home grounds to recent times and defends the South Italians from American charges of criminality. Mondello and Iorizzo trace and protest the growth of American press treatment of Italian crime from an early date. Most of these articles touch on the Black Hand without going into the subject in any great detail.

There is a good bit of biographical and autobiographical material bearing on the Black Hand. Dorothy Caruso, *Enrico Caruso, His Life and Death* (1945), and Pierce Van Rensselaer Key, *Enrico Caruso, a Biography* (1922), tell of the great singer's experience with the Black Hand in New York in 1910. Henry H. Curran, *Pillar to Post* (1941), describes the investigation of the New York Police Department by his committee of the Board of Aldermen in 1912-1913, revealing protection to Italian and other criminals. Michael Fiaschetti, *You Gotta Be Rough: The Adventures of Detective Fiaschetti of the Italian Squad* (1930), tells in lurid detail of this able detective's long war on the Black Hand. Martin A. Gosch and Richard Hammer, *The Last Testament of Lucky Luciano* (1976), deals chiefly with a later period, and its authenticity has been questioned; but it does stress this noted gangster's early alliance with Jewish criminals. John Kobler, *Capone: The Life and World of Al Capone* (1972), has considerable information on Italian gangs in New York in the early 1900s and later, with incidental treatment of the Black Hand. William McAdoo, *Guarding a Great City* (1906), has high praise for Petrosino and takes satisfaction in the author's creation of the Italian Squad. Hank Messick, *Lansky* (1971), stresses the Jewish-Italian alliance in organized crime, chiefly in a period later than that of the Black Hand. Arrigo Petacco, *Joe Petrosino* (1974), first published in Italy, is the only biography of this great detective. It is particularly strong on the assassination and its aftermath in Palermo.

A number of other works in this category help to clarify the political and administrative background of law enforcement in New York City during the Black Hand period. Among these, in addition to Curran's autobiography, noted above, are Alfred Connable and Edward Silberfarb, *Tigers of Tammany: Nine Men Who Ran New York* (1967); Edwin R. Lewinson, *John Purroy Mitchel, the Boy Mayor of New York* (1965); Louis H. Pink, *Gaynor: The Tammany Mayor Who Swallowed the Tiger* (1931); Lincoln Steffens, *The Autobiography of Lincoln Steffens* (1931); Harold C. Syrett, ed., *The Gentleman and the Tiger: The Autobiography of George B. McClellan, Jr.* (1956); Lewis J. Valentine, *Night Stick: The Autobiography of Lewis J. Valentine, former*

Police Commissioner of New York (1947); Nancy Joan Weiss, *Charles Francis Murphy, 1858-1924: Respectability and Responsibility in Tammany Politics* (1968); and Captain Cornelius W. Willemse, *A Cop Remembers* (1933). Sadly lacking to date is a biography of "Big Tim" Sullivan, Tammany boss of the lower East Side of Manhattan at the turn of the century and later.

Secondary works treating of Italy and the background of Italian immigration, with more or less material on brigandage and criminal societies in the homeland, include Luigi Barzini, *The Italians* (1964); Luigi Barzini, *From Caesar to the Mafia* (1971); Shepard B. Clough and Salvatore Saladino, *A History of Modern Italy* (1968); Leonard Covello, *The Social Background of the Italian-American School Child* (1972); Robert F. Foerster, *The Italian Emigration of Our Times* (1919); Major Arthur Griffiths, *Mysteries of Police and Crime: A General Survey of Wrongdoing and Its Pursuit* (1899); Charles W. Heckethorn, *The Secret Societies of All Ages and Countries* (1875 and 1897); Norman Lewis, *The Honored Society: A Searching Look at the Mafia* (1964); Michele Pantaleone, *The Mafia and Politics* (1966); and Denis Mack Smith, *Italy: A Modern History* (1959).

Books dealing more or less incidentally with the Black Hand and Italian crime in the United States include Grace Abbott, *The Immigrant and the Community* (1917); Paul M. Angle, *Bloody Williamson: A Chapter in American Lawlessness* (1952); Herbert Asbury, *The Gangs of New York: An Informal History of the Underworld* (1928); Herbert Asbury, *Gem of the Prairie: An Informal History of the Chicago Underworld* (1940); Francesco Cordasco, ed., *Studies in Italian-American Social History* (1975); Federal Writers' Project, Works Progress Administration, *The Italians of New York* (1938); William J. Flynn, *The Barrel Mystery* (1919); John Higham, *Strangers in the Land: Patterns of American Nativism* (1955 and reprint 1965); James G. Huneker, *New Cosmopolis: A Book of Images* (1915); Alfred Henry Lewis, *The Apaches of New York* (1912); Lloyd Lewis and Henry Justin Smith, *Chicago: The History of Its Reputation* (1929); Eliot Lord, John J. D. Trevor, and Samuel J. Barrows, *The Italian in America* (1905); Denis Tilden Lynch, *Criminals and Politicians* (1932); John Horace Mariano, *The Second*

Generation of Italians in New York City (1921); Michael A. Musmanno, *The Story of the Italians in America* (1965); Humbert S. Nelli, *Italians in Chicago, 1880-1930: A Study in Ethnic Mobility* (1970); Robert E. Park and Herbert A. Miller, *Old World Traits Transplanted* (1921); Virgil W. Peterson, *Barbarians in Our Midst: A History of Chicago Crime and Politics* (1952); Lawrence F. Pisani, *The Italian in America: A Social Study and History* (1957); R. A. Schermerhorn, *These Our People: Minorities in American Culture* (1949); Giovanni E. Schiavo, *The Italians in Chicago: A Study in Americanization* (1928); Craig Thompson and Allen Raymond, *Gang Rule in New York: The Story of a Lawless Era* (1940); Arthur Train, *Courts, Criminals and the Camorra* (1912); and Morris R. Werner, *Tammany Hall* (1928).

Since the revival of interest in the Mafia, there has been a steady flow of books more or less centering around it and the Italian criminal stereotype in general. As a rule, works by Italian-American scholars, naturally, tend to be rather defensive. Books on the subject by others, chiefly journalists, stress the more recent period and refer to the Black Hand only briefly, commonly identifying it with the Mafia. Among recent works in this field, not listed above, are Joseph L. Albini, *The American Mafia: Genesis of a Legend* (1971), which holds that criminal syndicates have no inherent ethnic basis, that the Mafia never took root in America, and that the Black Hand was not a mere transplant of the Mafia or the Camorra; David L. Chandler, *Brothers in Blood: The Rise of the Criminal Brotherhoods* (1975), which finds the Mafia at work in the United States from an early date but insists that neither it nor the Camorra was related to the Black Hand; Fred J. Cook, *Mafia!* (1973), alarmist and chiefly on the later period, but with some reference to Petrosino and the Black Hand; Donald R. Cressey, *Theft of the Nation* (1969), chiefly on the later period and the Mafia, but with brief reference to the Black Hand and not sure of its connection with the Old World Mafia; Nicholas Gage, ed., *Mafia, U.S.A.* (1972), chiefly on the period since 1920 and equating the Black Hand with the Mafia; Richard Gambino, *Blood of My Blood: The Dilemma of the Italian-Americans* (1974), highly defensive over the revived Mafia legend, discounting Mafia impact on the United States, and referring incidentally to the Black Hand and Petrosino;

Francis A. J. Ianni with Elizabeth Reuss-Ianni, *A Family Business: Kinship and Social Control in Organized Crime* (1972), which traces the history of an Italian crime family, under a pseudonym, from the Black Hand period to the present, with its evolution to respectability and social acceptance; Luciano J. Iorizzo and Salvatore Mondello, *The Italian Americans* (1971), which deplores the criminal label but has a good bit on the Black Hand; Ed Reid, *The Grim Reapers: The Anatomy of Organized Crime in America* (1970), very much alarmed at the Mafia and equating the Black Hand with it; Andrew F. Rolle, *The Immigrant Upraised: Italian Adventurers and Colonists in an Expanding America* (1968), essentially a success story but mentioning the Black Hand and simply equating it with the Mafia; Ralph Salerno and John S. Tompkins, *The Crime Confederation: Cosa Nostra and Allied Operations in Organized Crime* (1969), devoted almost wholly to the period since 1930, stressing Jewish-Italian combination in organized crime and noting the process of ethnic succession in the field; Giovanni E. Schiavo, *The Truth About the Mafia and Organized Crime in America* (1962), reviewing theories about the Black Hand and finding the Mafia a myth in the United States; Dwight C. Smith, Jr., *The Mafia Mystique* (1974), chiefly on the later period and discounting the Mafia as a factor in American crime, but with an interesting section on Petrosino and the Black Hand; Frederick Sondern, *Brotherhood of Evil: The Mafia* (1959), highly sensational on the menace of the Mafia and equating the Black Hand, in its day, with Mafia; Silvano M. Tomasi and Madeline H. Engel, eds., *The Italian Experience in the United States* (1970), very reticent about the Italian community's crime problem, but mentioning briefly "blackhanders and other lawbreakers" as exploiting compatriots.

A considerable number of the earlier studies listed above dealing with the Italian-American community, with others, have been reprinted in the Arno Press collection, *The Italian American Experience* (1975), under the editorship of Francesco Cordasco. A convenient general bibliography on the Italians in America is Francesco Cordasco, *Italians in the United States: A Bibliography of Reports, Texts, Critical Studies and Related Materials* (1972). A more detailed analytical listing is Francesco Cordasco, *The Italian-*

American Experience: An Annotated and Classified Biblio-graphical Guide (1974), and his *Italian Americans: A Guide to Information Sources* (1977).

In the field of fiction, Norman Douglas, who spent most of his life in South Italy, in *South Wind* (n.d.) implies strongly that the term *Black Hand* was another name for the Camorra of Naples in the early part of this century. Mario Puzo's *The Godfather* (1969), a best-selling novel later made into a sensationally successful movie, is based on very considerable research. It deals chiefly with a later period, but portrays a Black Hand operator who turned out to have no organization at all back of him. Adolfo Valeri, an Italian scholar then in New York, in *La "Mano Nera"* (1905) describes the Black Hand as founded there by a former Camorra chief fleeing from justice in Naples. While the work is in the form of a novel, the author, who seems to be well informed, wants to be taken seriously in portraying the Black Hand as a direct offshoot of the Camorra. Arthur B. Reeve's detective thriller, "The Black Hand," in *Cosmopolitan Magazine* (1911), has his hero, Craig Kennedy, in conflict with the infamous Paoli gang of Black Handers in New York City. They are all rounded up, of course, after a thrilling battle. The story no doubt helped to keep the public interested and alarmed, as Mafia fiction has done in our own time.

INDEX

260